SERGEI O. PROKOFIEFF, born in Moscow i
and art history at the Moscow School of Art. I
posophy in his youth, and soon made the decisi⌐..
Since 1982 he has been active as an author and lecturer. In 1991 he
became a co-founder of the Anthroposophical Society in Russia, and
since Easter 2001 he has been a member of the Executive Council of the
General Anthroposophical Society in Dornach. Eighteen of his books are
currently published in English translation, including his recent major
work *May Human Beings Hear It!*

THE FOUNDATION STONE MEDITATION

By the same author:

THE FOUNDATION STONE MEDITATION

A Key to the Christian Mysteries

Sergei O. Prokofieff

TEMPLE LODGE

Translated from German by Maria St. Goar

Temple Lodge Publishing
Hillside House, The Square
Forest Row, RH18 5ES

www.templelodge.com

First English edition 2006

Originally published in German under the title *Die Grundsteinmeditation, Ein Schlüssel zu den neuen christlichen Mysterien* by Verlag am Goetheanum, Dornach, in 2003

A catalogue record for this book is available from the British Library

ISBN-10: 1 902636 82 1
ISBN-13: 978 1 902636 82 5

Cover by Andrew Morgan featuring Rudolf Steiner's 'seal' from his Mystery Drama *The Portal of Initiation*
Typeset by DP Photosetting, Neath, West Glamorgan
Printed and bound by Cromwell Press Limited, Trowbridge, Wilts.

Contents

Introductory Note

The present work represents both a supplement and an extension of what was stated in the book *May Human Beings Hear It! The Mystery of the Christmas Conference* published in German by Verlag Freies Geistesleben in 2002 and subsequently in English by Temple Lodge, Great Britain in 2004. The lecture I gave under the title 'The Foundation Stone Meditation and the Hierarchies' during the summer conference of 2001 at the Goetheanum was the occasion for the further development of the theme. It finds expression in the second and third chapter. The remaining chapters deal with aspects of the main theme that for one reason or another were not included in the above-mentioned book, or merely referred to briefly.

The entire book is an attempt to introduce the nature of the new Christian Mysteries that Rudolf Steiner established at the Christmas Conference.

Following a study of this work, the question might arise in the reader of how it is possible that one and the same text of the Foundation Stone Meditation can be explained in such different ways. An answer is found if one considers that, due to its spiritual-mantric form, the text represents the characteristics of an *archetype* and for that reason represents a kind of *key* to the most diverse areas of world and human existence. Or, put metaphorically, depending on which spiritual portal is opened with this key, one arrives at one result or another, and one and the same line of the meditation becomes a reply to the most varied questions. In the following, several results of an actual application of this method in the most diverse dimensions of spiritual science are illustrated.

Like my other books, this one too is meant above all to serve as an incentive for the further deepening of a theme that without a doubt belongs among the most important themes of Anthroposophy.

Goetheanum, Dornach, 15 April 2003   *Sergei O. Prokofieff*

1. The Foundation Stone Meditation and the Being Anthroposophia

People who encounter Anthroposophy for the first time frequently ask, 'How can I best acquire a broad and comprehensive understanding of it?' If they want to grasp Anthroposophy more on the level of thinking, they should be directed to Rudolf Steiner's book *Occult Science, an Outline*. In the last edition of that book, published during his lifetime, he himself wrote, 'The book does, after all, contain the outlines of Anthroposophy *as a totality*.' (GA 13, p. 31) In that work the reader can indeed discover a comprehensive explanation of all basic insights of modern spiritual science, or the 'Science of the Grail' as Rudolf Steiner termed it on occasion. From the standpoint of the Christ Impulse and the central deed, the Mystery of Golgotha for the purpose of which the Christ entered Earth evolution, *Occult Science* describes: the scientifically viewed composition of the human being; man's earthly evolution and after-death life in the spiritual world in accordance with the laws of karma and reincarnation; the activity of the higher hierarchies and the cosmic development carried out by them (including the spiritual-hierarchical evolution of humanity); and finally the modern Christian-Rosicrucian initiation and the perspectives of future Earth evolution. Rudolf Steiner describes this in the following manner:

'For the anthroposophical world view, the Christ Being enters as a very centre into the whole tableau of reincarnation, the being of man, the consideration of the cosmos, and so on. One who in this sense deliberates on the anthroposophical world view, tells himself, I can consider all this but I can begin to understand it only when the whole picture points to the mighty focal point, the Christ. From various perspectives I have drawn the teaching of reincarnation, the teaching of the human races, of the planetary development, and so forth. But here I have drawn the nature of the Christ from one viewpoint. And thereby light is cast over everything else. It is a picture that has a main figure and everything else is related to it; I only comprehend the significance and expression of the other figures when I understand the main figure.' (GA 112, 30 June 1909)

Aside from this more thought-imbued (but not abstractly intellectual) approach to Anthroposophy, its nature can be grasped in a purely artistic manner as well. If we wish to pursue this direction we can turn to the architectural forms, the sculptural metamorphoses, the windows and paintings of the First Goetheanum. For in them we actually have the whole content of *Occult Science, an Outline* translated from the language of thought into that of Imagination. Here the images of the First Goetheanum address above all the artistic sensibility of the viewer, as does every work of art. Thus, in the totality of the inner configuration of the building, the above-cited main themes of Anthroposophy can easily be recognized in the language of art. In accordance with humanity's origin out of the spiritual forces of the cosmos, as well as the steps of modern initiation that lead to a true insight into the human being, an Imaginative depiction of the supersensible structure of man can therefore be discovered in the windows. The *complete* cosmic evolution from Saturn to Vulcan was pictured in the architraves and capitals. The spiritual-historical evolution of mankind was presented in the cupola-paintings, from ancient Lemuria to the coming sixth cultural epoch. On the other hand, the reproduction of the Christ Entity as the Representative of Humanity and its higher 'I' was supposed to be the very centre of the whole structure.

Rudolf Steiner spoke about this secret of esoteric Christianity in a lecture of 24 June 1909, (GA 112) and in so doing referred to the Rosicrucian stream as the guardian of this Mystery: 'The higher "I" that can be born in every human soul points us to the rebirth of the Divine "I" in the evolution of the whole of humanity through the Event of Palestine. Just as the higher "I" is born in every single person, in Palestine the higher "I" of all mankind, the Divine "I", is born and it is preserved and further developed in what is concealed in the sign of the Rose Cross.' In the First Goetheanum this mystery appeared in the painted main motif of the small cupola and likewise came to expression in the so-called 'Sculptural Group' where Christ is depicted as the 'Representative of Man'. It was supposed to be placed in the eastern part of the stage.

These two stages of experiencing Anthroposophy on the level of thinking and feeling are followed by the third and highest experience, the experiencing of it on the level of the will. This becomes possible through the will-like strengthening of thinking and feeling during meditative reflection into the esoteric nature of Anthroposophy. The best path to this goal is inner work with the Foundation Stone Meditation, because this meditation is the quintessence of the whole of Anthroposophy that was given in meditatively inspired form by means of earthly words. In such a form the meditation moreover unites within itself the two other elements, that of thought and the artistic (Imaginative) one. However, its linguistic expression merely represents the outer sheath of its spiritual content that emerges directly out of the spiritual world, namely out of that world's highest sphere, the *Word of Worlds* Itself. Rudolf Steiner characterized the content of the Foundation Stone Meditation—and this applies equally to all of Anthroposophy—as having been spoken by him 'out of the will of the spiritual world', as 'verses heard from the Cosmic Word'. (GA 260, 26 December 1923, morning)

From experiencing Anthroposophy through thinking in *Occult Science, an Outline,* then with the aid of artistic feeling in the First Goetheanum, and ultimately through meditative immersion in its being through the inner work on the Foundation Stone Meditation,[1] we discover in this threefold metamorphosis significant degrees of spiritualization of the three main forces of the human soul: thinking, feeling, and willing. Their spiritualization leads to the purification of the astral body. This in turn signifies this body's gradual transformation into the microcosmic Sophia.[2]

That is the significance of this metamorphosis for the inner life of a human being. On the other hand the three stages have a different significance for the development of mankind. Through them, proceeding from the Christ Impulse and directly out of the spiritual world, Rudolf Steiner could renew science, art, and religion, the three main areas of the cultural development of humanity.[3] In so doing he actualized the lofty ideal of true Rosicrucianism, the most important stream of esoteric Christianity. For 'it is indeed the most profound goal of Rosicrucianism ... to unveil ... the intentions of the *living Christ* ... in the absolute forms of wisdom, beauty, and action'. (GA 262, 'Manuscript of Barr' III; emphasis by Rudolf Steiner)

For persons who try to experience these metamorphoses in accordance with the consistently pursued path of modern Christian-Rosicrucian initiation as described by Rudolf Steiner in classic form in the corresponding chapter of *Occult Science, an Outline,* these stages turn out to be three tasks that a student of spiritual science can only fulfil by proceeding in freedom, meaning from his own inner exertions. The first task consists in transforming the *thought*-substance of Anthroposophy as presented in *Occult Science* into an *Imaginative* one. For each thought in this book was shaped in such wise that through corresponding meditative work it can be transformed into a picture, an Imagination. Rudolf Steiner did not offer anthroposophical wisdom immediately in Imaginative form, since a presentation *without* the mediating effect of earthly thinking, coming as it does directly out of the spiritual world, would inevitably exert an influence on the freedom of a human being, and this is something that is inadmissible from the standpoint of modern initiation. Rudolf Steiner therefore chose a wholly scientific-intellectual form for Anthroposophy so that a person can remain free in regard to the spiritual facts transmitted to him or her.[4] Consequently it is with this intellectual form of presenting Anthroposophy that the first of the three tasks of the modern path of initiation is given, namely the transformation of its thought–content into an Imaginative one, meaning in turn the experiencing of *Occult Science, an Outline* through pictures (Imaginations) formed independently and freely in the soul.[5]

The second task in the sense stated above consists in living with the *Imaginative* forms of the First Goetheanum that were given to us in such a way that they can be transformed through the inner activity of soul into *Inspirations*. Then the very building will begin to speak with man in the language of the gods. Rudolf Steiner pointed to this task of the First Goetheanum when he described its forms as 'organs . . . for the language of the gods' (GA 286, 17 June 1914) through which 'they are supposed to speak to us from all sides of the universe'. (ibid.) 'The house of language, the speaking house, the house that is alive in all its walls', (ibid.) this is what Rudolf Steiner called the First Goetheanum, and in saying so he emphasized that it was built in every detail in a 'musical' manner, meaning, that in all its Imaginative forms it harboured Inspirations everywhere, but Inspirations that an individual can only unlock and experience through his own inner work, and this once again means: proceeding out of his own freedom.

Finally, the third task is connected with the Foundation Stone Meditation that was originally given as a spiritual content that we are above all supposed to *hear*. 'First, however, may our ears be touched by these words', is the way Rudolf Steiner began the cultic act of the Laying of the Foundation Stone. (GA 260, 25 December 1923 in the morning) And he concluded it with the accompanying words: 'Hear it [the words of the Foundation Stone Meditation], my dear friends, thus resound in your own heart.' This is likewise why the third task consists in lifting oneself based on one's own freedom through meditative effort from an Inspirative experience of Anthroposophy as presented in the Foundation Stone Meditation to its *Intuitive* perception.

For the Foundation Stone Meditation is shaped in such a way that in every resounding (Inspirative) element, meaning in every resounding form of the content, the potential is hidden to rise to Intuitive experience of the higher spiritual reality *behind* this meditation; to actual entities of the spiritual world.

From the standpoint of anthroposophic insight it must be emphasized here again that in reality the spiritual world does not consist of some fantastic forces or energies, or a refined 'spiritual' matter, of a substance that so many materialists dream about today in a number of pseudo-spiritual 'New Age' movements. It consists solely and purely of *spiritual beings* (the hierarchies)—good and evil ones. Thus the third task on this path implies experiencing those *spiritual entities* who open up access for the human being today to all those beings of the spiritual world of whom mention is made in the Foundation Stone Meditation and find actual expression in it. Here it is a matter of a direct *encounter* with that being of the spiritual world who is a personified bearer of the Inspirative content of the Foundation Stone Meditation. The highest and ultimate level on this path therefore consists in the ascent from the Inspirative content of the Foundation Stone Meditation to the Intuitive perception of the super-sensible entity standing behind it.

Having begun with the *study* of Anthroposophy in its initial purely thought-filled form, the first stage of the modern path of initiation, (see GA 13) we have gradually approached the heights of the threefold metamorphosis through the inner work with the Foundation Stone Meditation, namely the encounter with an actual entity of the spiritual world.

This can be summed up as follows:

The stages of metamorphosis ★	The originally given form ★	The spiritual tasks ★
'Occult Science, an Outline'	— *Thought-filled* form of Anthroposophy	— Transition to *Imaginative* stage
The First Goetheanum	— The *Imaginative* form of Anthroposophy	— Transition to *Inspirative* stage
The Foundation Stone Meditation	— The *Inspirative* form of Anthroposophy	— Transition to *Intuitive* stage (Encounter with a supersensible entity)

Now what sort of spiritual entity is it whom we encounter on this path? In lectures of the year 1923 directly preceding the Christmas Conference, Rudolf Steiner determinedly referred to 'her'. This first occurred in Dornach in the lecture cycle *The Anthroposophic Movement* and subsequently in particularly concrete manner, merely five weeks before the Christmas Conference, in The Hague at the conclusion of the cycle, *Supersensible Man.*[6] In both cycles Rudolf Steiner spoke directly of an actual supersensible being who stands behind the development of Anthroposophy on Earth. In so doing he particularly stressed in the first instance that every single anthroposophist must feel the 'greatest possible responsibility' for 'her', that he must always 'seek "her" council first in all

actions he undertakes in life'. This would be particularly important so
long as the Anthroposophical Society only 'consists of a small number of
persons'. (GA 258, 16 June 1923) In the second cycle Rudolf Steiner
spoke of the fact that this supersensible being 'knocks on the portal of our
hearts' with the words 'Let me in', (GA 231, 18 November 1923), and he
pointed to the actual possibility of encountering her 'when we allow
Anthroposophy to enter into our hearts'. (ibid)

Seen as a whole, we have here a fourfold process. First in the summer of 1923 Rudolf Steiner speaks in Dornach of the responsibility in
regard to this supersensible being without mentioning its name. In
November of the same year he takes a further step and speaks of the
necessity that as a real being of the spiritual world it should enter into
the heart of every anthroposophist, again without mentioning its name.
If on the first level of this process reference is made to the questions
anthroposophists can pose to it, on the second level this being itself
turns to them with words that they can hear with their hearts. Then,
on the third level (during the Christmas Conference) Rudolf Steiner
refers to this being by name ('Anthroposophia') and at the same time
describes the next step that consists in enlivening the ether forces of the
human heart through this being. Finally, at the conclusion of the
whole process at the fourth stage, Rudolf Steiner once again calls this
being by name and asserts the nature of the *main task* of human beings
who have not only allowed it to enter their hearts but have moreover
allowed it to fill them with new life forces. Henceforth such a human
being is not merely an esoteric pupil of Anthroposophia, but likewise
her *co-worker* in order to reach those goals for the realization of which
she herself requires the earthly union of anthroposophists (the Anthroposophical Society).

This whole path can be pictured like this:

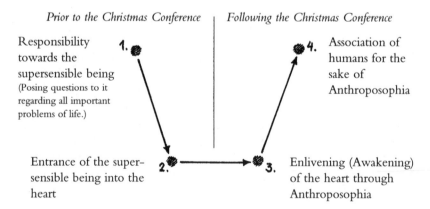

Prior to the Christmas Conference | *Following the Christmas Conference*

Responsibility   **1.**   **4.** Association of
towards the   humans for the
supersensible being   sake of
(Posing questions to it   Anthroposophia
regarding all important
problems of life.)

Entrance of the super-   **2.** ⟶ **3.** Enlivening (Awakening)
sensible being into the   of the heart through
heart   Anthroposophia

As an entity who stands directly behind the substance of the Foundation Stone Meditation, Anthroposophia is an intercessor between the human being and all the spiritual beings who are mentioned in the meditation. She desires to be a contemporary guide to them. Thus it is she from whose Inspirations the fundamental insights evolve concerning the world of the hierarchies and their working together with the highest spiritual Powers, with the divine Trinity, of whom mention is made in the Foundation Stone Meditation. Here the most significant characteristic of the existence of spiritual beings in the higher worlds is depicted in its highest and most sublime form in the *working of beings through beings*: the working of the Father-God through the spirits of the First Hierarchy, the Seraphim, Cherubim, Thrones; the working of the Son (the Christ) through the spirits of the Second Hierarchy, the Kyriotetes, Dynamis, Exusiai; and the working of the Holy Spirit through the spirits of the Third Hierarchy, the Archai, Archangeloi, Angeloi. It is particularly important here to note that this working of the three personages of the Trinity comes to expression here through the three categories of the spiritual hierarchies in their relationship to the central event of Earth evolution, namely the birth, death, and resurrection of the divine Christ-Being (the Rosicrucian words). And this is then affirmed in the meditation three more times by the choir of the ether world's four categories of elemental spirits.

Anthroposophia thus guides us to a comprehension of the interaction of the highest spiritual powers in the universe, an interaction whose focal collective point is the central Christ-Mystery. In so doing she offers a reply to human beings of the present time concerning the question that Rudolf Steiner formulated in a lecture given about three years earlier on the evening preceding Christmas day of 1920 as follows: 'It is not the Christ we lack, the knowledge of the Christ ... what is lacking is *the Sophia of the Christ.*' (GA 202, 24 December 1920) This wisdom of the Christ or the Sophia of the Christ made her appearance in full measure in the Foundation Stone Meditation as a direct expression of her supersensible nature.

If out of gratitude for all that we have received from the being Anthroposophia we wish to create a soul-spiritual sheath for her on earth, meaning that, as the Anthroposophical Society, we have the will to become 'a true alliance of human beings for Anthroposophia', this can only be realized if, as members, we actually immerse the Foundation Stone of the Christmas Conference into the ground of our hearts, and if the words of her meditation turn into an inseparable part of our life so 'that they cannot leave us'. (GA 260)

2. The Foundation Stone Meditation and the Cosmic Working of the Hierarchies

Having lifted the veil in the preceding chapter from the supersensible being whose direct revelation is the Foundation Stone Meditation, we can now turn to the contents of the meditation itself and this also means, to the theme of this chapter, the meditation's relationship to the world of the hierarchies. In order to do this we shall first study the general structure of the Foundation Stone Meditation whose first three parts consist in each case of an interconnected microcosmic and macrocosmic segment. As was already demonstrated in another work, their connection is possible only on the basis of the contents of its fourth part, which means, only through the Mystery of Golgotha that took place at the Turning-point of Time and has for all future times connected the microcosm with the macrocosm; the human being with the world. Rudolf Steiner pointed to this 'mystical fact' throughout the whole process of the cultic Foundation Stone Laying.[7]

In this union of the above-mentioned parts of the meditation we furthermore have an expression of the blending of the two main streams of the ancient Mysteries, the southern and northern one, as a result of the Mystery of Golgotha. One is the stream that sought for a connection with the spiritual world by means of the mystic path through sinking into the depths of the human soul; the other strove in ecstatic manner for union with the spirit-cosmos outside the body. In a lecture on 19 December 1910 (GA 124) Rudolf Steiner spoke of how, on the aforesaid path, the one about to be initiated must initially overcome the temptation of Lucifer's powers in his soul in order then, having safely lived through the encounter with the Lesser Guardian of the Threshold, to enter the spiritual world. Conversely, on the second path, the one who is to be initiated must first overcome the powers of Ahriman in order then, following the encounter with the Greater Guardian of the Threshold, to enter into the spirit-cosmos. These two ancient Mystery-paths were represented at the Turning-point of Time by the Shepherds and Kings. In the pivotal event of the mystery of Earth evolution, the Mystery of Golgotha, they were then linked and at the same time lifted to a higher level.

One result of their blending is the modern Christian-Rosicrucian path of initiation which is described in Rudolf Steiner's books, *Knowledge of the Higher Worlds and Its Attainment* and *Occult Science, an Outline,* (GA 10 and 13) where the spirit disciple experiences the encounters with the Lesser as well as with the Greater Guardian of the Threshold. The first of these two encounters unlocks for man the path into the depths of his own being (the microcosm), the second leads the way into the heights of the spiritual world that exist outside the human being (the macrocosm).

The union of these streams in thinking, feeling, and willing (in life itself) was given in mantric form in the first three parts of the Foundation Stone Meditation. This is the reason why meditative work with the microcosmic segments leads to true *self perception* and this means, to the encounter with the Lesser Guardian of the Threshold. On the other hand, meditative work with the macrocosmic segments leads to true *world perception,* which means to the encounter with the Greater Guardian of the Threshold.

On a number of occasions Rudolf Steiner gave his pupils the following short verse as a meditation. It is a verse that accurately describes the modern path of spirit perception (of initiation):

> If you want to perceive your own being,
> look around in the world in all directions.
> If you truly want to see through the world,
> look into the depths of your own soul. (GA 40)

The Foundation Stone Meditation likewise follows this basic principle of the new initiation. Three times, the process of self perception passes over into that of world perception, and the process of world perception into that of self perception corresponding to the threefold structure of man and the threefold ordering of the world to which man belongs.[8]

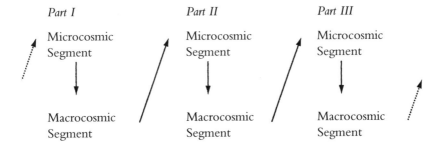

Part I	*Part II*	*Part III*
Microcosmic Segment	Microcosmic Segment	Microcosmic Segment
Macrocosmic Segment	Macrocosmic Segment	Macrocosmic Segment

Here the transition from the perception of man to that of the world aids the one who meditates in overcoming the one-sided activity of the forces of Lucifer, an activity that lures human beings to the various forms of egoism; to being caught up only in themselves and their own inner world. The transition from the perception of the world to that of man, on the other hand, helps one who meditates to overcome the one-sided influence of the forces of Ahriman who by all means available to him tries to dull human consciousness upon entrance into the spiritual cosmos. Now, the forces of the Christ contained in the fourth part of the meditation make it possible for the spirit disciple to withstand both dangers, inasmuch as he unites both Mystery streams in his soul: the path of the Shepherds that helps overcome the temptations of Lucifer, and the path of the Kings that leads to the overcoming of Ahriman's temptations.

The structure of the Foundation Stone Meditation as a totality (but particularly its fourth part) corresponds to the Sculptural Group which depicts the 'Representative of Man' between Lucifer and Ahriman. However, the names of the opposing powers are not actually mentioned in the meditation, since their alluring forces have already been subdued on the path described in it in the twofold manner.

★

Turning now to the content of the first three segments of the meditation, it must be kept in mind that there exists one characteristic they all have in common, namely the same relationship to the stream of time. Both segments of the first part refer to the past, both segments of the second part to the present, and those of the third part to the future. Therefore, to the human activity of (microcosmic) *recalling* ('Practise Spirit-recollection') corresponds the creative working of the 'Father-Spirit' in the macrocosm, an activity through which at the beginning of world evolution the earthly world came into being. To the human faculty of *pondering* ('Practise Spirit-pondering') corresponds the working of the 'Son-God,' the Christ, as the highest leader in the whole subsequent evolution ('For the Christ-Will in the encircling Round holds sway / In the Rhythms of Worlds, blessing the Soul'). Finally, to the human faculty of *beholding* ('Practise Spirit-vision') corresponds the working of the Holy Spirit in the macrocosm, that Spirit who awakens in all beings of the world ever higher states of spirit awareness. For the human being the next state of such a higher consciousness will be Imaginative cognition which, beginning in our age, will develop in humanity.

This threefold relationship to the stream of time can moreover be found in the fourth part of the meditation. Here, three segments can be clearly recognized; the first that relates to the Turning-point of Time (the past), the next to the current working of the 'Christ-Sun' in the earthly world (present), and the third to the coming creating of the Good through the human soul that has taken into itself the 'Light Divine' ('That good may become . . .').

The question now arises: What is the relationship between this evolution of the cosmos in time (which, according to the macrocosmic parts of the meditation, passes through the Father's epochs of creation in the past, the Christ's in the present, and the Holy Spirit's in the future) and the activities of the hierarchies serving the Trinity? What is the relationship of the First Hierarchy (Seraphim, Cherubim, Thrones) to the past of the universe, of the Second Hierarchy (Kyriotetes, Dynamis, Exusiai) to the present of the universe, and of the Third Hierarchy (Archai, Archangeloi, and Angeloi) to the future of it?[9]

The description of the primordial Saturn-condition of our cosmos that we find in a lecture of 4 January 1924 (GA 233a) can serve as a starting point for an answer to this question. Here Rudolf Steiner speaks of how the warmth nucleus of Ancient Saturn was formed through the joint activity by all three categories of spirits of the First Hierarchy. 'The choir of the Seraphim, Cherubim and Thrones works together. This is done inasmuch as the Thrones establish a core; the Cherubim let stream their own light-illumined being from out of this core; the Seraphim ensheathe the whole in a mantle of enthusiasm that radiates far out into cosmic space . . . Such an association of entities of the First Hierarchy once came into existence in the universe and it formed the Saturn existence.'

Another aspect from an earlier lecture needs to be added to this description of Ancient Saturn's origin. In the lecture cycle, *Spiritual Hierarchies and Their Reflection in the Physical World*, Rudolf Steiner first depicts how, during the Ancient Sun-condition, the Cherubim approached the Sun-planet from the four corners of cosmic space (from the direction of Bull, Lion, Eagle and Man) and gradually created the twelve parts of the zodiac around it. 'What today is so tangibly called 'the zodiac' has to be traced back to the ring [Ger.: 'Reigen'—in the sense of a round dance] of the Cherubim who from the cosmic surroundings worked down upon Ancient Sun.' (GA 110, 13 April 1909-II) In the same lecture Rudolf Steiner moreover points out that this working of the Cherubim already took place 'in a certain sense' on Ancient Saturn. 'Picture to yourselves each of the four Cherubinian figures attended by two companions each, and you have twelve forces and powers in the surroundings of the Sun. A certain indication of them was present as early as on Ancient Saturn.' In the following lecture he speaks once again about the connection of the processes of Ancient Saturn he had described: 'Now you have to picture how these Cherubim who are working in the environs of the Ancient Sun existed still earlier in the periphery of Saturn. Then, however, they were not yet called upon, in a manner of speaking, to engage in their activity.' (GA 14 April 1909-II) Now, since Rudolf Steiner on other occasions spoke more than once of the active *creative working* of the Cherubim even on Ancient Saturn, it has to be assumed that the words quoted above do not refer to the overall activity of the Cherubim, only to their forming of the zodiac. For the latter only came into being in its present form on Ancient Sun. On Ancient Saturn, on the other hand, it merely existed in a germinal state, and that in the form of the raying out of the Cherubinian forces from the *four directions* of cosmic space.[10]

Seen as a whole, one can try to imagine the activity of the beings of the First Hierarchy on Ancient Saturn as follows: The emergence of every new forming (of a cosmos) in the universe is preceded by a process of self-restriction by the highest deity (the Trinity). The result is that a 'location', a 'space', or 'spherical space' arises in the universe[11] that is enclosed 'from outside' through the working of the highest spirits, the Seraphim, 'bearers of the goals of the [new] cosmic system', goals that the latter receive from the 'divine Trinity'. (ibid.) Then the Cherubim approach this new 'space' or 'location' of the future cosmic system. They are the spirits whose task it is to 'work out' the goals they have received from the Seraphim, and this means, to transform them into real 'feasible plans'. During this 'trans-formation' the Cherubim create a sort of force-field in the space of the future cosmic system as a source of Inspirations that motivate the next category of hierarchical spirits, the Thrones, to begin with their creative activity. They receive the plans of the Cherubim—plans filled with cosmic wisdom—in the form of highest Inspirations. Then they transform them 'into reality' and in so doing they bring about the beginning of the creation of a new cosmic system in the sense of the words: 'Out of their very own being the Thrones let flow the primordial fire into this spherical space.' The actual development of our cosmos began with this sacrifice out of the substance of their own being that the Thrones offered up on the altar of cosmic evolution.

Put briefly: In the origination process of the new cosmic system, the Seraphim bring into being a sheath as the 'location' of the future creation; the Cherubim fill the thus created 'spherical space' with their forces by causing a kind of spiritual 'high pressure' which in turn has the effect of an Inspiration. Under its influence the Thrones then start with their creative activity. This brings about the Ancient Saturn as well as the foundation for the future physical body of man:[12]

Seraphim—creation of the sheath
Cherubim—forming of a force-field (or field of Inspirations) in the
    sheath
Thrones—beginning of the creation-process.

These three forms of activity by the entities of the First Hierarchy who stand at the very fount of our cosmic system possess the significance of a highest spiritual *archetype* for the subsequent development of the seven planetary systems (from Saturn to Vulcan). This is why these three forms of activity are repeated as the primary condition in all the following planetary stages of evolution of our solar system. The only difference is that each time new hierarchical beings participate in them, beings who during their own evolution have at that point in time reached the corresponding stage.[13]

Thus it is not the Seraphim, who on the Ancient Sun form their own sheath, but the Cherubim who have ascended to their [the Seraphims'] evolutionary level. The force- (or Inspiration) field within the sphere of Ancient Sun is now represented by the Thrones who have attained the next-higher stage of their development (the stage of the Cherubim). Now they not only work as direct creators but moreover as inspirers of creators. On Ancient Sun these are the Spirits of Wisdom (the Dominions or Kyriotetes), who through the offering of substance of their own being fashion Ancient Sun in the cosmos and on it likewise the seed for the human ether body.

On Ancient Moon the Thrones then create the outer sheath of the new planetary condition of the solar system. The Spirits of Wisdom fill this outer sheath with the forces of lofty Inspirations; following them in turn, the hierarchy of the Spirits of Movement [or Dynamis] rise to the level of creators. Through their offering of substance from their own being a new planetary body, Ancient Moon, came into being and on it the seed of the human astral body.

On the Earth this process is repeated, but with one essential difference. For the first time *only* spirits of the Second Hierarchy participate in the origination of our solar system[14]: Spirits of Wisdom [Kyriotetes] create its sheath, Spirits of Movement fashion its Inspiring force-field, and for the first time, following their Inspirations, the Spirits of Form begin *creating independently* in the universe. These spirits who are called Elohim in the Bible, are the true creators of earth and man. They endow the human being with the principle of the individual ego through offering up substance of their own being.[15]

This moreover explains why it is above all the Second or Sun-hierarchy (see GA 236, 27 June 1924) that occupies a central position in Earth evolution.[16] This likewise is the reason why, at a certain point of World evolution, they had to admit the second personage of the Trinity into their midst, the Son of God, the Christ, who on His path to Earth from the highest spirit sphere initially united with the Sun domain, for out of it the spirits of the Second Hierarchy carry out the guidance of our solar system.

The various stations of this, the Christ's macrocosmic path, first to the Sun and from there to Earth was described by Rudolf Steiner in many lectures. In one such lecture on 24 April 1922 he referred to this descent into the Sun sphere out of still higher regions of the spiritual world ('the Christ descended from still more elevated heights to the Sun', (GA 211) and on 13 April 1912 he stated that the Christ 'entered this sphere through the portal of the Sun Spirit of Wisdom'. (GA 136) Subsequently, having passed in the Sun sphere through the hierarchy of the Spirits of Motion, the Christ then united with the seven Sun-Elohim (the Spirits of Form) who guide Earth evolution, and led them. (See GA 103, 20 May 1908) Since then the Christ was revered in all the Mysteries of antiquity as the highest spirit of the Sun and leader of the whole domain of the Sun.[17]

Thus in today's present cosmic epoch the spirits of the Second Hierarchy, the Kyriotetes, Dynamis, and especially the Exusiai, play a central and fundamental part in the evolution of the Earth and humanity. Their connection with the Christ as the highest Sun-Spirit is brought to expression in the Foundation Stone Meditation as follows:

> For the Christ-Will in the encircling Round holds sway
> In the Rhythms of Worlds, blessing the Soul.
> Kyriotetes, Dynamis, Exusiai!
> Let there be fired from the East
> What through the West is formed.

These words point on the one hand to the connection of the spirits of the Second Hierarchy with the Christ, and on the other to their connection with the Sun (their apparent movement in the firmament in the direction from East to West speaks of this). In addition it is principally the Sun-spirits of the Second Hierarchy at whose head stand the Spirits of *Wisdom* who, together with the spirits of the Third Hierarchy that minister to them, form the new entity common to them all, the Heavenly Sophia[18] through their joint working in the macrocosm. From this is borne the significance of the Divine Sophia for the development of the Earth aeon, at the end of which the Sophian Mysteries are to turn into the central Mysteries, for only with their help will the Christ be comprehended in His cosmic (Sun-)significance.

As was explained in the first chapter of another work by the author,[19] the spiritual being who links the Heavenly Sophia with mankind is

Anthroposophia. Thus, with the establishment of Anthroposophy in the first quarter of the twentieth century, the unveiling of the Mysteries of the Heavenly Sophia began.

If we now turn to the creation-activities of the First Hierarchy on Ancient Saturn, proceeding from this primal image we can trace the subsequent activity in the world aeons following the earthly aeon. Thus, in the Jupiter aeon, the hierarchies leading it will work in the ensuing direction: the sheath of the Jupiter cosmos will be fashioned by the Spirits of Motion, the Spirits of Form will create the Inspirative field, and the actual creators of Jupiter will be the Spirits of Personality (Archai). Further on in the Venus aeon, the Spirits of Form will mould its form, the Inspirations will come from the Spirits of Personality, and the Archangeloi will be the creators. Finally in the Vulcan aeon the Spirits of Personality will forge the outer sheath, the Archangeloi the field of Inspiration, and the Angeloi will create Vulcan. With that the Vulcan aeon, which concludes this entire sequence of cosmic stages of developments, will be led by all three categories of spirits of the Third Hierarchy, even as all three categories of the Second, the Sun-hierarchy, jointly lead our present Earth aeon, and as all three categories of the spirits of the First Hierarchy led the aeon of Ancient Saturn together.

The Foundation Stone Meditation refers us to such activity on the part of the hierarchical entities in the course of world evolution. 'Practise Spirit-recollection' in its first segment extends all the way to the activity of the Seraphim, Cherubim and Thrones in the creation-process of Ancient Saturn; 'Practise Spirit-pondering' in the second segment reaches to the creation-activity of Kyriotetes, Dynamis and Exusiai as leaders of the Earth aeon and cosmic servants of the Christ Entity, the leading Sun-Spirit, connected with them; and the 'Spirit-vision' of the third segment points to the future evolution of our cosmos all the way to its seventh and final incarnation, the Vulcan-aeon, that will be led by the Archai, Archangeloi, and Angeloi.

This can be summarised as follows:

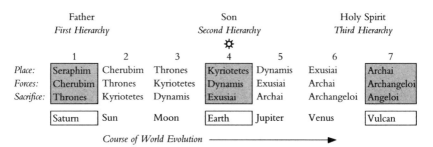

		Father *First Hierarchy*			Son *Second Hierarchy* ☿		Holy Spirit *Third Hierarchy*	
		1	2	3	4	5	6	7
Place:		Seraphim	Cherubim	Thrones	Kyriotetes	Dynamis	Exusiai	Archai
Forces:		Cherubim	Thrones	Kyriotetes	Dynamis	Exusiai	Archai	Archangeloi
Sacrifice:		Thrones	Kyriotetes	Dynamis	Exusiai	Archai	Archangeloi	Angeloi
		Saturn	Sun	Moon	Earth	Jupiter	Venus	Vulcan

Course of World Evolution ⟶

★

Another question is: What might the next stage of this world process be like? Naturally it could not be answered if Rudolf Steiner had not given us a few indications from his spiritual research concerning the subsequent evolution *after* the Vulcan condition.[20] In the above-mentioned cycle, *The Spiritual Hierarchies and Their Reflection in the Physical World,* he stated: 'In the Vulcan development, all the beings that emerged as it were from modest beginnings of the Saturn existence [these words refer primarily to human beings] are spiritualized to the highest degree; all of them together have become not only sun but super-sun. Vulcan is more than sun and with that has attained to the maturity of sacrifice, the maturity to dissolve itself ... The sun [of Vulcan] will dissolve, will ray out its beingness.' And further on: 'When a sun has advanced so far that it has once again united with its planets, it turns into circumference; it turns into a zodiac', in order then to move on to new creating in the universe. 'What had formerly developed within a solar system can now send down its effects out of cosmic space and out of itself can give birth to and create a new solar system.' (GA 110, 14 April 1909 - II) If we now take what Rudolf Steiner stated here and consider it from the standpoint of how the above-described primal image worked in evolution, then we can say: After the Vulcan-existence the Archangeloi will begin the new world evolution and create a new 'space' (zodiac) in the cosmos; the Angeloi will then fill this space with their cosmic Inspirations. And into this stream of world evolution the actual creators of the new solar system will enter, and they will be the *human beings.* Henceforth they will arise as the final part of the hierarchical totality to the level of the 'mighty cosmic sacrificial service'. (ibid.)

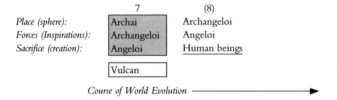

Course of World Evolution ⟶

It goes without saying that the solar system, which will then be created by human beings, will differ fundamentally from the cosmos of Ancient Saturn. For in that time mankind will have turned into the *tenth hierarchy* which Rudolf Steiner characterized as the Hierarchy of Freedom and Love. (GA 110, 18 April 1909 -II) This hierarchy will then create a solar system, the foundation of which for the first time in all of world evolution will be the power of the Christ, of Love, and the power of the Holy Spirit, the Light of Wisdom (of the highest perception) that can be bestowed on the soul that through its own endeavours will have attained complete inner freedom.

> Where the eternal aims of Gods
> World-Being's Light
> On thine own I
> Bestow
> For thy free Willing.

Out of the combination and joint activity of the two forces, the *Love* of the Christ and the *Wisdom* of the Holy Spirit, will emerge the creative *Deeds of Good* from the soul, deeds of Good out of which the tenth hierarchy will create the new solar system.

The three above-mentioned elements out of which such a solar system will emerge are germinally contained in the last, fourth, segment of the Foundation Stone Meditation. These truly exalted aims of world and humanity's evolution can, however, only be attained if the warmth and the light of the 'Christ-Sun' are received into the soul in the present Earth aeon; the warmth of His love that entered into Earth existence through the Mystery of Golgotha and the Holy Spirit's light sent down by Him at Whitsuntide.[21] For in the 'Christ-Sun' that is mentioned in the fourth part of the meditation, we already have a *germ* of that Super-Sun which eventually is intended to emerge out of the creative deeds of humans at the end of the Vulcan aeon. Similarly the *archetype* of the great sacrifice that humans will then achieve, together with the spirits of the Third Hierarchy by sacrificing the 'Super-Sun' so that it may transform into a new zodiac, can be discovered as early as in the deed of Christ on Golgotha. This is moreover why He is called the 'Great Sacrifice' or the 'Mystical Lamb' in Christian esotericism. (GA 102, 27 January 1908)

As we saw, the foundation for the creative activity of mankind, for the Hierarchy of Freedom and Love, is brought about in the macrocosm particularly by the two hierarchies standing above humanity, the Archangels and Angels. This is why, when speaking of the tenth hierarchy, simultaneously with it Rudolf Steiner mentioned these two categories of hierarchical beings. 'And how are we to speak of humans when we rank them among the hierarchies? After the Archangels and Angels (the arch-messengers and messengers) there will have to be added to the sequence of the hierarchies the spirit of freedom and the spirit of love. Counting from the top, this is the tenth of the hierarchies that is, however, engaged in development, yet it does belong to the spiritual hierarchies.' (GA 110, 18 April 1909 – II)

3. The Foundation Stone Meditation and the Inner World of the Hierarchies

Working meditatively with the Foundation Stone, one can gain the impression that it contains not only a description of the *outward activity* of the divine-spiritual hierarchies during the cosmic development from Saturn to Vulcan and even beyond, but also quite concrete indications of the nature of the *inner life* of the hierarchies.

This inner life was described by Rudolf Steiner in detail in the lecture cycle, *Spiritual Beings in the Heavenly Bodies and in the Kingdoms of Nature*. (GA 136) There he initially draws our attention to the life of the earthly human being, a life that consists of two opposite experiences: the connection with the external world through outer perceptions, and the inner life that is independent of the exterior world with its thoughts, feelings, and will impulses. A quite similar polarity, but in a completely different form, is likewise experienced by the beings of the Third Hierarchy, the Angels, Archangels, and Archai. They too have a kind of inner and outer life in the higher worlds. For them, however, the life in perceptions, contrary to that of earthly man, which takes its course merely in passive surrender to outer impressions, signifies dynamic creative activity. As Rudolf Steiner depicts it, for them 'all perception is at the same time a revelation of their own being'. Or put differently, the Third Hierarchy is formed by entities 'who perceive inasmuch as they reveal, inasmuch as they bring to expression what they themselves are'. (5 April 1912) Their self-awareness is moreover linked with this peculiarity of their existence: 'They possess feeling of self so long as they reveal themselves to the outside.' (ibid.) The opposite of this condition consists of their turning to their own inner world. A special form of inner life arises in which, immersing themselves in themselves, they become capable of perceiving the revelations of the higher hierarchies (the Second and First ones). These revelations then imbue their whole inner being like a mighty spiritual vision.

This inner life of these beings of the Third Hierarchy has nothing in common with our own egotistical interests that we harbour in most cases for our thoughts, emotions, and will impulses. Rather it consists above all in an opening up of their inner world in regard to the higher hierarchical beings. 'Something then enters into their own being like the revelation of spiritual worlds that are higher than they themselves', 'where they find they are filled by other entities who are higher than they.' (ibid.) Rudolf Steiner called this, their second state of consciousness, 'being filled with spirit' (ibid.) that is like a 'spiritual light' pouring into them.

A second peculiarity of both stages of consciousness on the part of these beings of the Third Hierarchy is that they are incapable of lying! For every falsehood would indicate for them a revelation to the outside of something that does not correspond to their inner content (being filled with spirit). At the same time, since the revelation of their own nature to the outside is for the spirits of the Third Hierarchy the basis of their self-awareness, any lie would inevitably extinguish this awareness of self, meaning they would lose themselves, something that would be equal to a radical denial of their own nature. 'Thus, these beings must dwell in the realm of absolute truth if they wish to experience themselves at all.' (ibid.) The beings of the Third Hierarchy can therefore become lofty teachers of *Truth* for earthly humans.

★

The two states of consciousness of the entities of the Second Hierarchy, of the Exusiai, Dynamis, and Kyriotetes, manifest in a completely different way. In the activity corresponding to human perception, they also reveal their own being to the outside. But in contrast to the entities of the Third Hierarchy 'this revelation of their own being is sustained as something independent that becomes separated from these entities themselves'. (6 April 1912) In so doing what separates from them possesses a quality of beingness, meaning it is *being* as well. 'They not only reveal their self as do the entities of the Third Hierarchy; they separate this being from themselves so that it remains as an independent entity.' (ibid) During their cognitive activity the spirits of the Second Hierarchy therefore continually create replicas or images of their own being in the outer world, replicas that objectively survive there.

If on the other hand these spirits contemplate themselves, their inner life consists in filling the objective (being-imbued) replicas they have fashioned with life forces: 'The arousing of life is always the result of such creation of one's self.' (ibid) And when 'being filled with spirit' in the case of the Third Hierarchy is revealed to Imaginative vision as an in-streaming of 'spiritual light' into their inner being, the above process of 'arousal of life' in the now self-sustained replicas of the spirits of the Second Hierarchy is connected with the Inspirative cognizing of 'spiritual resounding' or the 'harmony of the spheres'. (ibid) Just as the entities of the Third Hierarchy dwell in the realm of absolute Truth, so do the entities of the Second Hierarchy in the dominion of absolute beauty. For the independent beings created continually by the Second Hierarchy are a replica of this hierarchy's inner world, filled as this world is by highest beauty and harmony. It is in the resounding of the music of the spheres, the most perfect expression of the beauty and harmony of their objectivated inner world, that the spirits of the Second Hierarchy are revealed in the macrocosm. This is the reason they can moreover be the lofty teachers of *beauty* and harmony for human beings on earth.

★

As to the First Hierarchy of the Thrones, Cherubim, and Seraphim, their cognitive life consists not only of the creation of new beings— replicas of their own being who are thus dependent on their creators. Their cognitive life also consists of the creation of new worlds capable of leading a self-sustained life completely independent of their creators. If therefore the creatures of the Second Hierarchy fall victim directly to death and dissolution as soon as they are abandoned by their creators, the creations of the First Hierarchy continue on even if the spirits who have created them separate from them because they assume other tasks in the universe. 'They therefore do not bear their creation along with them; this creation remains even when they [the spirits of the First Hierarchy] leave them behind.' (7 April 1912) This in turn signifies that the spirits of the First Hierarchy rise up to what Rudolf Steiner calls 'world-creating', something through which new worlds come into existence in the cosmos. 'These entities of the First Hierarchy can move away from this [activity]. Nevertheless it remains as something self-sufficient and objective.' (ibid.) The worlds created by the First Hierarchy thus have the ability to con- tinue evolving independently.

Now when the spirits of this hierarchy move on to an experiencing of their own inner life, then during this activity they create new spirits who inhabit the worlds created by them; worlds that exist independently in the universe. 'For these entities of the First Hierarchy, their inner condition of consciousness, their inner experiencing lies in creating, in making beings self-sufficient ... To create beings—this is their inner life.' (ibid) Such creation of new worlds with self-reliant entities is possible for the spirits of the First Hierarchy only by bestowing on their creation such a mighty impulse of Good that the worlds created by them become capable of existing independently of their heavenly creators, and of evolving further. For this reason, these spirits of the First Hierarchy can be great teachers of the *Good* for earthly humankind.

All this has a direct relationship to what is described in the Foundation Stone Meditation as the working of the three hierarchies. In the third part of this meditation mention is made of the connection of the Third Hierarchy to the impulse of the Holy Spirit who fills their inner being with 'Thoughts of Worlds', meaning with the thoughts of Truth. These Thoughts of Worlds that bear within them 'eternal aims of Gods' are unveiled to Imaginative consciousness as an in-streaming of 'World-Being's Light' which evokes 'being filled with spirit' in the Third Hierarchy. Their whole inner being strives to attain this condition. And this is why it says in the meditation:

> Archai, Archangeloi, Angeloi,
> Let there be prayed in the Depths
> What from the Heights is answered,
> Speaking:
> Per Spiritum Sanctum reviviscimus.

This unceasing entreaty by the beings of the Third Hierarchy that is directed to the Holy Spirit represents an inseparable part of their inner being. This is why in the Middle Ages they were often represented in the form of beings who were praying, singing hymns and praising God. In regard to human beings it is the task of the Third Hierarchy to bring to man's earthly consciousness the *Light of Truth* ('World-Being's Light'), received by them from the Holy Spirit, and thus to make it possible for men to recognize the 'Thoughts of Worlds' of the hierarchies corresponding to which the cosmos and man were once created. These 'Thoughts of Worlds' indwell all things and beings of the material world, but are to be liberated through the active doings of human consciousness from their bondage to matter. Through recognition of the spirit-grounds of the world, man's own 'I' can once again reconnect the 'Thoughts of Worlds' resting in all things with their primal fount, the *Light* of the Holy Spirit. This is the beginning of their resurrection-process—'Per Spiritum Sanctum reviviscimus'. This is why it says in the meditation that the 'Thoughts of Worlds' in the 'depths' of the world 'beseech Light', which means the Light of Truth with which they can unite through man's perceptual activity. This in turn signifies that such a resurrection of 'Thoughts of Worlds' interred in all things is possible with the aid of the Light of Truth only when man has attained the faculty 'truly' to 'think' in his 'foundations of the Spirit'. In our time this is only possible through the study of the communications of spiritual science, the study that stands for the first level of the modern path of initiation. In order however to take in the Light of Truth one must not only fill one's thinking with the spirit-content of spiritual science; one must moreover attain the next level which consists of the Imaginative experiencing of man and the world. To develop this Imaginative faculty in oneself is one of the most important tasks of the present fifth post-Atlantean epoch. To this end, true thinking attained on the preceding level must be brought to complete stillness so that Imaginative beholding of the Spirit can slowly dawn in the soul. This is indicated in the third segment of the meditation with the words:

> Practise *Spirit-vision*
> In quietness of Thought,
> Where the eternal aims of Gods
> World-Being's Light
> On thine own I
> Bestow
> For thy free Willing.

Through such meditative work a person can grasp 'World-Being's Light' which, originating from the sphere of the Holy Spirit, is brought towards him or her by the entities of the Third Hierarchy. And when one receives this into one's consciousness, one will in full freedom turn into a co-worker of the higher hierarchies in the attainment of their 'eternal aims'.

This transition of the human soul from thinking spiritual scientific thoughts to their Imaginative perceiving is the beginning of the gradual *soul-awakening*. In so doing the soul ascends from earthly thoughts to their archetypes in the spiritual world—to the Third Hierarchy's Universal Thoughts. In the published version of the Foundation Stone Meditation Rudolf Steiner translated the third part of the Rosicrucian verse 'Per Spiritum Sanctum reviviscimus' with the words, 'In the Spirit's cosmic thoughts, the soul awakens.' Its third segment guides the student of spiritual science to such an awakening of the human soul in the domain of the Third Hierarchy. The actual awakening occurs in his soul by experiencing in microcosmic form something that is similar to what the entities of the Third Hierarchy carry within their being macrocosmically: the [state of] 'being filled with the Holy Spirit'.[22]

★

Just as the third part of the meditation describes the inner life of the Archai, Archangeloi and Angeloi, so does its second part characterize the inner life of the Kyriotetes, Dynamis, and Exusiai. And just as the activity of the Holy Spirit is the highest ideal and archetype for the spirits of the Third Hierarchy, an activity that awakens higher consciousness in all entities, (the reason why the spirits of the Third Hierarchy are moreover called 'Spirits of Soul' in the meditation for they work inwardly in the human soul) so, for the spirits of the Second Hierarchy, the Christ as the creative Word of Worlds is the highest ideal and archetype for their activity in the cosmos.

As has been described earlier, the inner activity of the Second Hierarchy consists in filling the beings created by them with life. This activity can be compared with the cosmic music or the harmony of the spheres. And just as the Word of Worlds that created the cosmos by means of the hierarchies does not abandon its creation but remains united with it, the spirits of the Second Hierarchy, emulating the Logos, maintain an indissoluble connection with their creation. The descent of the Christ into our world represents the highest expression of such a connection of the Logos with the cosmos: first Its union with the Sun, meaning the domain of the Second Hierarchy's activity, and then with the Earth and humanity. For the Christ Himself this deed was an act of His divine free will. (See GA 131, 14 October 1911) All this can be found in the words:

> For the Christ-Will in the encircling Round holds sway
> In the Rhythms of Worlds, blessing the soul.
> Kyriotetes, Dynamis Exusiai . . .

These words indicate that the highest archetype for the spirits of the Second Hierarchy is the Christ Being whom they serve and whose *will* they try to fulfil. These words moreover characterize the true nature of their own inner life that is connected with the harmony of the spheres or the 'Rhythms of Worlds' that fill the universe. In the microcosmic segment of the second part of the meditation they are mentioned as the 'surging / Deeds of the World's Becoming'. Moreover, the words of the meditation, 'Thine own I / unite / unto the I of the World', point to the fact that the spirits of the Second Hierarchy never abandon their creation but furthermore 'unite' their own being with it ever and anew and thereby with the all-encompassing domain of the Sun Logos.

As beings who essentially indwell the Sun sphere, the spirits of the Second Hierarchy stand behind all phenomena of *light* in our world as well as any of the manifold colours brought forth by the light. Everything we attribute to the sphere of *beauty* becomes visible in the earthly world through the effect of light whose source is the Sun that moves from East to West across the firmament. The following words in the meditation point this out:

Kyriotetes, Dynamis, Exusiai,
Let there be fired from the East
What through the West is formed.
Speaking:
In Christo morimur.

When we now call to mind that in the speech of esotericism 'East' always signifies the spiritual world and 'West' the material world, we can find in the quoted lines a reference to the mission of true art. For its mission consists in creating new forms in the world of matter—in architecture, sculpture, painting, music, poetry and so on—for a content that the artist has received from the spiritual world. This creative activity of man moreover contains the wellspring of *beauty* in the earthly world. In all this the forces of the Spirits of Form are more involved in the spatial arts and the forces of the Spirits of Motion in those involving time, whereas the forces of the Spirits of Wisdom penetrate *all* forms of art and bestow on them the attribute that we experience as *beauty*.

Put differently, beauty originates in the earthly world when, through the creative activity of man, the spirit that emerges out of the sphere of the Spirits of Wisdom begins to light up in matter. These spirits are essentially of a *Sophia-like* nature[23] and this appearing of the spirit represents the first level of the future spiritualization of matter. The fact that the ultimate spiritualization of the world (its 'salvation') begins with beauty was experienced particularly powerfully by F. M. Dostoevsky, and he brought this to expression with the well-known words, 'Beauty shall save the world.' This truth is proclaimed to every human soul by the Sun rising in the morning and in the spiritual world by the spirits of the Second Hierarchy who stand behind the Sun.

Rudolf Steiner translated the Latin Rosicrucian words that form the centre of the second component of the Foundation Stone Meditation in the published version as: 'In Christ, death becomes life.' The overcoming of death through cosmic life, something that is possible only on Earth in the physical body, corresponds to the fact that in the Sun sphere of the Second Hierarchy all beings created by this hierarchy are gifted with life. These life streams of the Second Hierarchy pour through all the spirits unceasingly from the Sun, awakening and enlivening everything that is alive on the earth during the year's course.

What becomes reality out of the Sun through this hierarchy every Easter; what was celebrated during all ages in the Mysteries as a symbolic festival of the dying and re-rising god in nature (the cults of the Sun-gods: Baldur, Adonis, Mithras, Attis, Osiris, and others), became reality on the physical plane only once in the Mystery of Golgotha, not as a symbol but as an actual *fact* of human history. Thus was the foundation laid in Earth evolution for the future union of the Earth with the Sun. Viewed esoterically, the words 'In Christ, death becomes life' signify that through the deed of Christ on Golgotha the Earth has received the spiritual force that will lead it to becoming a new sun. Moreover mankind has been given the potential to acquire eternal life, the beginning of which is represented in the conscious co-operation with the spirits of the Second Hierarchy as the leaders of the Earth aeon. For the death forces work in matter, whereas the life forces come from out of the Sun sphere.

Rudolf Steiner referred to this connection between the death of Christ on Golgotha and the beginning of the shining forth of a new sun in the Earth's depths with the words: 'The first impetus for our Earth's becoming a sun was given at the time when the blood flowed from the wounds of the Redeemer on Golgotha ... Then a new cosmic centre was created.' (GA 112, 6 July 1909) And he continued: 'But this is what we must understand: We stand before the inception of a newly forming sun when we consider the dying God.' (ibid)

★

In the first segment of the Foundation Stone Meditation a description is contained of the inner life of the highest hierarchy, that of the Seraphim, Cherubim and Thrones. As mentioned before, the distinctive aspect of their activity is that they not only create new worlds and beings dwelling on them, but moreover bestow on them the potential for complete independence. This implies that such beings are given the possibility to exist autonomously once the hierarchical beings have left to move on to new deeds in the universe. The First Hierarchy's highest ideal and archetype in this creative activity is the working of the Father-God. At the beginning of His world-creation, out of His own free will, God limited His presence in His own realm so as to allow our world-all to come into being. In so doing God created a 'space' in this universe that could arise as the stage for the creative activity of the spirits of the First Hierarchy (see above). The lines of the first part of the meditation refer to this creative activity of the First Hierarchy out of the forces of the Father-God:

> For the Father-Spirit of the Heights holds sway
> In Depths of Worlds, begetting Life.
> Seraphim, Cherubim, Thrones!
> (Spirits of Strength!)
> Let there ring out from the Heights

What in the Depths is echoed,
Speaking:
Ex Deo nascimur.

Through the three categories of the First Hierarchy's spirits, the Father-God in this way allows a new cosmos to come into being through an act of creation that in the Foundation Stone Meditation is characterized as one that 'in Depths of Worlds [is] begetting *Life*'. In accordance with the first line of the Rosicrucian verse, the world is 'born' in the actual sense of these words from out the womb of the father-like primal ground of all existence. In the published version of the meditation Rudolf Steiner then translated 'Ex Deo nascimur' as 'From God, Mankind *has Being*'. And in the sevenfold evolution of our cosmos (from Saturn to Vulcan) human beings will in the course of time attain to full emancipation from their Creator inasmuch as they gradually disengage themselves from the 'wielding World-Creator-*Life*', where in the beginning of their evolution man's 'own I' was linked in being with 'the I of God'.[24] 'Being' [Sein—in the sense of existence] manifests as the main attribute of the Father-God. And He can bestow this Being on His creation so that later on it is able to exist completely autonomously in the universe.

The word 'being' or 'has being' ['takes on being,' i.e. 'erweset'], mentioned twice in the first part of the meditation, indicates the evolution within the beings [in the sense of entities 'Wesen'] of the world that has come into existence, beings whom God from the beginning foreordained to full independence. Here in the first part of the first segment, this verb 'erweset' [or 'takes on being'] relates to the individual human being:

Thine own I
Comes to being
Within the I of God,[25]

in the second part it then relates to the whole of mankind as the tenth hierarchy:

From God, Mankind has Being.

The power on the other hand, out of which the Father-God bestowed on His creation the faculty for independent existence, is the *absolute Good* which in the whole universe is vested in God alone. For the only faculty of God's *Being* is the *Good*. This is why the Christ said to His disciples: 'Why do you call me good? No one is good. The good is with God alone.'[26] The first part of the Foundation Stone Meditation points us to this sphere of the absolute Good as the very source of the Creator-forces of the spirits of the First Hierarchy who in their deeds serve the Father-God and emulate Him.

4. The Foundation Stone Meditation and the Preparation of Anthroposophy in the Heavens

A further aspect of the activity of the hierarchies in our cosmos connects the Foundation Stone Meditation with the celestial development of Anthroposophy, something that Rudolf Steiner described in detail in the karma lectures of the year 1924. There he speaks of the fact that at the beginning of the fifteenth century, when below on Earth the period of the consciousness soul started in the year 1413, in the lofty Sun sphere the Archangel Michael proceeded to instruct a large number of human souls who found themselves in the spiritual world between death and their new birth.

Simultaneously with the beginning of this work, a powerful event took place in the higher worlds, an event that 'manifests only after long periods of time within the development of our cosmos'. (GA 237, 28 July 1924) This was a mighty occurrence that the spirits of the First Hierarchy accomplished, which was beheld by all the participants of the super-sensible school of Michael. Rudolf Steiner depicted it as follows: 'One sees the Seraphim, Cherubim and Thrones carry the spiritual element out of the realm of the Exusiai, Dynamis and Kyriotetes down into the physical and by their power implant spirit into matter.' (ibid.) Like a 'cosmic thunderstorm' these doings of the First Hierarchy permeate the whole spiritual world at this moment, and the souls who participated in this saw the Earth below 'flashed through by lightening flashes' and heard 'mighty rolling thunder'. 'One would like to say: What was taught by Michael to his own during that time was heralded down below in the earthly worlds amid lightning and thunder.' (ibid.)

Rudolf Steiner explained this cosmic event in the following way: 'This was because the Seraphim, Cherubim and Thrones were conveying the Cosmic Intelligence into that member of the human organization that is called the system of nerves and senses, the head-organization. *Once again* a great event had taken place that does not show itself distinctly as yet. It will only do so in the course of hundreds and thousands of years. But it means that humans are being utterly transformed. Formerly they were beings of heart; then they became beings of the head. The [cosmic] intelligence becomes their own. Seen from the supersensible, all this is of immense significance.' (ibid.)

The words 'once again' in the above-quoted excerpt indicate that this cosmic event which is referred to is part of a whole sequence of similar events, of which Rudolf Steiner mentions only one that preceded this one in ancient Atlantis. '*The last time*, during the ancient Atlantean Epoch, when the Cosmic Intelligence still remained cosmic but had taken possession of human hearts, something like this also occurred which, for the present region, the earthly region, now once more displayed itself in spiritual lightning and thunder.' (ibid.) The words 'the last time' speak again of the fact that the event which occurred in ancient Atlantis was likewise not the first one in the referred-to sequence but that at least one preceded it, namely in the Lemurian Epoch. In that far-distant time the Cosmic Intelligence pervaded man's system of limbs and the metabolism, and with that entered the human being for the first time. When we now recall that humans accepted their individual 'I' as a gift of sacrifice from the Spirits of Form (Elohim), it becomes comprehensible that (along with receiving the Cosmic Intelligence into the system of limbs and metabolism) we have the most important prerequisite for man to become an 'I'-being. This is moreover confirmed through the fact that in awakening from sleep the entry of the 'I' into the physical body occurs through the limbs, whereas the 'I' departs the physical sheath through the head when falling asleep.[27]

The *first* cosmic event was thus connected with the fact that the human being in ancient Lemuria took in the 'I'-principle; in the second event during the Atlantean Epoch man entered upon the solid ground of the Earth. With this, Earth development as such now began (and at the same time reached its midpoint).[28] Finally the event at the beginning of the fifteenth century signified the third and most significant prerequisite for attaining the actual goal of Earth evolution: man became a free being. For only in the head-system can Cosmic Intelligence be changed into human intelligence, something that is essential for the development of the consciousness soul during which time the ego is supposed to attain its highest bloom, full of freedom and greatest awareness. The fundamental transformation, which since the fifteenth century has occurred in humanity with the beginning of the so-called 'modern age', is a concrete outcome of this fact.

In the third event described earlier the participation of *all three* hierarchies can therefore be demonstrated, even though in variable forms. The First Hierarchy doubtlessly plays the most important and active part in this. The Second on the other hand is the guardian of the spiritual substance (the Cosmic Intelligence) which the First Hierarchy imprinted out of its sphere—the Sun sphere—into the earthly world (into the human head system). For it took place under the effect of the First

Hierarchy that this spiritual substance left the Sun sphere, the domain of the Second Hierarchy's activity, and united with the human being on Earth. Aside from Michael and human beings belonging to his super-sensible school, the witnesses to this grandiose process were all the categories of spirits from the Third Hierarchy that were linked with his activity as well as those elemental spirits who are mentioned in the Foundation Stone Meditation: 'All those beings from the hierarchy of the Angeloi, Archangeloi and Archai who belonged to the Michael stream, participated [in the supersensible school]. Numerous elemental beings likewise participated.' (GA 240, 27 August 1924)

This is why any anthroposophist who truly works intensively with the Foundation Stone Meditation (which as we have seen contains a kind of quintessence of the whole of Anthroposophy as taught in the super-sensible Michael School in the midst of the cosmic thunderstorm's 'thunder and lightning') can today become convinced, based on personal experience, of the reality of Rudolf Steiner's words: 'This should be understood, my dear friends, for these thunder and lightning flashes must become enthusiasm in the hearts and minds of anthroposophists! And one who really has the impulse towards Anthroposophy ... bears in his soul today after-effects of having received in Michael's surroundings at that time the *heavenly Anthroposophy* which preceded the earthly one. For the teachings given by Michael were then preparing what is now to become Anthroposophy on earth.' (GA 237, 28 July 1924)

In a more direct manner—there in mantric form—this 'heavenly Anthroposophy' is mentioned in the microcosmic parts of the Foundation Stone Meditation in words that bring to expression the activity of the three hierarchies; an activity through which the Cosmic Intelligence could gradually take hold of *all three systems of man*: The limb system during the Lemurian Epoch, the heart and lung system during the Atlantean Epoch, and beginning with the events in the fifteenth century the system of head and nerves. For the human limbs unfold their activity in that realm in which only the highest first beings of the hierarchy can imprint the spirit inasmuch as they turn the spiritual impulses 'into the creative element of the physical'. (ibid) This is why it says in the medi-tation concerning the limbs that they bear man 'through the world of Space / into the *ocean-being of the Spirit*', which means into the ocean of the highest spirituality of the Seraphim, Cherubim, and Thrones who later are referred to by name in the same segment of the meditation. The perception of their presence and activity in the limb system is, however, laid open to man only when, through personal efforts, one is capable of extending one's faculty of recollection ('Practise spirit-recollection') to that primordial condition where one's 'own I' still 'comes into being' in the womb of 'the I of God' or 'God's I'. Furthermore it says concerning the beat of heart and lung that it 'leads' a human being 'through the rhythmic tides of Time into the feeling' of its 'own Soul-being'. Now, the source of all rhythms in our cosmos is the Sun with all the spirits of the Second Hierarchy who exist there. This is why Rudolf Steiner pointed out that the Christ, descending as He did from the Sun, likewise brought along the true impulse of the age to Earth; an impulse that is capable of overcoming the soul-deadening forces of space, thus returning to man his original 'soul-being': 'Then came the Christ and once again brought human beings that which is of time. Inasmuch as the human heart, human soul, and human spirit unite with the Christ they attain once more to the stream of time from eternity to eternity.' (GA 236, 4 June 1924) Yet in addition to what the Christ brought in this way objectively to Earth, the human being today is moreover supposed to attain his own individual relationship. But this can come about only when, through intensive meditative work, an individual finds access to the Christ Being ('Practise spirit-pondering') in the sense of the meditation's words concerning the union of man's 'own I' with the 'I of the world'.

Finally it says in the meditation concerning the system of head and nerves that this system opens to man 'the Thoughts of Worlds' from the 'ground of the Eternal'. This however can come about only when a human being out of freedom and in full consciousness carries back into the spiritual world the Cosmic Intelligence ('Thoughts of Worlds' by the hierarchies) which has become human in man's head system. By so doing a person can moreover rise up to what Rudolf Steiner calls 'intellectually becoming clairvoyant'. (GA 130, 18 November 1911) Then man's thinking too becomes an organ of perception for events and entities in the spiritual world ('Practise . . .'). And 'on the fact that a person's ideas not only remain in a thinking mode but in thinking become capable of "seeing"—on this depends immeasurably much'. (GA 26, p. 68) For in this way man learns consciously to perceive the 'World-Being's Light' that proceeds out of the 'eternal aims of Gods' in the supersensible world.

Now, in the macrocosmic segments of the meditation, we have the description of the participation of all nine hierarchies in the cosmic event of the fifteenth century. First the Seraphim, Cherubim, and Thrones are addressed: 'Let there ring out from the Heights / what in the Depths is echoed.' This activity, through which they are able to inscribe the spiritual substance of the Sun sphere into the human being on Earth, corresponds exactly to the essential part they play in that cosmic event. Furthermore, it says in the meditation about the Kyriotetes, Dynamis, and

Exusiai who work on the Sun: 'Let there be fired from the East / what through the West is formed.' Here the reference is to the 'forming' of a specific substance in the Sun sphere (from East to West), the same substance which is then imprinted into the human being through the spirits of the First Hierarchy. Finally, of the spirits of the Third Hierarchy (the Archai, Archangeloi, and Angeloi) it says that they remain in continual prayer. This in turn is coined in the words: 'Let there be prayed in the Depths / what from the Heights is answered.' These lines contain the totality of hope entertained by the spirits of the Third Hierarchy who beheld the cosmic thunderstorm from out of the Michael School. It is the hope that, with their help, human beings who have received the 'heavenly Anthroposophy' might be in a position, once they have gone back to Earth, to return the Cosmic Intelligence (the Cosmic Intelligence that has been individualized in their heads) to the gods of the cosmos. Such human beings will moreover arise in full freedom to conscious co-operation with the spiritual hierarchies, something for which instruction in the supersensible school of Michael intended to prepare them.

As we saw, the main role during the inception of the 'cosmic thunderstorm' is played by the spirits of the First Hierarchy whose effects reach from the spiritual heights all the way to the worlds' depths, meaning to the material world itself, inasmuch as they imbue it with the loftiest spirituality.[29] The transformation of man's being undertaken by them at the transition to the consciousness soul was a necessary prerequisite for the then following celestial and quite specifically earthly Anthroposophy. For owing to this change human nature became capable of receiving anthroposophical thoughts on earth. To bring about such a transformation extending even to the physical sensory world was something that only the highest and mightiest First Hierarchy was able to do. (GA 26, Leading Thought 71) Thus the first segment of the meditation is above all connected with the activity where mention is made of the working of this hierarchy in the cosmos.

The second part of the meditation is connected with the Second Hierarchy, as well as the first and most important stage of the divine preparation for Anthroposophy. This stage was described above as the supersensible Michael School that had its location in the Sun sphere, the abode of the Second Hierarchy. The second segment of the meditation contains the actual nature of this school's teaching in briefest form. Here, Michael presents the development of the ancient pre-Christian Mysteries on earth to the spirit-eyes of human souls, and hierarchical entities connected with him, but particularly those Mysteries that were linked with the secrets of the various planets of our solar system. But from the

very beginning of those Mysteries' existence, the most important ones
stood out, those Mysteries of Earth evolution connected with the Sun
secret. For the Sun is the location where the cosmic Christ sojourns. (See
GA 240, 20 July 1924) In the course of his instructions Michael thereafter
laid the groundwork to what later was to become 'the new Christianity'
(GA 240, 18 July 1924) in Anthroposophy on earth. This Anthroposophy
is the first to be in a position, with the help of the Michaelic Intelligence
that has descended to man, to grasp the whole cosmic-telluric significance
of Christ's arrival on the Earth and the Mystery of Golgotha. In the lines
of the second part of the meditation, we find a reference to this central
substance of the supersensible Michael School:

> For the Christ-Will in the encircling Round holds sway,
> In the Rhythms of Worlds, blessing the soul.
> Kyriotetes, Dynamis, Exusiai!
> Let there be fired from the East
> What through the West is formed,
> Speaking:
> In Christo morimur.
> (In Christ, Death becomes Life.)

Here the last two lines point to the main task of the Sun Mystery of all
ages. For in them was celebrated—although to start with merely in
symbolic-prophetic form—the process of death and resurrection by
borrowing from the year's spiritual-natural course. Particularly in the
Mysteries that were linked with the fate of Baldur, Adonis or Osiris, we
have Mysteries in which initiates were still preparing in pre-Christian
times for their next task, namely to bring down out of the spiritual world,
the Second Hierarchy's sphere of activity, the spiritual impulses (East)
which can then be realized on earth (West). The fulfilment of this task
became possible in full measure, and then not merely for initiates but for
all human beings through the death and resurrection of the Christ.

The movement from East to West together with the Sun described in
this segment of the meditation furthermore points to the spiritual-
geographic placement of the Mysteries during the Fifth Post-Atlantean
Epoch—from the ancient Indian period, the ancient Persian to the
Egyptian-Assyrian-Chaldean, then to the Greco-Latin and on to our
present fifth one. And through all the post-Atlantean Mysteries of the pre-
Christian time, the Christ Being worked *out of the Sun sphere*, 'bestowing
grace' upon human souls in the course of the cosmic and historical
evolution of earth humanity. Thus the holy Rishis in ancient India

revered the Christ under the name Vishva Karman; Zarathustra called Him Ahura Mazda; the Egyptians worshipped Him under the name Osiris; the Greeks under the name Apollo.[30] But after the Christ had passed through the death on Golgotha during the fourth post-Atlantean period (In Christo morimur—In Christ, Death becomes Life), He works as the new Spirit of the Earth in its spiritual encircling round out of the forces of His *will*, forces that at the Turning-point of Time had caused the resurrection of His physical body: 'For the Christ-Will holds sway in the *encircling Round* of the Earth. Through the resurrection the Christ once again restores the physical body of man to its original form, the way it was created on Ancient Saturn by the Spirits of Will (the Thrones).' (See GA 131, 11 October 1911) Since the substance that these spirits sacrificed for its coming about was *will*-substance, there exists a direct connection between the Mystery of the death and resurrection of the Christ and the working of His will.

Since the Mystery of Golgotha this 'Christ-Will' holds sway in all spiritual-physical processes which Rudolf Steiner has described in the lectures on the cycle of the year as processes of the earth's breathing and its four great festivals. (See GA 223 and 229) During the cultic Foundation Stone Laying, Rudolf Steiner pointed directly to this activity of the Christ by saying: '... the Christ force that works everywhere in the *encircling round*, that weaves with the air's currents, circling around the Earth ...' (GA 260, 25 December 1923). What will eventually form the centre of the Christian Mysteries of the future—namely the experience of the Christ who as leader of the whole evolution of mankind works 'in the Rhythms of Worlds, blessing the Soul', but now (in contrast to the ancient Mysteries) not out of the far-distant Sun sphere but out of the new Spirit of the earth, directly into the earth's supersensible encircling round—all of this is contained in these few lines of the meditation and represents the basis of the 'new Christianity' that Michael prepared in his supersensible school.

The next stage of the celestial preparation of Anthroposophy is formed by the so-called 'heavenly cultus' at the transition from the eighteenth to the nineteenth century in the spiritual region adjacent to the Earth, meaning in the sphere of activity of the Third Hierarchy, which therefore has the most direct relationship to this cultus. In it, 'what the Michael-disciples had learned in that supersensible school of instruction was developed in mighty Imaginative pictures'. (GA 237, 28 July 1924) 'With mighty actual Imaginations there was presented what is to be established again in a spiritual form *in the new Christianity of the twentieth century*.' (GA 240, 19 July 1924) This 'new Christianity in the twentieth century' is

Anthroposophy. What the disciples of Michael had received in the supersensible school to a greater extent into their spiritual forces of insight was inscribed in the course of the supersensible cultus into their individual will as the Imaginative expression of the 'eternal aims of Gods' whose representative is Michael in regard to humanity. Following the incarnation of these souls on earth, the substance of this cultus could then turn into a living fount of Inspirations in them that now made it possible for these souls to work also in the physical world in the sense of these aims. In unusually concentrated form the lines of the third segment of the Foundation Stone Meditation point to this:

> Where the eternal aims of Gods
> World-Being's Light
> On thine own I
> Bestow.

With the help of the supersensible cultus the 'eternal aims of Gods', which concern the whole cosmic-earthly evolution of humanity,[31] could enter in the form of the 'World-Being's Light' of the (Imaginative) wisdom into the individual consciousness of a number of human souls who then discovered Anthroposophy on earth as an earthly expression of these aims; souls who were dedicated in full devotion to this Anthroposophy. In this sense the last two lines of the microcosmic part of the meditation's third segment refer to the earthly insight of Anthroposophy:

> And thou wilt truly *think*
> From the ground of the Spirit of Man.

It is Anthroposophy, the timely science *of the Spirit,* that leads us today to such 'true thinking'; a thinking extending even to the 'ground of the Spirit of Man' which is referred to below in the macrocosmic segment of the meditation's third part. In the twentieth century, the *'new Christianity'* was established out of this Spirit, a Christianity that owing to this Spirit's presence links up directly with the Mystery of Golgotha and therefore cannot be distorted by any subsequent additions, human imperfections, and historical traditions. This is that *cosmic Christianity of the future* of which mention is made in the fourth and final part of the Foundation Stone Meditation.[32]

Although Rudolf Steiner spoke merely of a presence of the 'elemental spirits' in Michael's Sun-school, there is no doubt that they furthermore participated in this school's continuation in the Imaginative cultus, especially because this school took its course in the spiritual world adjacent to Earth (the Moon sphere), meaning in their particular habitat.[33] And when we note that while they participated in the Michael School, they moreover were witnesses of the cosmic thunderstorm that was caused by beings of the First Hierarchy, then the reference to them (at the end of all three macrocosmic segments of the meditation) can gain full significance for us. For it is the desire of these elemental spirits that human souls, who were instructed in the supersensible school of Michael, would hear the call of the Time Spirit and might dedicate themselves to the fulfilment of his tasks. Altogether, the connection of the heavenly-earthly development of Anthroposophy with the entire content of the Foundation Stone Meditation can be summed up as follows:

Part 1	—	*1st Hierarchy and elemental spirits*	— The 'cosmic thunderstorm' as macrocosmic prerequisite of the celestial preparation of Anthroposophy (Beginning of fifteenth century)
Part 2	—	*2nd Hierarchy and elemental spirits*	— Celestial preparation of Anthroposophy in the supersensible Michael School in the Sun's domain (Fifteenth to eighteenth century)
Part 3	—	*3rd Hierarchy and elemental spirits*	— Celestial preparation of Anthroposophy in the supersensible cultus in the spiritual world adjacent to the earth (Eighteenth to nineteenth century)
Part 4	—	*Earthly humans*	— Establishment of Anthroposophy in the twentieth century and development of a new Christianity from it.

5. The Foundation Stone Meditation and the Forming of Human Karma

A further aspect that links the Foundation Stone Meditation with the world of the hierarchies concerns their participation in the forming of human karma. Rudolf Steiner unveiled this secret of karma in full measure only *after* the Christmas Conference in the karma lectures of the year 1924. The Christmas Conference itself chiefly had two consequences, the founding of the Michael School on earth as the direct continuation of the celestial development of Anthroposophy and the unveiling of the karma Mysteries as an immediate result of the fact that beginning from the twentieth century the Christ has become the Lord of Karma.

Concerning the participation of all nine hierarchies in the developmental process of human karma Rudolf Steiner said: 'This human karma is, after all, initially a background, a curtain; it is like a veil. If we look behind this veil we see the weaving, working, influencing, and doing of the Archai, Archangeloi, Angeloi; Kyriotetes, Dynamis, Exusiai; Seraphim, Cherubim, Thrones.' (GA 239, 8 June 1924)

Now, according to the Foundation Stone Meditation, each of these three hierarchies are guided in their cosmic activity by different principles or primal archetypes which, for the First Hierarchy, go back to the Father-God; for the Second Hierarchy to the Son-God, the Christ; for the Third to the Spirit-God or the Holy Spirit. This results in a quite different participation in the forming of cosmic and human karma.

Thus in the karma sphere, the spirits of the highest hierarchy, the Seraphim, Cherubim, and Thrones represent the forces of the Father-God, forces that are connected with the will of world-justice in the universe. This is moreover why their participation in the shaping of karma brings it about that its laws work with the force of nature or cosmic necessity. As an example, if a person is destined by his karma to encounter another person on earth, even if that one was born in New Zealand and he himself in Paris or Berlin, this notwithstanding, his life will take its course from birth in such a way that this encounter will absolutely occur at the very location and time as demanded by the necessity of their joint karma. Not only the external circumstances but likewise the activity of muscles and limbs will be such that the person in question, whether he wants to or not, will at the specific moment be at the very bus stop where he cannot but meet the other person who is karmically connected to him, even if the possibility of this happening amounts to seconds and from the standpoint of the theory of probability is equal to zero. This deepest level of karma resting in the depths of the spiritual-physical human being is under normal conditions inaccessible to day-consciousness. Only an initiate can gain entry into the activity-sphere of these karma forces, and from the highest level of initiation at that, the stage of Intuition.[34] In the Foundation Stone Meditation the following lines of its first segment indicate such a 'karma of necessity':

> For the Father-Spirit of the Heights holds sway,
> In Depths of Worlds, begetting Being.
> Seraphim, Cherubim, Thrones,
> Let there ring out from the Heights,
> What in the Depths is echoed.

These words state that this level of karma belongs among the facts of human *existence* and cannot be changed through any outward powers any more than the laws of nature can be altered by the wishes of human beings.[35]

Through the actions of the beings of the First Hierarchy, the Will of the Father in the heights inevitably turns into existence in the world's depths, meaning this Will becomes reality extending even to Earth's physical matter. The Creator-Word spoken by the spirits of the First Hierarchy rings out in the world's depths as a mighty *echo* and forms the totality of mankind's earthly destiny. One can therefore say that the whole of terrestrial destiny is a kind of 'echo' of the First Hierarchy's activity in the region of world karma.

When we view this process not from the standpoint of the higher hierarchies but from that of the human being we can characterize it best in the words of the meditation:

> Thine own I
> Comes to being
> Within the I of God.

In the realization-process of this karma of the depths the human ego takes on being even to this day in the 'I' of God, just as it comes to expression in the words of the Lord's Prayer. 'Thy will be done, as in heaven so also on earth,' (Mt.6, 9–13), meaning, as in the heights of the world [universe] so in its depths. This is why the only proper mental

attitude in regard to this part of karma is that 'recollection' of the forces of
the Father-God is practised in it according to the words by the Christ:
'But not my will, but thy will be done.' (Lk. 22, 42) As a result of such an
attitude regarding one's own karma the human soul can attain to the truth
based on its own experience that the human 'I' in its own deepest essence
cannot be separated from God. And then it will feel the whole significance of the meditation's words: 'From God, mankind has being.'

★

The entities of the Second Hierarchy, the Kyriotetes, Dynamis, and
Exusiai, work completely differently in the sphere of karma. As we have
seen, their loftiest archetype or ideal is the creative activity of the Son-
God or the Word (Logos) in the world. This is why it is their task to form
a quite different aspect of karma, namely that karma which does not work
in human life with nature's necessity but in such a way that a person is
able, under certain circumstances and within specific limitations, to
recognize and transform it. Beginning in our age, completely new possibilities are opening up in this direction for human beings. For the main
consequence of the Christ's return in etheric form, which had its
beginning in the thirties of the twentieth century, is that He became Lord
of Karma at the end of that century. Rudolf Steiner indicated this in
prophetic terms: 'Towards the end of the twentieth century yet another
important event shall occur ... This event will have as fundamental a
significance for the development of humanity as had the Event of
Palestine at the beginning of our Christian era.' (GA 131, 7 October
1911) The only difference is that this time it shall not take its course on the
physical plane but in the supersensible world closest to earth. 'What kind
of event is that? This event is none other than that in regard to human
evolution a certain office in the universe passes over to the Christ—is
handed over in a more enhanced sense than had been the case until now.
In fact, occult clairvoyant research teaches us that in our age the important
event that occurs is Christ's becoming the Lord of Karma for humanity's
development.' (ibid.)

In another lecture Rudolf Steiner referred in almost biblical terms to
this central event of our time: 'In truth this is something that begins in the
twentieth century and continues on to the end of the Earth. Judgement
starts in our twentieth century, meaning the ordering of karma.' (GA 130,
2 December 1911) And he described the Christ's working as Lord of
Karma in the following manner: 'To fit our karmic compensation into
general earthly karma (the general progress of mankind) will in the future
be the task of the Christ.' (GA 131, 14 October 1911) Now this parti-

cipation of the Christ in the forming of humanity's karma is one side of this process. The other is to be the ever increasing participation of human beings themselves in that process. For only in this way can the fundamental nature of today's era of the consciousness soul be maintained, a process that is supposed to lead to the highest possible development of a free and independent human 'I'. Rudolf Steiner pointed to this aspect of the transformation of karma, saying: 'That our karmic account shall be so balanced in the future, meaning it be placed into a world-order in such a way, that in future time (*once we have found the path to the Christ*) the form of our karmic compensation can bring about the greatest possible benefit to humans for the rest of Earth evolution: This shall be the concern of Him who, beginning in our time, shall be the Lord of Karma. It will be the concern of the Christ!' (GA 130, 2 December 1911)

'Once we have found the path to the Christ', this is in truth decisive in the whole process. The following words of the Foundation Stone Meditation indicate this aspect:

> Do thine own I
> Unite
> Unto the I of the World.

For today it depends purely on a person's free will whether he wants to find the Christ in order to unite his own I with His cosmic I in the sense of the Pauline words: 'Not I but the Christ in me', or whether he excludes this possibility and is forced to await his next incarnation to catch up with what he has left undone, but then under much less favourable conditions. Thus we have to say: Whether the Lord of Karma is unveiled to a person as the divine archetype of his I and the ultimate ideal of the whole of Earth evolution, or whether 'the Lord of Karma appears like a terrifying punishment' (GA 131, 14 October 1911) will depend on that person himself as well as on his viewpoint regarding modern spiritual science. For it is spiritual science that brings to human beings today the necessary insight of the Christ and the events just described: 'The purpose of disseminating the anthroposophical world view in our age is that man can be prepared on the physical plane ... or on higher planes [meaning, after death] to be capable of perceiving the Christ Event.' (ibid) 'Beholding the Christ Event does not depend on whether we are incarnated in a physical body, but on the preparation for it.' (ibid)

In this way two karma elements are connected in the Christ's new karmic working: on the one side the *necessity* to equalize karma in accordance with universal justice, and on the other side the *freedom* to choose the direction of its realization. For one and the same karmic activity can be pursued in numerous ways: By striving only for one's own development, or the greatest possible benefit of a specific group of people, or a whole nation, or even the whole of mankind. We can say: If bringing karma into order takes place by means of the Christ's guidance so that the balancing required here promotes the greatest possible benefit of all humanity, then this has a 'blessing' effect on man individually.

The second part of the meditation speaks in the following lines about this activity of the Christ in the realm of karma which has a 'blessing' effect on the human soul:

> For the Christ-Will in the encircling Round holds sway
> In the Rhythms of Worlds, blessing the Soul.

In this activity it is above all the spirits of the Second Hierarchy, the Sun hierarchy, who help the Christ realize His impulses in humanity. Continuing on, it says of this in the meditation:

> Kyriotetes, Dynamis, Exusiai,
> Let there be fired from the East
> What through the West is formed.

Here we have an indication that is connected with the fact that the Christ becomes Lord of Karma to do with all of Earth evolution, an indication of the metamorphosis which, beginning in our time, will be undergone by human conscience. In the lecture of 2 May 1910 Rudolf Steiner gave a detailed description of the origin and development of the impulse of conscience viewed from a spiritual scientific standpoint. The special aspect of this impulse is its connection with the appearance of the Christ on Earth: 'Thus we see how on Earth, over in the East, love [the Christ] emerges, and here in the West conscience. These are two things that belong together: how the Christ appears in the East, and how in the West conscience awakens so as to receive the Christ as conscience. In this simultaneous emergence of the fact and comprehension of the Christ Event, and the preparation of these two aspects at various points on Earth, we see an infinite wisdom holding sway that is present in evolution.' (GA 116, 2 May 1910)

It is to this connection of the impulse of conscience with the Christ Impulse in its spiritual–geographic–reciprocal relationship of East–West, that the above-quoted words in the Foundation Stone Meditation point. At the same time these words characterize the activity of the beings of the

Second Hierarchy. Here mention is first made of the all-warming (kindling) arising of the Spirit Sun *in the East* due to the Christ's coming down to Earth and then of the form which His activity receives *in the West* by means of the fact that there the conscience awakens as an organ of perception of the Christ Being.[36] For only with the help of conscience as the organ of Christ perception can a human being grasp the meaning of the most important deed of the Christ on Earth, the Mystery of Golgotha as the central event of the whole of Earth evolution: 'In Christ Death becomes Life.'

As the result of the fact that the Christ becomes Lord of Karma, the impulse of conscience will undergo a major change in the course of the next three thousand years within humanity's evolution. From a more or less unclear inner voice it will be transformed into clairvoyant perception of actions which human beings will have to carry out in the future in order to balance their karma in the direction of the greatest possible good for all mankind. Rudolf Steiner described this future effect of the forces of conscience in the following way: 'Beginning in our time, from the middle of our century and continuing on through the next few thousand years, more and more human beings will have the following experience: Persons will have done this or that. They will *ponder* it. They will have to look up from what they have done—and something like a dream image will arise before them ... The time is beginning when, the instant they have done a deed, they will have a presentiment, even a clear picture, a feeling about what the karmic compensation of this deed will be ... These will be mighty incentives for man's morality. These incentives will signify something quite different from what the preparation for these incentives has been, namely the voice of conscience.' (GA 131, 14 October 1911)

Yet in order to arrive initially at an undefined presentiment and then at a more distinct feeling and finally a concrete picture of the karmic consequences of actions, it is necessary to 'practise Spirit-pondering' of one's own actions and make the effort to comprehend them from the standpoint of how modern spiritual science speaks about the working of the law of karma. All this is indicated by the second part of the Foundation Stone Meditation. The first part describes the working of the Father-God's forces through the spirits of the First Hierarchy, where in the realm of karma unalterable *being* is 'begotten' by the 'World-Creator-being' that 'wields' throughout the world all the way to earthly matter. The second part points to the nature of the 'Deeds of the World's Becoming' in which the Creator-Being of the Son (of the Word of Worlds) is revealed. Working through the spirits of the Second Hierarchy who sojourn in the Sun sphere, the greatest fountainhead of all creative rhythms of the cosmic structure, He weaves together unchangeable and changeable karma by means of the 'surging Deeds of the World's Becoming'.

The first two lines of the macrocosmic segment of the meditation's second part refer even more clearly to this working of the Christ where direct mention is made of the Christ-Will that bestows blessing on souls *in the Rhythms of Worlds*. From the standpoint of forming human karma, it is the goal of these 'world-rhythms' to bring about the greatest harmony or 'blessing-bestowing' union of the unalterable parts of karma coming from the Father's sphere with those parts that can and must be altered so that their later actualization, by being lived out in life, might serve the greatest possible benefit of humanity.

If we term karma that comes from the sphere of the Father the karma of necessity, the karma that is formed in the sphere of the Son is best described as transformed karma or the karma of metamorphosis. In the formative process of the latter the present working of the Christ as Lord of Karma finds its most perfect expression. The second part of the Foundation Stone Meditation indicates this working in mantric form.

★

A further aspect of the forming of human karma is depicted in the third part of the meditation. Here we have a characterization of the third karma aspect that refers to the future. The working of the Holy Spirit in Earth evolution will actualize this future aspect through the beings of the Third Hierarchy, the Archai, Archangeloi, and Angeloi.

The forming of new karma, which is referred to in the third part of the Foundation Stone Meditation and which is required so that mankind might become the tenth hierarchy, is something that humans are supposed to carry out based on conscious co-operation with the entities of the Third Hierarchy. This co-operation will be possible for them through the experience of the Etheric Christ. Only when we pay heed to this can we truly understand the nature of forming future karma. For while the new conscious clairvoyance that is connected with the Second Coming of the Christ develops among human beings, in the next three millennia people will gradually learn to become cognisant of the entities of the *Third* Hierarchy in the surroundings of the Christ. Cognition of them will begin simultaneously with the beholding of images of future actions that will be compensation for past deeds. 'But something else will come about', is how Rudolf Steiner described it. 'Human beings will know: I am not alone; everywhere around me live spiritual beings who have a connection with me. And humans will learn to have dealings with these beings, will learn to live with them.' (GA 131, 14 October 1911)

This new cognitive faculty for the beings of the Third Hierarchy, which must be developed during the time that begins now and will extend to the middle of the sixth cultural period, was referred to by Rudolf Steiner in another lecture. There he particularly emphasized the decisive importance of this faculty for the social life of human beings. Moreover he described how this faculty will gradually lead to the possibility 'of sensing, of grasping through an encounter with another person, his or her relationship to the Third Hierarchy; to the Archai, Archangeloi, Angeloi'. (GA 185, 26 October 1918) For since the Mystery of Golgotha the Christ works through the ranks of the higher hierarchies in quite a new form. He inspires our fifth post-Atlantean period through the Angeloi and causes the third Egypto-Chaldean period to reawaken again, but now in Christian form. Through the Archangeloi ministering to Him, He will work in such a way in the sixth cultural period that the spirit-substance of the second ancient Persian period can take on life. Finally in the seventh cultural period, the re-arising of the first ancient Indian cultural period inaugurated by the seven holy Rishis will come to pass. It will be the age when, in the midst of the 'War of All Against All' along with the decline of earthly civilization, the 'Christ-Sun' will shine forth with special force and bequeath the spiritual strength to human beings, something that is needed to make the transition to the new great spiritual epoch (the Sixth Epoch).

Rudolf Steiner indicated these future perspectives in lectures of the year 1911 and even then used the term 'Christ-Sun,' an expression through which he linked the development depicted there with the Foundation Stone Meditation given twelve years later: 'The Holy Rishis will once again arise in the radiance of the *Christ-Sun* in the seventh cultural period of post-Atlantean humanity.' (GA 129, 21 August 1911) And Rudolf Steiner continued: 'Thus we see that for the beings of these *four* hierarchies, for the human beings but likewise for the Angels, the Archangels, and the Archai, the Mystery of Golgotha (the Christ Event) in all regards signifies the utmost that we can speak about in our cosmic evolution as humans.' (ibid.) Owing to this connection between earthly humans and the beings of the Third Hierarchy with the Mystery of Golgotha, and the necessity resulting from this of working together, it will furthermore become possible to bring to realization what the third part of the Foundation Stone Meditation refers to and will then cause the shining forth of the 'Christ-Sun' in Earth evolution (fourth part).

In accordance with the microcosmic segments of the Foundation Stone Meditation we therefore have three sorts of karma:

Part 1: 'And thou wilt truly live' — Karma of the past as spiritual basis of
                                          our present existence[37]

Part 2: 'And thou wilt truly feel' — Image of actions that must be carried
                                          out so as to compensate for past karma

Part 3: 'And thou wilt truly   — Conscious participation of man in
         think'   forming new karma

And in accordance with the macrocosmic parts we can say:

Part 1: Father   — *Karma of necessity* (result of past actions)

Part 2: Son   — *Karma of metamorphosis* (present matters
                                          as synthesis of those of past and future)

Part 3: Holy Spirit   — *Karma of the future* (creation of new
                                          karma).

★

From all this it becomes evident that the basis for forming new karma is
not merely the beholding and the subsequent realizing of actions which
are necessary for compensating *past* karma, but likewise the perception
and actualization of what the third part of the Foundation Stone Meditation represents with the words:

> Practise *spirit-vision*
> In quietness of Thought
> Where the eternal aims of Gods
> World–Being's Light
> On thine own I
> Bestow
> For thy free Willing.

Here it is no longer just the transformation of past but creation of *new
karma* that we are supposed to form out of freedom together with the
beings of the Third Hierarchy; beings who are mentioned by name in the
third part of the meditation:

> Archai, Archangeloi, Angeloi,
> Let there be prayed in the Depths
> What from the Heights is answered.

As we behold activity such as that of the beings of the Third Hierarchy,
we should also learn to carry it out. In the depths of Earth where, from the

standpoint of the spiritual world, our earthly evolution takes place, we are to accomplish what then can be received in the heights of the divine-spiritual hierarchies as a transformation and extension of their own experiences. For that, man has to learn consciously to perceive the 'World-Being's Light,' the Light which in the spiritual worlds proceeds from 'the eternal aims of Gods' and brings to human beings the knowledge of these aims.

One form of this 'World-Being's Light' is the so-called 'astral light', bearer of the wisdom of the divine-spiritual hierarchies. From it, man is supposed to learn to receive the motivation for his creative deeds on earth, deeds that only he can accomplish in their purely human form. The spiritual fruits of these deeds on the other hand, can then be received by the spiritual world so that, as cosmic deeds, that world can continue working in them. This is therefore a matter of the spiritual world passing through man and thereby being able to raise itself to a new level of development. For as to its own evolution, the spiritual world depends on the human being.[38] Rudolf Steiner described this process in the following manner: 'He (the spirit disciple) knows that the supersensible existed first and that all sensory things developed out of the supersensory ... But this previous supersensible world needed the passage through the sensory. Its further development would not have been possible without this passage. Only when in the sensory kingdom beings with corresponding faculties will have developed, can the supersensible realm continue onward once again, and these beings are the human beings.' (GA 10, p. 206/207)

The metamorphosis of the cosmic forces that to begin with become human forces, but afterwards turn into cosmic forces again in a completely metamorphosed form, is connected with Michael's activity in the spiritual worlds.[39] 'When out of his freedom and motivated through the reading in the astral light man consciously or unconsciously does one thing or another, then Michael bears this human deed out into the cosmos so that it turns into cosmic deed.' (GA 233a, 13 January 1924)

The spirits of the Third Hierarchy, however, are only ready to allow this astral light (revealing the lofty aims of the gods) to stream into man when he has started to become a free being on Earth and then turns his freedom towards conscious perception of the spiritual world. This means when man begins to lift Michael's cosmic intelligence, that has become earthly, back into the Archangel's domain. Only then will the perception of these aims become accessible to human beings, and along with them the possibility to work together with the gods on the actualization of these aims, something that signifies the beginning of the fashioning of an entirely new karma.

We might now ask: How can a human being participate even now in such a process when in our age conscious reading in the astral light is possible only for an initiate? An answer is given through the existence of spiritual science or Anthroposophy. For its content, encompassed by the more than 350 volumes of the complete edition of Rudolf Steiner's work, is the result of his spiritual research that unlocked for him, reading in the astral light, the secrets of the cosmos he then presented in the form of thoughts comprehensible today to every human being. It follows from this that anyone who takes in the thoughts of spiritual science does even now read in the astral light, even if this reading initially occurs merely in the *form of thoughts*.[39a] Nevertheless, by means of the comprehension of man and world thus gained, this is the beginning of the once Michaelic cosmic intelligence being carried upwards again into the kingdom of Michael.

This is why the above-quoted words (namely that Michael admits the deeds of humans, which were motivated by reading in the astral light, into the spirit cosmos where they turn into cosmic deeds) also relate in full measure to those deeds that were inspired by *thoughtful reading* in the astral light. For the *study* of the communications of spiritual science which is the first stage of the modern path of initiation (see GA 13) is *such a reading*. Put differently, what we carry out today on the basis of a comprehension of the spiritual world turns into *cosmic deeds* through the activity of Michael; deeds that in the spiritual world serve the founding of the new cosmos of which Rudolf Steiner speaks at the end of his book, *Occult Science, an Outline*.

★

Here another question needs an answer: What kind of 'eternal aims of Gods' are referred to in the third part of the Foundation Stone Meditation? Rudolf Steiner gives an answer in a lecture on 10 April 1914. There he speaks of what he calls the 'religion of the gods' in the spiritual world, something that is the *highest* goal of their creative activity. 'As the aim of their creation, the gods have in mind the ideal of the human being. It is that human ideal which certainly is not expressed in the way physical man is now, but the way the most sublime soul-spiritual life could come to expression in the perfectly developed potentials of this physical human being.' (GA 153, 10 April 1914) Here the unfolding of the soul-spiritual principles in man's physical foundations is mentioned, meaning the highest development of that threefoldness about which it says in the Foundation Stone Meditation:

Then in the All-World-Being of Man Thou wilt truly live.	*Perfect Body*
Then 'mid the weaving of the Soul of Man Thou wilt truly feel.	*Perfect Soul*
Then from the ground of the Spirit of Man Thou wilt truly think.	*Perfect Spirit*

And then Rudolf Steiner continues: 'As the *goal*, as a highest ideal, as the religion of Divinity, the gods have in mind an image of humanity. As though on the distant shore of divine existence, there hovers before the gods the *temple* which, as the most sublime artistic accomplishment by gods, presents the replica of divine existence in the image of man.' Thus man himself is the highest aim of the gods as a temple not created by human hands, a temple in which one day the Holy Spirit—referred to by the third part of the meditation—will be able to dwell. The Apostle Paul likewise spoke of this ideal when he called the human body the temple of the Holy Spirit: 'Do you not know that you are a temple of God and that the Spirit of God would dwell in you?' (1 Cor 3, 16 JM) And further down in the same epistle: 'Do you not know that your body is a temple of the indwelling Holy Spirit in you? You have received it from God: you do not belong to yourselves.' (6, 19 JM)

In this sense, seen as a whole, the Foundation Stone Meditation is the timely path to the supersensible Temple of the New Mysteries[40] in which a person can consciously have interchange through the mediation of the Holy Spirit with the higher hierarchies and the 'chosen living dead'.[41] The possibility for this was given along with the Mystery of Golgotha in the Mystery of the Resurrection of the Christ of which He Himself stated prophetically: 'Demolish this temple, and in three days I will raise it up anew.' (Jn 2, 19) In this central deed by the Christ we have an archetype of what will in the future be actualized as the highest ideal of the gods' religion when earthly humanity shall ultimately be the hierarchy of freedom and love, and will stream into the hierarchical totality of our cosmos. But for this actually to occur it is necessary even beginning in our age, meaning from the time that the Christ is becoming Lord of Karma, to start with the forming of the *new karma* under His guidance. This is the karma of the joint working of men and the gods, of mankind and the spiritual entities, initially the Third Hierarchy and later the higher ones.

That such activity is only possible in our time as a result of the events around the Turning-point of Time, is attested to in the fourth and last part of the Foundation Stone Meditation. Here the three kinds of karma are mentioned, namely, in a spiritual-historical context. The words that refer to the two main streams of Mystery development, the northern and the southern one (represented at the Turning-point of Time by the Shepherds and the Kings in the East), point to the karma of the *past* or the karma of the pre-Christian Mysteries where the law of iron necessity still prevailed:[42]

> At the Turning-point of Time
> The Spirit-Light of the World
> Entered the stream of Earthly Being.
> Darkness of Night
> Had held its sway;
> Day-radiant Light
> Poured into the souls of men:
> Light
> That gives warmth
> So simple Shepherds' Hearts;
> Light
> That enlightens
> The wise Heads of Kings.

Here we deal with events on earth not brought about by the will of men but by the higher will of cosmic guidance.

Careful consideration of the above-quoted lines of the meditation shows that the last six lines—in contrast to the first seven—are not in the past but the present tense. This results in a sort of transition from the karma of the past (or the karma of necessity) to the karma of the present on which we can consciously work. This is also why the text of part IV (in the eurythmic performance of the Foundation Stone Meditation) is presented in turn by two groups of eurythmists. The second starts its movements with the word 'light' (eighth line).[42a]

Further on, in the second part, the karma of the *present* is mentioned, meaning the present activity of the 'Christ-Sun' in Earth existence, or the *possibility*—since today humanity has entered the age of freedom—that human hearts and human heads may receive the Christ-Sun's light today as the indispensable prerequisite for their work of transforming the karma of the past into karma of the future.

> O Light Divine,
> O Sun of Christ!
> Warm Thou

Our Hearts;
Enlighten Thou
Our Heads.

The light of the Christ-Sun that warms our hearts leads to the awakening of an attribute of the tenth hierarchy, namely to *love*, that connects man to the whole hierarchical cosmos. The light that illuminates our heads through world-wisdom helps us attain the other faculty of the tenth hierarchy, namely full inner *freedom* sustained on comprehension of cosmic relationships (in the perspective of the astral light and the reading in it), and goes into action proceeding from these relationships.

Finally, the third and last segment of the fourth part indicates the future karma of humanity, the karma of *absolute good*:

That good may become
What from our Hearts we would found
And from our Heads direct
With single purpose.

Here the shaping of that karma is referred to proceeding from which in due time humans will be able to accomplish two things. First, as the tenth hierarchy, they will themselves be able to 'create' a 'new cosmos' of freedom and love in the universe (the cosmos that Rudolf Steiner spoke of at the end of the book, *Occult Science, An Outline*, (GA 13); secondly, they will be capable of 'directing' this new cosmos. With that, we humans will attain the *goal* of our evolution and, realizing the ideal of the 'religion of the gods', enter the hierarchical totality of the cosmos.

Here it is necessary to add that any actual work on karma always takes place between human beings, meaning within a social community. That is likewise the reason why, from the beginning of his anthroposophical activity until the end of his life, Rudolf Steiner devoted so much energy and time to establishing and then developing first the German section of the Theosophical Society (1902), which he led, secondly the independent Anthroposophical Society (1913), and finally the General Anthroposophical Society founded at the Christmas Conference (1923).

Rudolf Steiner moreover pointed to this social element as an unalterable prerequisite for the work on karma in part IV of the Foundation Stone Meditation, where two polar groups (the Shepherds and Kings) are referred to who stand for the two main streams of pre-Christian Mysteries. At the Turning-point of Time they represent an *archetype* for the work on karma today for our age through the collaboration and mutual fructification of the two main karmic streams in the Anthroposophical Society, mentioned by Rudolf Steiner in the karma lectures of the year 1924. (See GA 237 and 240)

At the Christmas Conference where the founding took place of the General Anthroposophical Society that was needed for the union and joint work of the two karmic groups, Rudolf Steiner created the super-sensible Foundation Stone (that consists of spiritual substance, Imaginative form, and a radiant thought-aura). (See GA 260, 25 December 1923) The three kinds of karma are easily recognizable in these three elements of the Foundation Stone. For substance is always provided with a certain con-sistency that corresponds to the karma in which the forces of the Father are effective. On the other hand, although it has a certain shape, the Imaginative form is nevertheless capable of undergoing the most varied transformations and in that way corresponds to the karma filled by the forces of the Son. Finally, the thought-light that depends on the forces of man bears within itself the possibility for a completely new karma in which the forces of the Holy Spirit can work. This is why the Spirit manifests in the light-aura of the Foundation Stone, the Spirit mentioned by Rudolf Steiner at the conclusion of the Mystery-act of the Foundation Stone's creation. (ibid.)

★

If we now try to bring what has been said in this chapter concerning the threefold forming of human karma into connection with what was described in the previous chapter as the supersensible preparation of Anthroposophy, the following relationship is the result. When on the first level during the 'cosmic thunderstorm' the spiritual-physical constitution of earthly man was objectively changed, then this is a typical actualization of the karma of necessity, or karma of the Father, independent of the human being. On the second level in his supersensible school, Michael initially outlined the substance of the ancient pre-Christian Mysteries in which the karma of necessity still held sway. Then, however, he pointed to the central significance of the Mystery of Golgotha in earthly and cosmic evolution as the fulfilment of the highest expectations of all ancient Mysteries so as to create the basis for the new Christianity from this synthesis of past and future. (See GA 240).

In the Michael School the past was thus linked with the future due to the Mystery of Golgotha, and the ancient Mysteries re-emerged in new form by posing the possibility for human beings to continue working on their own in this direction proceeding from the karma of metamorphosis, or the karma of the Son. Ultimately in the supersensible cultus, the very content of 'new Christianity' was immersed into the depths of human will as an impulse of the future. The work for actualization of this future is at the same time the creation of new karma, the karma of the Holy Spirit.

A foundation for the third kind of karma was laid in the supersensible cultus inasmuch as a human soul who participated in this cultus made the decision to work on this karma during its incarnation on Earth. In a quite special way Rudolf Steiner referred to such a decision made still prior to incarnation: 'This is actually inscribed in the karma of every anthroposophist: Become a man of initiative.' (GA 237, 4 August 1924) And continuing: 'This is something that should be kept in mind as if inscribed in golden letters in the soul of anthroposophists, namely that initiative is inherent in their karma' and they should 'become conscious of it by an act of will'. (ibid.)

What is meant by such 'initiative' in the first place are our free deeds on Earth that we carry out based on the motivations we receive from the astral light that is given us in thought-form through Anthroposophy. We offer up the fruits of these deeds to Michael. And if they were carried out on the basis of free and selfless insight, in the spiritual world they can turn into cosmic deeds out of which, comparable to building blocks, the new cosmos will gradually come into being.

As we found in the previous chapter, the spirits of the First Hierarchy or 'Spirits of Strength' play the main role in the 'cosmic thunderstorm'; the Michael School then took its course in the Sun sphere, the actual locality of the Second Hierarchy or 'Spirits of Light'; and the supersensible cultus was conducted in the spiritual sphere closest to the Earth (the Moon sphere), the sphere of the working of the Third Hierarchy or 'Spirits of Soul'. In one form or another all nine divine-spiritual hierarchies, who in their totality are guiding the karma of our cosmos, thus participated in the preparation for Anthroposophy proceeding from the impulses that they receive from the Trinity itself, something that is depicted in the Foundation Stone Meditation. Still, even as in the centre of the meditation stands the 'Christ-Sun' around which is grouped the meditation's essence, so the service for the Christ as Lord of Karma forms the centre and goal of the karmic working of the hierarchies.

This also explains why the new *Christian* teaching of reincarnation and karma stands in the centre of Anthroposophy's proclamation, a teaching that Rudolf Steiner began to develop in full measure following the Christmas Conference, meaning after the establishment of the new Christian Mysteries.

★

To sum up, we can say: In the Foundation Stone Meditation we have the key for comprehending the various aspects of activity by the nine hierarchies in man as well as in the cosmos and their own realm. It is a working in the service for the divine Trinity and (emerging from the latter) the Christ Being as the Word of Worlds. For according to the testimony by Rudolf Steiner, the Christ is the 'leader and guide ... of *all* the beings of the higher hierarchies'. (GA 129, 21 August 1911)

This is pointed out in the Foundation Stone Meditation inasmuch as there He is revealed as the 'Christ-Sun' in the centre of the cross formed by the nine hierarchies in the universe. The First Hierarchy works from above to below, the Second from East to West, the Third from below to above, inasmuch as each follows the Will of the world-creating divine Logos, the Logos who guides them out of the middle of the cross as the 'Christ Will.'

Rudolf Steiner concluded the Christmas Conference on the evening of 1 January 1924 by reading the meditation's middle segment of part IV which in the sphere of karma-working represents the transition from past to future. Then, as reported by eyewitnesses, he drew the sign below into the air:

This is none other than a symbolic depiction of the cosmic cross with the Spirit Sun of the cosmos in the middle:

In so doing Rudolf Steiner once more pointed to the relationship of the Christ with the activity of the three-times-three hierarchies in the way this comes to expression in the main anthroposophical meditation, the Foundation Stone Meditation.

6. The Merging of the Rosicrucian and the Michaelic Stream in the Foundation Stone Meditation

What has been described in the previous chapter as the continuing development of mankind in the course of the last three cultural periods (the fifth, sixth, and seventh) within the *large* fifth post–Atlantean epoch, must be prepared already today during our age of the Michael rule. Rudolf Steiner pointed to this task of the present age in the karma lectures dedicated to the cosmic Michael Mysteries. Here, addressing the anthroposophists, he said: 'Human beings have to work together with the gods, with Michael himself.' (GA 240, 19 July 1924) In other words, already now anthroposophists must learn to co-operate spiritually not only with Michael, the leading Time spirit, but also with the hierarchies serving him in spiritual worlds; with Archangels and Angels as well as the human souls that are united with him; souls who after their death are working in the Temple of the New Mysteries.

This in turn signifies that within humanity there has to be a group of people, be it ever so small, who are ready to dedicate themselves consciously to the preparation of the decisive transition from the large fifth period of Earth evolution (encompassing all seven post–Atlantean cultural periods) to the large sixth epoch that will begin after the 'War of All Against All'. Anthroposophists are meant to become such a group. As Rudolf Steiner stated, the *call* of the Masters of Wisdom and Harmony of Feeling is directed today especially to them, just as at the end of the Atlantean time a similar call went out to a small number of human beings from Manu, who was the leading initiate of the central Sun oracle.

Just as the [fifth] large post–Atlantean epoch with its central point, the descent of Christ to the Earth in the fourth cultural period, had to be prepared through this small group of humans for all mankind, so, in the course of the preparation of the transition to the sixth large [post–Atlantean] epoch, full comprehension for the being of the Christ and His mighty deed, the Mystery of Golgotha, has to be attained through a small group of anthroposophists under the leadership of the Masters of Wisdom and Harmony of Feeling.

Comparing today's situation with the one at the end of the Atlantean epoch, Rudolf Steiner said: 'Today there resounds a call out of the spiritual world to a similarly small group, one that we characterize as the *call of the Masters of Wisdom and Harmony of Feeling* ... These human beings who today come from all segments of society with a longing in their hearts for spiritual life that is to establish the future cultures, these people whom we find everywhere are in fact the true theosophists [anthroposophists].' (GA 109/111, 6 April 1909) And 'just as humanity ... who gathered on Atlantis at that time as a small scorned group around the great initiate [Manu], after many generations produced the material that made possible the Christ's incarnation on Earth, so today's anthroposophical humanity has to make it possible *fully to understand the Christ*'. (ibid.) In other lectures Rudolf Steiner emphasized this call by stating that today's spiritual science has the task to prepare the sixth cultural period within humanity. During that period the nucleus of humans will ultimately have to be formed that will then lead over into the transition from the fifth to the sixth large epoch.[43] For if a new spiritualized *comprehension* of the Christ Being is above all necessary for the preparation of the sixth cultural period, then the Mystery of the Living Christ will be unveiled fully in the sixth large epoch of humanity. As a result 'Christianity will only come to expression fully in the sixth root race.[44] Only then will it truly be present.' (GA 93, 11 November 1904) But so as to have access to this reality of Christianity human beings not only have to acquire a spiritual understanding of the Christ, they have to become aware of His actual presence in their own souls: 'This in turn is the advance as compared to the earlier Atlantean time when in an insignificant locale a community of people developed, whereas *among us* [among us anthroposophists] there is the opportunity that all across the Earth and out of all ethnic backgrounds those who really hear *the call of the Earth's mission* are chosen. These are people who understand how *to make the Christ come alive in themselves,* who unfold the principle of brotherhood all across the Earth, not in the sense of the Christian confessions but in the sense of true esoteric Christianity that can emerge out of all cultures. Those who understand this Christian principle will be present in the time that will follow after the great War of All Against All.' (GA 104, 24 June 1908)

A dual task follows from this for the Anthroposophical Society in our time. For one, a Rosicrucian comprehension of the Christ Being and His most significant deed—the Mystery of Golgotha. For the effort towards such an understanding is the response that anthroposophists can offer to the *call* addressed to them by the Masters of Wisdom and Harmony of Feeling, and among these Masters above all to the leader of the stream of esoteric Christendom, Christian Rosenkreutz.[45] Here Rudolf Steiner remarked: 'Out of this spiritual stream that is linked with Christian Rosenkreutz comes the greatest help for making the Christ Impulse comprehensible for our present age.' (GA 130, 20 November 1911) The reason is that in one of his previous incarnations the founder of the Rosicrucian stream was a contemporary of Jesus and '*was there*' at the Mystery of Golgotha. (GA 130, 27 January 1912)

For another, a no less significant task of the Anthroposophical Society is to strive towards the attainment of those objectives which were posed by Michael in his supersensible school to the future anthroposophists and then immersed into their will during the Imaginative cultus. Rudolf Steiner connected these objectives in the first place with the founding of the 'new Christianity' on Earth. He spoke of this in connection with the description of Michael's supersensible school. In an earlier lecture he indicated this by saying, ' . . . through Michael's spirit coming to Earth [referring here to the beginning of his present period of rule among humanity], through his Inspiration, mankind [could] gradually begin . . . to understand all that the Christ Impulse, the Mystery of Golgotha, signifies.' (GA 152, 2 May 1913) This Inspiration by Michael is revealed in full measure to human beings in Anthroposophy.

The Christ Mystery thus stands from the very beginning in the centre of Rosicrucian, as well as Michaelic, Christianity. Here Rosicrucian Christianity can be understood from the standpoint of Earth development and Michaelic Christianity from that of cosmic evolution.

The sources of Rosicrucian Christianity must therefore be sought on Earth where the Mystery of Golgotha was accomplished and where, incarnating in nearly every century, Christian Rosenkreutz works as do the other Masters of Wisdom and Harmony of Feeling. The secret of the Christ as the Son of God, who descended to the Earth and passed through death and resurrection in order to bestow on mankind 'a new member of human nature' (GA 131, 11 October 1911) or the *resurrection body,* is the secret that genuine Rosicrucianism wishes to unveil in the course of the centuries.

The sources of Michaelic Christianity on the other hand, are to be sought not on Earth but on the Sun. This is why Michael today discloses to humanity a completely different side of that Mystery. It is first and foremost the cosmic aspect of the Christ secret. As the divine Word that belongs since the ultimate beginning to the Holy Trinity, the Christ on His path to Earth initially united with the Sun sphere and there turned into the Sun Logos or leading Sun spirit. Later on however, at the Turning-point of Time, *He departed from the Sun* and moved down to Earth.[46]

He departs from the Sun Sphere: 'He leaves.' This was Michael's fundamental experience and that of all human souls belonging to his stream, souls who at the Turning-point of Time between death and rebirth were abiding in the Sun sphere. He descends to the Earth: 'He comes.' This was the primary experience of the first witnesses of Christ's appearance on Earth amongst whom, above all, belonged the future founder of the Rosicrucian stream.[47]

What both groups experienced as the most important outcome of the Mystery of Golgotha was just as different. At the moment when the blood of the Christ flowed down from the Cross on Golgotha and was received by the Earth, Michael and the human souls staying with him on the Sun could behold how a complete transformation of the Earth's aura occurred whereby the foundation was laid for its eventual union with the Sun. 'Viewed spiritually, since the Event of Golgotha the Earth once again has the power within itself that will lead it back together with the Sun,' is how Rudolf Steiner described it. (GA 103, 26 May 1908) Henceforth the Earth was the centre of our cosmos.

The main experience of the first Christians on the other hand, was their connection with the Resurrected Christ, and linked with it the potential to receive, extending even into the physical body, the forces of His Phantom, something that bestows eternal being (immortality) on the earthly ego of man.

★

Here a brief historical supplement has to be fitted in. The first as yet prophetic reference to the future union of the Rosicrucian and the Michaelic stream can be found in the well known *Fairy Tale of the Green Snake and the Beautiful Lily* by Goethe. The whole symbolism of the temple, lost (concealed below Earth's surface) and then rediscovered, likewise the figures of the three kings who represent the ideals of wisdom, beauty, and power as well as other elements, bears witness to Rosicrucian Inspiration. In the *Fairy Tale*, says Rudolf Steiner, one can find much 'of Rosicrucian wisdom'.[48] Its relationship to the Imaginative cultus at the end of the eighteenth century as the second stage of the celestial preparation of Anthroposophy attests to its connection with the cosmic Michael stream.[49] Both streams were then united through Rudolf Steiner in Anthroposophy for the first time in Earth evolution.

This union was preceded by his encounters with the Rosicrucian master in Vienna between the ages of eighteen and twenty-one and the supersensible encounter with Michael during his work on the *Philosophy of Freedom* in Weimar.[50]

In this connection the fact must be heeded that Rudolf Steiner's first spiritual scientific lecture was dedicated to the esoteric contemplation of Goethe's *Fairy Tale*. It took place on Michaelmas Day, 29 September

1900, in Berlin. Thus, already at the very beginning of Rudolf Steiner's activity, this extremely important aspect of his mission within the stream of esoteric Christianity became evident.

In the early period however, the two directions within the Anthroposophical Movement did not develop simultaneously but one after the other. Initially Rosicrucian esotericism emerged in the foreground. This became particularly clear beginning from 1904 when Rudolf Steiner started organizing his own esoteric activity; first in the framework of the esoteric school which existed at that time within the Theosophical Society. At the same time he began to publish articles in the magazine *Lucifer-Gnosis* that described the modern Rosicrucian initiation and later came out in book form under the title *Knowledge of the Higher Worlds and Its Attainment*. (GA 10)

The next level was reached in 1907. It was then that Rudolf Steiner finally separated his esoteric school from that of Annie Besant, orientated as that was on the Eastern path of initiation. In so doing he emphasized that his school was under the leadership of the two leading Masters of esoteric Christianity, namely Master Jesus (Zarathustra) and Master Christian Rosenkreutz.[51]

Only now, subsequent to the final separation, Rudolf Steiner began to unveil the Michael Mystery. In the esoteric lesson on 9 October 1907, he mentioned for the first time the significance of the year 1879 as the beginning of the present Michael period. Moreover he referred to the important changes connected with this particular year in the spiritual world as well as in the development of earthly culture. In the same [esoteric] lesson he referred for the first time to the year 1250 as the beginning of the Rosicrucian stream. In this way he linked both themes, the Rosicrucian and Michaelic one. 'In 1250 a spiritual stream had its start that reached its high point when Christian Rosenkreutz was elevated to Knight of the Rose Cross in 1459. Then (in 1510) the age began which in occultism is called the age of Gabriel. In 1879 began that of Michael.' (GA 266/I, p. 251) During the ensuing lessons Rudolf Steiner then spoke of all seven Archangels and of Michael's pivotal position in their circle, a position that gains its forces from the Sun.

The next phase in the afore-mentioned direction is the writing of Rudolf Steiner's main work, *Occult Science, an Outline* which, as he put it, 'is after all a summary of Anthroposophy as a whole'. (GA 13, p. 31) The book was written in 1909 and published in 1910. Even though the names Christian Rosenkreutz and Michael are nowhere mentioned in it, the presence of their impulses is obvious. In the sevenfold path of initiation described there, which leads to the experience of the Christ Being and a comprehension of the significance of the Mystery of Golgotha for all of Earth evolution, the Rosicrucian impulse comes to expression. The Michael impulse is present in the grand panorama of cosmic evolution, at the centre of which the secret of the Christ's relationship to the Sun is found together with the future genesis of the new Cosmos of Love out of the forces that flowed into Earth evolution from the Mystery of Golgotha.

Thus in the year he wrote *Occult Science, an Outline*, Rudolf Steiner pointed out that for a spiritual researcher 'there [exist] the two elements ... of mankind's future spirit evolution. What is immersed into [man's] inner being as the Christ Life will be the first element. The second will be what, as spiritual cosmology, will bring about an understanding for the Christ in a comprehensive way. Christ Life in the innermost being of the heart, understanding of the cosmos that leads to understanding of the Christ—those will be the two elements.' (GA 113, 31 August 1909) The whole content of *Occult Science, an Outline* rests on these two fundamental elements of modern Christian esotericism. They are additional proof of the fact that the Rosicrucian as well as the Michaelic impulse was active in the Anthroposophical Movement from the very beginning.[51a]

The disclosure of the Michael Mysteries for all anthroposophists and not merely for the narrow circle of members of the Esoteric School did not take place until three years later after the separation from the Theosophical Society.[52] Up until then the Michael Mystery remained in the background in a manner of speaking and the main accent was directed to further development of the Rosicrucian theme. Then on the day prior to Michaelmas in 1911 there followed the well known lectures in Neufchâtel in which mention was made for the first time of Christian Rosenkreutz's initiation in the thirteenth century, as well as the subsequent spiritual activity by the Rosicrucians, for strengthening his etheric body. (GA 130, 27 and 28 September 1911) Then in 1912, in the third lecture in Neufchâtel, Rudolf Steiner described how Christian Rosenkreutz 'sent his student and friend', the Gautama Buddha, to Mars. (GA 130, 18 December 1912) During the interval between the first two lectures and the third one in Neufchâtel, Rudolf Steiner made the attempt to inaugurate an organization named the 'Society for Theosophical Ethos and Art'. He intended to detach this society from himself at a later date and place it directly under the leadership of Christian Rosenkreutz. For just as the Michael school founded at the Christmas Conference was under the direct leadership of the Time Spirit, so this group was likewise supposed to have a similar relationship to the leading Master of esoteric Christianity.[53]

The development of the Michael theme itself was introduced in the independent Anthroposophical Society, established at Christmas of 1912, in a form accessible to all members in three lectures, on 2 May 1913 in London and on 18 and 20 May of the same the year in Stuttgart. (GA 152)[54] Thereby in both cities, the Michael theme was linked to the appearance of the Etheric Christ.[55]

Later, at the beginning of the First World War, the Michael theme emerges once more into the foreground. In the lecture of 9 November 1914, Rudolf Steiner speaks about Michael not merely in connection with the etheric appearance of the Christ but likewise in relation to events of the war. (GA 158) Yet it is only in the year 1917 that the Michael theme really turns into a pivotal subject. This new stage in its development begins with the lecture cycle *The Fall of the Spirits of Darkness*. (GA 177) In the same year when in Russia the Bolsheviks, possessed by the spirits of darkness (who had been cast down into the earthly world by Michael), assumed power, and in the West the United States under the leadership of President Woodrow Wilson (who was gripped by an ahrimanic spirit) entered the war, there resounded out of the spiritual middle of central Europe the voice of the Christian initiate who spoke of the impulse of Michael and this being's *spiritual* victory over the ahrimanic dragon.

In the autumn of 1919 the Michael theme was then continued with the lecture cycle, *The Mission of Michael* (GA 194) and later in 1923 with the lectures dedicated to the Michael festival.

With this we have drawn near to the Christmas Conference which on its part signifies the culmination of the whole process of dealing with the joining of Michaelic and Rosicrucian Christianity in Anthroposophy. This union found its concrete expression in the dual structure of the Foundation Stone and its meditation serving as the foundation of the newly established Anthroposophical Society. Thus the microcosmic segments of this meditation lead initially to the transformation of man's thinking, feeling, and willing; then to transformation of his spirit, soul, and *body,* something that enables him in a purely inner meditative way to attain the very objective that the medieval Rosicrucian strove for through his alchemistic experiments, when in his laboratory he studied the processes of the forming of salt, its dissolving, and combustion.[56] The macrocosmic parts of the meditation conversely speak of the descent by the Christ out of the sphere of the Trinity through all nine hierarchies to His union with Earth and its elemental world in the Mystery of Golgotha. Witness and guardian on the other hand, of the knowledge concerning this macrocosmic path of the Christ from heaven down to Earth through all the spiritual spheres, is Michael, the 'Sun countenance of the Christ'.

The secret of the transformation of the physical body (a body that consists of three systems—the limb and metabolic system, the one of heart and lung, and that of the head and nerves) is contained in the microcosmic parts of the meditation as the highest goal of Rosicrucianism (the attainment of the Stone of the Wise). The three exercises likewise lead to this goal, exercises connected with the developmental process of the human 'I' which, when ultimately having reached full maturity, will be capable of transforming the astral body into the microcosmic Sophia. This in turn comes about when man will have learned how to think, feel, and will 'truly'.[57] The threefold mention of the 'I' in the microcosmic segments of the meditation moreover points to its salvation in the course of evolution through the transformation of the physical body, and that means through the union of the 'I' with the forces of the resurrection body of the Christ (the Phantom).

The origin of those cosmic forces that the Christ, owing to the Mystery of Golgotha, linked with Earth evolution, is contained in the macrocosmic segments of the meditation, where this secret is described from the standpoint of Michael, the 'arch-strategist' of the heavenly forces. The fact that in the macrocosmic parts of the meditation the Rosicrucian lines were enclosed, lines that point to the Mystery of Golgotha as the central event of earthly and cosmic evolution, confirms once again the union of Rosicrucian and Michaelic Christianity which represent the esoteric and the cosmic aspect of the all-encompassing Christ Mystery.[57a]

One can moreover say that in the microcosmic segments of the meditation we have the path from the Rosicrucians to Michael, the path that in its final lines reaches a culmination where mention is made of the trichotomy of man, of a being that consists of body, soul, and spirit to which, in the macrocosm, correspond the three worlds, the physical, soul, and spiritual world. (See GA 9) The guardian of the secret of this trinity is Michael in the spiritual worlds. Thus the microcosmic segments of the meditation form a kind of chalice which, created out of Rosicrucian impulses, receives the Michael revelation and then is supposed to bring it to man.

The macrocosmic segments on the other hand, stand for the path from Michael to Rosicrucianism. Here, as 'arch-strategist' and representative of all the hierarchies, Michael creates out of their forces a chalice into which the three Rosicrucian sayings were immersed that harbour the secret of the Mystery of Golgotha.

In this way the microcosmic segments of the meditation lead from man to the world, or from the microcosm to the macrocosm. They begin with the call to the individual human soul and the description of the threefold formation of the physical body. They end with the reference to the 'All-

World-Being of Man', the 'weaving of the Soul of Man', and the 'ground of the Spirit of Man'. Conversely, its macrocosmic segments lead from the macrocosm to the microcosm; they begin with the sphere of the Trinity, meaning the description of the highest macrocosmic spirituality, and end with the call of the elemental spirits that is directed to man: 'May human beings hear it!'

★

A further aspect of the working together of both streams consists in the following: The microcosmic or Rosicrucian segments of the meditation describe the steps of ascent into the spiritual world that comprise modern initiation, the basis of which is the process of self-knowledge as well as man's inner work on himself. This is the path of the Son of Man that leads from below to above. It leads out of the earthly world, where the three systems of the physical body of man are active, to experiencing himself as a threefold being consisting of body, soul, and spirit. The macrocosmic parts of the meditation on the other hand, describe the descent of the Son of God through all the spiritual spheres of the hierarchies to Earth, even to the elemental world and earthly humanity. And this coming-to-Earth of the Son of God is 'heard' by the elemental spirits 'in East, West, North, South / May human beings hear it!'

These two principles, the principle of the Son of Man and that of the Son of God, unite in the fourth part of the meditation inasmuch as the working of the Michaelic as well as the Rosicrucian stream can be traced. Where mention is made of the cosmic aspect of the Turning-point of Time, independent of the will of earth-humanity, the activity of the Michael impulse predominates:

At the Turning-point of Time,
The Spirit-Light of the World
Entered the stream of Earthly Being.
Darkness of Night
Had held its sway;

Particularly the following words affirm this:

Light Divine
Sun of Christ

whose mystery lies at the basis of the 'new Christianity' that was taught in the supersensory Michael school.

In the words of the fourth part of the meditation that relate more to Earth evolution, on the other hand or, put more accurately, to the Mystery streams of the Shepherds and Kings (streams that represent the two main streams of earthly wisdom), the Rosicrucian direction is addressed. For both Mystery streams, the Shepherds' as well as the Kings' stream, later on flowed into the Rosicrucian Mysteries.[58] Their centre was, however, formed from the very beginning by the insight that it was due to the Mystery of Golgotha that 'Day-radiant Light / Poured into the souls of men', and that it is this light that 'gives warmth to simple Shepherds' hearts' and 'enlightens the wise Heads of Kings'. (In these lines the two verbs are in the present tense, something that points to the working of these Mystery streams even into our own age.)

The last two lines of the fourth part that follow directly after the reference to the 'Christ-Sun' point even more clearly to the synthesis of the Michael and Rosicrucian stream:

Warm Thou
Our Hearts,
Enlighten Thou
Our Heads
That good may become
What from our Hearts we would found
And from our Heads direct
With single purpose.

For the *truly Good* shall in future arise only out of the ultimate and full integration of the two streams in the ether-heart of man,[59] meaning the very space into which the supersensible Foundation Stone of the General Anthroposophical Society was placed at the Christmas Conference.

The *first* lecture cycle that Rudolf Steiner gave immediately following the Christmas Conference was likewise dedicated to the theme of Rosicrucian and Michaelic Christianity. Its title was *Rosicrucianism and Modern Initiation. Mystery Centres of the Middle Ages.* (GA 233a) Doubtlessly the final lecture represented its culmination. It was given on the twelfth day after the end of the Christmas Conference. (More on this, see below.)

Finally in the 'Last Address' given in 1924 by Rudolf Steiner on the evening prior to Michaelmas Day, which he concluded with the meditation for the Time Spirit, the link between the two streams emerges in the reference to the sequence of incarnations of an actual individuality (Rosicrucian principle) and the description of its passage through the various planetary spheres following death (Michaelic principle).[60]

Moreover it is most likely that the 'Last Address' was to form the beginning of the karma-unveiling of those individualities who had directly participated in the events of the Turning-point of Time and for this reason were connected later on in one way or another with the Rosicrucian stream.

With this, a second group of karma lectures was supposed to be added to the first,[60a] the centre of which consisted of the description of the supersensible school of Michael and his Imaginative cultus. The second part was to consider the karma of humanity from the viewpoint of the Mystery of Golgotha as well as the karma of those persons who were linked with this event. Parallel to it Rudolf Steiner intended to inaugurate a *second* class of the School of Spiritual Science in the ritualistic forms of which the 'royal art' of the Rosicrucians[61] and the content of the Imaginative Michael–cultus (which had taken place at the end of the eighteenth century in the spiritual sphere adjacent to the Earth) were to find their synthesis.[62]

Finally it can be assumed that in the *third* class Rudolf Steiner would have laid the foundation for a form of spiritual work that would have been connected directly with the work by the Christ as Lord of Karma whom both streams (the Rosicrucian as well as the Michaelic) serve in equal measure starting in our time. On this level their ultimate union would have been achieved.

One can therefore say that in the totality of his spiritual scientific activity Rudolf Steiner initially renewed the Rosicrucian initiation based on the Michael impulse and then, with the aid of this initiation, created a spiritual chalice that is capable of receiving into itself the revelation of the Christ–Sun directed to all mankind.

In this drawing we have a symbol of the Holy Grail that depicts the nature of the totality of Rudolf Steiner's activity during almost forty years. All this found its highest expression and culmination in the forming of the Foundation Stone during the Christmas Conference.[63]

★

Let us now more closely consider the relationship of Michael as well as that of Christian Rosenkreutz with this esoteric centre of the Christmas Conference. From a spiritual-historical standpoint the Foundation Stone is indissolubly connected with the central Mysteries of Rosicrucianism. What in them was the work on the Philosopher's Stone, has become in the new Mysteries the inner work on the Stone of Love.[64] The very essence of Rosicrucianism therefore has undergone a complete metamorphosis through Anthroposophy in order, in this new form, to unite with Michael's cosmic Christianity.

This metamorphosis on its part is the beginning of the telluric-cosmic process that Rudolf Steiner described at the end of *Occult Science, an Outline* as the gradually proceeding transformation of the ancient Cosmos of Wisdom into the future *Cosmos of Love* through the free creative activity of the human 'I'. But since this process involves not only the human being but likewise the whole cosmos, Michael too participates in it. Now the forming of the Foundation Stone was already such a free creative activity by the ego-forces of Rudolf Steiner, a deed in which Christian Rosenkreutz as well as Michael were present and participated in a supersensible manner.

The spiritual presence of both Christian Rosenkreutz and the Archangel Michael is affirmed twice at the Christmas Conference and particularly at the forming of the Foundation Stone on 25 December 1923. For one it was through words by Rudolf Steiner, words he uttered in a private conversation to Ita Wegman, namely 'that on the occasion of the Christmas Foundation Stone Laying Christian Rosenkreutz and his hosts entered into the "Carpentry Hall".'[65] For another it was through the way the esoteric substance of the Mystery act of the Foundation Stone Laying must be understood in the light of what Rudolf Steiner said in the lecture on 13 January 1924.

In this lecture that was given exactly twelve days after the conclusion of the Christmas Conference, on the very day of the first publication of the Foundation Stone Meditation's whole text in the *Newsletter*, the main motif was the unification of the Rosicrucian and the Michaelic streams. Just as it took place in the development of the Anthroposophical Movement, so in this lecture too, mention was first made of the Rosicrucian stream. Rudolf Steiner initially described in detail the most important fruit of Rosicrucian initiation: the faculty to inscribe the results of modern-day science in the warmth ether in order then to receive them back from the gods in completely changed form out of the spiritual world.

Rudolf Steiner followed this path of Rosicrucian initiation from the very beginning and its most important fruit subsequently was the description of world evolution as represented by him in the book, *Occult Science, an Outline*. Moreover he reported in the lecture above that this work had emerged out of the practice of modern Rosicrucian initiation as depicted, for example, in the book *Knowledge of the Higher World and Its Attainment*.[65a] He furthermore referred to the facts that it was initially Christian Rosenkreutz who succeeded in solving the esoteric problem of how research-results of modern science, transformed by the gods through the warmth ether, can be received out of the spiritual world, and that it was only after this that it became possible for other Rosicrucians to unite with him in this activity. Still, Christian Rosenkreutz himself was able to find the path to this goal only 'based on inspiration from a higher spirit' by using his consciousness that was subdued for this purpose and placed into a dream state.

From the additional content of the same lecture one can conclude that this higher being of the spiritual world was the Archangel Michael. For Rudolf Steiner describes how the Rosicrucians always sought the encounter with Michael in the spiritual world. But they could do this only in a subdued dream-like state of mind at that time. This was the case even for their 'most illuminated spirits' among whom belonged Christian Rosenkreutz above all. He likewise could only approach Michael in a subdued state of consciousness: 'Rosicrucianism is distinguished by the fact that its most illustrious spirits had a powerful longing to experience Michael. They could do so only as if in a dream.' (ibid.)

Now this situation changed radically in the year 1879 with the beginning of the present Michael epoch. Due to the change in his relationship to humanity since that date it has become possible for the first time in Earth evolution to experience him consciously. 'This is what is unusual since the beginning of the Michael epoch (from the end of the seventies in the last third of the nineteenth century) that the same thing which during the time of old Rosicrucianism was attained through the manner described [in a subdued state of consciousness] can now be attained in a conscious way.' (ibid.) The *first* one who among the initiates of today reached the point of having such a fully conscious encounter with Michael in the spiritual world adjacent to the Earth was Rudolf Steiner. He then described later on in his lectures how this took place and what consequences it had for him personally and like-wise for Michael.

As a result, having achieved a conscious connection with Michael in his youth on the Rosicrucian initiation-path, Rudolf Steiner could bear the

'Stone of Love' as today's metamorphosis of the ancient Rosicrucians' 'Philosopher's Stone' into Michael's kingdom.[65b] With that he carried out the transition from the Rosicrucian to the Michaelic stream, not only on the occult but likewise on the world-historic stage, and united both in the New Mysteries founded by him at the Christmas Conference. Subsequently, in the lecture of 13 January 1924 (which in this way becomes a key for the esoteric nature of the Christmas Conference) he himself pointed out the significance of this event in the history of esoteric Christianity.

★

As described in another work by the author, Michael affirmed Rudolf Steiner's sacrificial deed at the Christmas Conference and received it into his cosmic sphere. Through this, what Rudolf Steiner had accomplished continued its effect in the Michael sphere, but now as a *cosmic deed*.[66] He pointed this out in the afore-mentioned lecture: 'Michael shall be the actual spiritual hero of freedom. He lets humans act but then takes what becomes of human deeds so as to carry it further in the cosmos in order to work with what humans as yet cannot accomplish in their working.' (GA 233a, 13 January 1924)

One can therefore say that in the presence of Christian Rosenkreutz and through the creative deed of his 'I', Rudolf Steiner transformed the Rosicrucian Philosopher's Stone in the sense of the concluding words of *Occult Science, an Outline* into a Stone of Love: 'Wisdom is the precondition of love, love is the result of wisdom that has been reborn in the "I".' (GA 13, p. 416) With this Rudolf Steiner showed for the first time in Earth evolution what the highest actualization of these words consists of in an actual human life. Then in accordance with the lecture on 13 January, he bore the Stone of Love he had created towards Michael, who in turn received it into his domain as the Foundation Stone for the new Cosmos of Love which in *Revelation* is depicted in the image of the heavenly Jerusalem.

This free creative deed by Rudolf Steiner had consequences even for Michael himself. For only then, as a response, could the Time Spirit establish his esoteric school on Earth where an additional metamorphosis of Rosicrucian initiation took place. This initiation now became a cosmic fact in the Michael School, a fact that concerns all the hierarchies. Through Rudolf Steiner Michael established a *new cosmic Rosicrucianism* on Earth.

We thus have the Rosicrucian and the Michaelic impulses working together as follows:

Rudolf	→ Transfor-	→ Surrender	→ Response	→ Transfor-
Steiner	mation of	of Philoso-	by Michael's	mation of
attains the	Stone of the	pher's Stone	Founding of	Rosicrucian
modern	Wise into	to Michael	the esoteric	initiation in
Rosicrucian	the Stone of		school (its	this school
initiation	Love		First Class)	out of the
				Michael
				impulse
				(Birth of
				cosmic Rosi-
				crucianism)

This is how the New Mysteries began through the deed by Rudolf Steiner during the Foundation Stone Laying in the presence of Michael, Christian Rosenkreutz, and his closest students. The centre of these New Mysteries is represented by the union of Rosicrucian and Michaelic Christianity on the foundation of the central impulse of Earth evolution—the Christ's Impulse and the Mystery of Golgotha.

*

In order better to understand the connection between the Foundation Stone and Michael, the leading Time Spirit and sun-like 'Countenance of Christ', we must pay heed to the words of Rudolf Steiner that he expressed on the eve prior to Michaelmas 1923 in Vienna: 'If in this way *confidence* in the spirit causes a state of mind where we reach the point of *sensing that this spirit is as real as the ground under our feet*, a ground of which we know that if it were not there we could not step on it with our feet, then we have a feeling in our heart and mind of what Michael actually wants from us.' (GA 223, 28 September 1923)

These words can arouse profound amazement in us when we realize that Rudolf Steiner actualized them less than three months later to the full extent when he bestowed on anthroposophists the *spiritual* Foundation Stone in such concrete and real form that henceforth the members of the Anthroposophical Society can find new ground under their feet. And the *Spirit* present in this ground and working in its aura can, for the members, become the leader for the actualization of spiritual tasks posed to them at the Christmas Conference.[67]

To lay the Foundation Stone into our hearts so as to stand on it as on our unshakable spiritual foundation and then to allow ourselves to be led by its spirit in all our actions in the world, it is this that, according to the above-quoted words, Michael *wills* for us today.[68] And if we are able in freedom and out of spiritual comprehension to live and do this, then by means of the Foundation Stone Michael will *enter into* our hearts and souls.

Now we will look at this process still more closely. During the cultic act of the Foundation Stone Laying, Rudolf Steiner spoke more than once of the necessity that every anthroposophist ought to immerse the Foundation Stone into the very ground of his or her soul and heart. In saying this he alternately referred both to the 'soul' (astral aspect) and to the 'heart' (etheric aspect). Thus Rudolf Steiner speaks of the Foundation Stone 'that we immerse in the ground of our souls', (GA 260) and 'the proper ground [for it] is our hearts'. (ibid.) In the first article dedicated to the cosmic Mystery of Michael eight months later, Rudolf Steiner referred in almost the same words to the soul and heart of man where, following his ascent to the rank of Time Spirit, Michael wishes to sojourn. 'Beginning from the last third of the nineteenth century he *wills* to live in the souls of men.' (GA 26, p. 61) Then, directly addressing the anthroposophists, Rudolf Steiner characterizes them as those who recognize 'that they are supposed to allow Michael to take up his abode in their hearts'. (ibid.) For today, in the present Michael epoch, 'man can live in soul-devotion to all that can be experienced in the *light of thought*'. (ibid., emphasis by Rudolf Steiner)

Rudolf Steiner likewise spoke about this 'light of thought' during the act of the Foundation Stone Laying. In the supersensible (etheric) world adjoining the Earth it surrounds the dodecahedric Stone of Love with its radiance and creates that light–aura in which the *Spirit* can manifest who with its presence consecrates the whole Christmas Conference, '. . . and then you will carry the Spirit (holding sway in the *radiant thought-light* around the dodecahedric Stone of Love) out into the world where it should give off light and warmth for the progress of human souls; for the progress of the world.' (GA 260, p. 69 G) It is this Spirit that since the Christmas Conference connects Rosicrucian and Michaelic Christianity in a new and inseparable oneness. It unites what Rosicrucianism is intended to accomplish for the forward development of the *human soul* and the world, and what the Michael impulse is meant to accomplish for the forward development of the *world* and the human soul.

In everything Rudolf Steiner accomplished after the Christmas Conference the impulse can be found that connects esoteric and cosmic Christianity. This is clearly demonstrated in the two essential outcomes of the Christmas Conference, namely the establishment of the Michael School on Earth and the karma lectures. The First Class of the Michael School is a direct continuation of the book, *Knowledge of the Higher Worlds and Its Attainment,* in which the modern form of the Christian-

Rosicrucian initiation is depicted.[69] This book ends with the description of the meeting by the student with the Greater Guardian of the Threshold who in one of his aspects is Michael. Rudolf Steiner once referred to this when he said of Chaldean religious traditions: 'On the other side, where through the tapestry of the sense world one finds the portal to the spiritual world, there stood the other Guardian [i.e. not the Lesser, but the Greater Guardian] Merodach or Marduk [Michael's name in Chaldean-Babylonian mythology], ... Merodach, whom we can compare with the [Greater] Guardian of the Threshold, with Michael.' (GA 113, 30 August 1909)

In the karma lectures given parallel with the First Class work, the two most important themes can also be traced: The description of the supersensible nature of the laws of karma from the standpoint of the cosmic activity of the hierarchies—namely the Michaelic aspect of the theme and consideration of actual cases of reincarnations of individual historical personalities—and the Rosicrucian aspect. The second aspect is linked to the fact that for many centuries the Rosicrucians represented the only occult stream in the West where concrete insights concerning reincarnation and karma were preserved within Christian culture.[70] This insight was unveiled to Rosicrucians, however, only on the highest levels of initiation. In that connection, Rudolf Steiner pointed out that students of the Rosicrucian Mysteries, even on the fourth and fifth level, were 'not yet [in a position] to attain full clarity about the most illuminating teachings of reincarnation and karma'. (GA 131, 6 October 1911) They were revealed in full measure only on the sixth and seventh level. For instance, it was known to the circle of the twelve sages, who in the thirteenth century participated in Christian Rosenkreutz's initiation, that in his person a lofty individuality had at that time come to the Earth, whose most important incarnation had taken place in Palestine.

The following likewise attests to the fact that from the very beginning Rosicrucians were bearers of the secret knowledge of reincarnation and karma. According to spiritual research by Rudolf Steiner, around the year 333 the four leading Masters, not only of esoteric Christianity but of Earth evolution met in a secret location. They were Manes, Zarathustra, Gautama Buddha (in his spirit body), and Skythianos. Although (with the exception of Gautama Buddha) they were all incarnated on Earth at that time, their encounter nevertheless took place on a higher plane. They came together 'in one of the largest gatherings that ever occurred in the spiritual world belonging to the Earth'. (GA 113, 31 August 1909) There they worked out a plan on how wisdom was supposed to flow gradually out of the circle of the Bodhisattvas in the sphere of Providence[71] into earthly humanity in order, with the support of this wisdom, to help the comprehension of the Christ Being and Mystery of Golgotha. (ibid) This wisdom of the Bodhisattvas, which to a large extent was the teaching of reincarnation and karma, was then 'brought across into those European Mysteries that are the Mysteries of the Rosicrucians'. (ibid.) This is moreover why the pupils on the highest levels of Rosicrucian initiation, where they could receive the Inspirations from the sphere of the Bodhisattvas, associated with Manes, Zarathustra, the Gautama Buddha, and Skythianos. For these 'were the teachers in the schools of the Rose Cross'. (ibid) And through these teachers flowed the insights concerning reincarnation and karma into Rosicrucian wisdom.[72]

In summary we can say: In the karma research of the year 1924 Rudolf Steiner gathered his insights out of both streams. This became particularly evident in the lectures that addressed the karma of the General Anthroposophical Society founded by him at the Christmas Conference.[73] The description of the supersensible Michael school in the solar realm in the above lectures points to the cosmic fount of the *Michaelic* stream. The research presented there concerning the two main karmic streams that form the Anthroposophical Society, as well as the two karmic groups connected with these streams (the Platonists, Aristotelians, and others) and their incarnations in the course of European history, go back more to Inspirations from the *Rosicrucian* stream.

Moreover, as we saw above, Rudolf Steiner was an associate of Michael in the earthly Michael school during the founding of the new *cosmic Rosicrucianism*. This was possible because he was the first human being who consciously encountered Michael in the spiritual world. Thanks to his initiation into the Michael Mysteries, he could then perceive the secret of the cosmic origin of human karma; something that signified above all the recognition of how all nine divine-spiritual hierarchies participated in the forming of this human karma. Rudolf Steiner then bore this cosmic *Michaelic* aspect of karma into the Rosicrucian stream as the spiritual substantiation of all research-indications concerning actual cases of reincarnation of individualities that he had earlier depicted.

★

As we saw, insight concerning the resurrection body, whose genesis belongs among the most significant consequences of the Mystery of Golgotha, represents the chief goal of the Rosicrucian Mysteries since their inception. According to Rudolf Steiner's spirit-research, the resurrection body likewise stands in direct relation to the redemption of the human 'I'. For this 'I' requires ego-consciousness for its existence in the human being. The ego-consciousness in turn is directly dependent on the physical body as an 'apparatus' that mirrors the forces of the 'I' and thereby awakens individual ego-consciousness. (GA 131, 11 October 1911) In Rudolf Steiner's formulation it says: '. . . that the "I" can only persevere in ego-consciousness' and that 'this "I" . . . emerges only by virtue of mirroring itself through the form of the physical body'. (ibid.) But because the 'decadence of the physical body had reached its highest point' by the time the Mystery of Golgotha occurred on Earth, the danger existed 'that ego-consciousness, the essential achievement of Earth evolution, could be lost'. (ibid.) The Mystery of Golgotha then led to the birth of the resurrection body as the most perfect form of body that is not only able to mirror the highest developed human "I" but likewise its most sublime archetype, the World-I of the Christ. Rudolf Steiner therefore could say that the Mystery of Golgotha is 'literally the salvation of the human "I".' (ibid.)

Furthermore, the connection with the Phantom body assures man a completely new 'I' consciousness after death, which in common Christianity is called 'personal immortality'. In the thirteenth century, the Realists among the Scholastics espoused this basic Christian principle over against the Arabian philosophers who negated it as did the Nominalists, who even then were inclined towards materialism. The reason for this difference of opinion was that under ordinary circumstances a person can maintain his individual ego-consciousness only thanks to the *memory* of his 'I' that he has taken along from his earthly life into the existence beyond. As does everything connected with memory, however, such ego-consciousness has only a more or less shadowy character. This is why the Greeks—through the mouth of their hero—stated that it is better to be a beggar on earth than a king in the realm of shades. The medieval Arabian philosophers refuted this Christian principle entirely.

Yet circumstances changed completely as a result of the Mystery of Golgotha. Henceforth every human being has the prospect of coming into contact with the Phantom of the Christ on earth and in this way to preserve his individual ego-consciousness on all levels of his after-death existence.[73a] In addition a person who has absorbed the forces of the Phantom into himself can not only completely overcome the shadowy nature of his ego-consciousness after death, but moreover develop those forces in himself, owing to which his ego-consciousness can become individually creative in the higher worlds. This in turn means being able to work out of one's own initiative in the spiritual world on bringing forth the new cosmos for which the foundation was laid through the Mystery of Golgotha.

★

The results of Rudolf Steiner's spiritual scientific research quoted here throw new light on the mission of Christian Rosenkreutz. During his initiation in the thirteenth century, he took in the forces of Christ's resurrection body and then (in a deathlike condition but finding himself still in the spiritual world with full ego-consciousness) experienced the encounter with the Christ.

This moment of Christian Rosenkreutz's initiation was described by Rudolf Steiner as follows: 'After a few days this thirteenth person's body, or the Christ's "Phantom", became completely transparent. For days he was as if dead.' But then something quite extraordinary occurred: His soul was utterly transformed by the Christ and returned into its body, which thereby '[became] enlivened in such a way that this enlivening of the completely transparent body cannot be compared with anything'. (GA 130, 27 September 1911)

The reason for the absolute uniqueness of this process is that here the physical body of a human being was for the first time revived by the forces of the Phantom and then once again took in its human 'I', which directly prior to its return had witnessed the whole above-mentioned process inasmuch as it had beheld this process fully consciously from the super-sensible world. Due to this the foundation was laid in Earth evolution for what was supposed to occur as a possibility later on, namely that a human being can receive a replica of the Christ-I into his human 'I'; a replica of the 'I' that the Christ imprinted into the sheaths of Jesus of Nazareth and which subsequently was reproduced in the spiritual world according to the laws of spiritual economy.

During the later centuries a majority of the Rosicrucians' esoteric work consisted in preparing humanity for this future. Christian Rosenkreutz himself was the first to reach this stage during the period of the con-sciousness soul. 'Starting with the sixteenth century the time begins when replicas of the Christ-"I" saw their way to be woven into the "I" of particular individualities. One of these was Christian Rosenkreutz, the first Rosicrucian. We owe it to this fact that a more intimate connection with the Christ became possible as revealed to us by esoteric teaching.' (GA 109/111, 28 March 1909) Viewed esoterically this 'more intimate connection with the Christ' signifies receiving a replica of His 'I' into oneself.

Thus, beginning in our time, every human being can receive the forces of the resurrection body on the path of modern Rosicrucian initiation as represented by Anthroposophy. For 'through what has been characterized as Rosicrucian initiation ... a bond of attraction [is] created between a human being, insofar as he is incarnated in a physical body and that which (as the actual archetype of the physical body) arose out of the tomb on Golgotha'. (GA 131, 14 October 1911) Such a connection with the resurrection body on its part brings about an attraction between the human 'I' and the replicas of the Christ-'I' that are preserved in the spiritual world. The reason is that the bodily form of the Phantom was originally linked with the forces of the Christ's World-'I' which guided this Phantom to the resurrection in the Mystery of Golgotha.

In this sense the Foundation Stone Meditation as a *whole* is a meditative path leading to a conscious connection with the resurrection body (the Phantom);[74] namely with the two aspects of this path: the microcosmic one that brings to expression the presence of the forces of the Son of Man in it, and the macrocosmic one that represents the working of the forces of the Son of God in it. Here the first aspect is linked with the taking in of the Christ-'I' into the 'I' of man as happened archetypally at the Turning-point of Time in Jesus of Nazareth; the second with the transformation of the Earth into a new sun, something for which the basis was created at the moment when the blood and flesh of the Christ's physical sheath was received by the Earth on the hill of Golgotha.

For us humans these two processes have their spiritual-historical archetype in the Ascension of the Christ and in the events of Whitsun; events that represent the direct consequences of the Mystery of Golgotha for man's etheric body, astral body, and his 'I'. Thus, by beholding the Ascension, the secret was unlocked for the Apostles in a prophetic way that it is possible from now on to unite with the spiritual-etheric forces of the Sun on Earth itself, without ascending into the Sun sphere.[75] Without this it would be impossible to transform the Earth into a new sun. Similarly we have in the Whitsun events a prophetic reference to what must gradually come to pass beginning in our age: the possibility that human beings can receive a replica of the Christ-'I' into their 'I'. Just as the Apostles at the Turning-point of Time were fructified by the forces of 'the individualized Holy Spirit', (GA 118, 15 May 1910) so in our age they can take the forces of the World-I of Christ into themselves in the sense of the 'reverse Whitsuntide'.

These two aspects, that on the one hand are connected with the development of mankind and on the other with that of the Earth, are moreover contained in the Foundation Stone Meditation. The inner work with this meditation's microcosmic segments leads to the afore-mentioned first goal, which in turn contains the genesis of the develop-ment of the 'I'.[76] Beginning from our time this work can prepare man to receive a replica of the Christ-'I' into himself. Viewed esoterically, the *whole* of the Anthroposophical Movement points from the very outset towards this goal.[77] However, the segments of the meditation mentioned above point quite directly to the realization of this goal, particularly the words:

Where the surging
Deeds of World's Becoming
Do thine own I
Unite
Unto the I of the World.

The comprehension of the Christ in His relation to the Sun as viewed from the cosmic viewpoint stands in the centre of the present Michael revelations for humanity. This likewise includes comprehension of the forces active in the resurrection body that as a result of the union by the Christ with the Earth can gradually transform the latter into a new sun. The macrocosmic segments of the meditation lead to the attainment of these lofty earth-goals and in them particularly the words about the 'Christ-Will' in the encircling spheres of the Earth,[78] meaning where the ether ring is forming as a first stage for Earth becoming a sun.[79] Michael as Archangel of the *Sun* is directly connected with the attainment of this goal.

What has been said here can moreover be described as follows. Just as the resurrection body can serve as a mirror-image on the microcosmic level (in man) for the replica of the Christ-'I' (goal of the Rosicrucian stream), so in future time the whole earth will play this role in the macrocosm when, through the work of human beings, it will have reached the highest stage of its spiritualization. Then, as the cosmic body of the Christ, it will become a perfect expression of His macrocosmic Sun-'I' that once was the spiritual centre of the Sun, a centre that was the necessary condition for the union of Earth with Sun (goal of the Michael stream).

Finally, as considered above in the fourth part of the meditation, the goals of both directions, the Rosicrucian and the Michaelic one, are connected. We thus have in Anthroposophy the union of the most intimate goals of Rosicrucian as well as Michaelic Christianity. This is the endeavour of the first to embed a replica of the Christ-'I' in the human 'I', and the striving of the second to transform the Earth into a new sun. The reason why such a union of Rosicrucian and Michaelic Christianity is only possible since the beginning of the present-day Michael-period, was explained by Rudolf Steiner in the above-quoted words, namely that only starting in this age can human beings reach a conscious relationship to Michael, something that in the past was unattainable even for highest initiated Rosicrucians.[80]

But what had unfolded up until the Christmas Conference in the Anthroposophical Movement alongside each other, moving alternately into the foreground and again into the background, was lifted in the New Mysteries, inaugurated during this conference, onto a higher stage and was guided into a completely new and henceforth inseparable unity. The result was that the coalescence of the path of Christian initiation in its modern spiritual scientific form (renewed Rosicrucianism) *rising* from below to above, with the Michael-revelation *descending* from above to below in the last third of the nineteenth century, was realized for the first time.[81] For only out of the flowing together of these two streams on Earth could the foundation be created for the Christianity of the future.

★

There is yet another, and for our age, perhaps the most important aspect of the joint workings by Christian Rosenkreutz, the leading initiate of esoteric Christianity, and the leading Time Spirit, Michael. This is their participation in the preparation of the central spiritual event of our time: the appearance of the Christ in etheric form.

Christian Rosenkreutz participates in this preparation with the help of his etheric body which came into existence as a result of his initiation in the thirteenth century. Concerning the present working of this etheric body, Rudolf Steiner made known the following: 'The twentieth century has the mission to allow this etheric body to become so powerful that it will even work exoterically', and that means outside the secret schools of the Rosicrucians. And 'those who are taken hold of by it [this etheric body] are privileged to experience the event that Paul experienced before Damascus ... In the twentieth century there will be more and more people who can encounter this effect and thereby will be allowed to experience the appearance of Christ in His etheric body'. (GA 130, 27 September 1911)

In this 'experience of Paul before Damascus' we deal with two aspects according to the Acts of the Apostles. The first is the appearance of the divine Christ *Light* and then, secondly, His own appearance as the divine *Sun* of the World. (See Acts 9, 3–4 and 17, 27) Likewise the words forming the centre of the fourth segment of the Foundation Stone Meditation, 'Light Divine / Sun of Christ' are a reference to the present revelation of the Christ out of the ether-sphere surrounding the Earth.

For today we have every reason to connect this 'Light Divine' with the etheric appearance of the Christ.[82] Furthermore, concerning Michael's participation in this spiritual event that is connected with the shining forth of the 'Sun of Christ' in the Earth aura, Rudolf Steiner stated: 'This event of the appearance of the Christ ... can only be brought about if the reign of Michael spreads out more and more. As yet it is still a process in the spiritual world. On the plane adjacent to our world, Michael in a manner of speaking battles in favour of the approach of the Christ ... Michael must fight the battle so that He does not appear in incorrect form in a subjectively [formed] Imagination by mankind, but appears in the proper Image ...' (GA 158, 9 November 1914)

Today therefore, preparation for the Second Coming takes place on two sides: From the microcosmic side, the etheric body of Christian Rosenkreutz illumines individual human souls and makes them receptive for the 'Light Divine' of the Etheric Christ. From the direction of the macrocosm, the Time Spirit Michael as Sun-Archangel serves the Second Coming and aids the shining forth of the 'Sun of Christ' among humanity. One could moreover say that Christian Rosenkreutz and with him all the Masters of Wisdom and Harmony of Feeling work from below to above, but from the other side, from above to below, Michael works in order to bring to realization the return of the Christ in the course of the next three millennia through their joint efforts.[83]

On the basis of these descriptions one can moreover understand why the most important task for Anthroposophy, which unites *both streams* in itself, the Michaelic as well as the Rosicrucian one, is the preparation and proclamation of the Etheric Coming in our time. Rudolf Steiner pointed out this task on more than one occasion in his lectures. Here we shall quote three of his statements:

'We now grasp spiritual science in a quite different sense. We learn that it is something that places a tremendous responsibility on us, for it is a *preparation* for the quite concrete event of the Christ's Second Coming.' (GA 118, 25 January 1910)

'Particularly in our age it is necessary that Christ is proclaimed. Therefore Anthroposophy too has the task to *proclaim* the Christ in [His] etheric form.' (GA 130, 4 November 1911)

'The Christ in all reality will be given to human beings who through spiritual science can strive upwards to the *comprehension*, the *beholding*, of the true Second Coming of the Christ.' (GA 118, 20 February 1910)

★

At the conclusion of this chapter the question shall be considered of how this union of the Rosicrucian and Michaelic stream in Rudolf Steiner's life's work relates to the Grail Mystery.

As we know, at the end of *Occult Science, an Outline*, Rudolf Steiner called Anthroposophy (which he had inaugurated) 'the science of the Grail'; and the initiates who tread the path depicted in this book he called 'initiates of the Grail' (GA 13, p. 407). It is Rudolf Steiner in the first place who belongs among these initiates of the Grail. This is why, in paying heed to these words, one can conclude that there exists a direct connection between the Foundation Stone and the nature of the Grail, as was in fact presented in the author's book, *Rudolf Steiner and the Founding of the New Mysteries* in the chapter, 'The Michael Age and the New Grail Event.'

When we turn to what has been said here, we can elucidate the question posed above through the drawing below:

The Michaelic Stream
(descending)

Spirit Research

Foundation Stone as
Centre of Modern Grail
Mysteries

The Rosicrucian Stream
(ascending)

Revelation

Here we have on the one side the stream *descending* to Earth out of the Sun-heights of Michael's new *revelations*, the Archangel who in 1879 rose to the rank of the leading Time Spirit. This is why, in his opening-lecture at the Christmas Conference, Rudolf Steiner pointed out that 'in the last third of the nineteenth century' a ' magnificent revelation, a revelation of something spiritual', was given to the world. (GA 260, 24 December 1923) In order to understand this revelation and to clothe it in thought forms that are accessible to every human being, the path of modern Christian-Rosicrucian initiation *ascends* towards this Spirit and bears towards the Michaelic revelation out of the spiritual world the faculty for *spirit research*, a faculty developed by man in himself consciously and freely. With the forming by Rudolf Steiner of the Foundation Stone as the modern centre of the Grail Mysteries in the spiritual world closest to the Earth, this unification process then attained its culmination.

Utilizing the image of the chalice, one can say that the ascending Rosicrucian stream creates its form. Into it pours the stream of the Michaelic revelation from above, filling it [this chalice] with spiritual substance and in so doing calling forth its radiance in the spiritual world, whereby man can find and experience in it the Foundation Stone and how, as the modern path to the Holy Grail, it is implanted into the ground of his heart.[84]

We can furthermore characterize what has been said above by starting out from the perspective of the *dual* creation of man, the being whom the Elohim, according to 'Genesis,' created according to their 'image' and 'likeness'. (See more on this in Chap 9) Later their paths separated as a consequence of the Fall of man. The 'image' remained in the higher worlds. The 'likeness' moved together with man to Earth after having lost its affinity to the divine-spiritual world. This is also why the restoration of man's original form ['Gestalt'] consists of two elements. From below, a human being gradually rises up through his own efforts while he slowly reacquires his 'divine likeness'. From above, to the degree that he completes this work, his divine 'image' (archetype) which had been retained in higher worlds descends to him like a divine manifestation. As to their ultimate union, that will occur as a result of the prevailing law according to which kin always strives to find access to what is originally its kin.[Tr.1]

In the sense of the stream of esoteric Christianity described in this chapter, one can say that in the Rosicrucian stream ascending to the spiritual world the forces of the 'likeness' or the Son of Man are at work, whereas in the Michael stream moving from above to below the forces of the 'image' or the Son of God are effective. At last in the Grail Mysteries, the union takes place between 'image' and 'likeness', something that signifies the beginning of the restoration of Spirit-Man in Earth-Man.

7. The Christmas Conference and the Supersensible Mystery of Golgotha

The experience of 'spiritually having stood before the Mystery of Golgotha' (described by Rudolf Steiner in Chap. 26 of *The Course of My Life*) also signified for him a conscious experience of this Mystery's inner essence in Intuition. This experience consists in the salvation of the individual human 'I' based on the forces of the original Phantom of the physical body (restored as it had been by the Christ). This central spiritual experience by Rudolf Steiner that completed his initiation process had a two-fold result for him: the penetration into the secret of the resurrection body and on this basis the intake of a replica of the Christ's World-'I' into his own ego.[85] For the latter is only possible as a result of the union with the forces of the Phantom which can serve as a 'mirror' for the Christ's cosmic 'I' in the human being, and this means as a portal for the entry of its replica.

As we saw already in Chapter 6, ego-consciousness originates as the experiencing of the individual 'I' that has become conscious in man only by means of the fact that it mirrors itself in the human body. In like manner, the replica of the Christ-'I' can be grasped by man in his consciousness only if this replica is mirrored by his physical body. No single human body can serve as a 'mirror' for the replica of the Christ-'I' however, if it has not previously received the forces of the Phantom that rose out of the tomb on Golgotha and can mirror such a replica. For while the replicas of the etheric and astral body of Christ Jesus were received unconsciously in past ages by specially chosen people and could be active in them without their knowing anything about it,[86] this is impossible in the case of the replicas of the 'I' by their very nature. The reason for this is that everything that is linked in man with the ego-principle must absolutely be grasped in our age by individual ego-consciousness.

After Rudolf Steiner had attained this experience he still had to wait twelve years before he could communicate to anthroposophists the secret of the Christ's Phantom and its relationship to the individual ego of man. This took place in October of 1911 during the lecture cycle, *From Jesus to Christ* (GA 131). Another twelve years went by before he could unveil the actual *path* to what he personally had experienced at the transition from the nineteenth to the twentieth century. He unveiled this actual *path* during the Christmas Conference by inaugurating the New Mysteries on Earth for all human beings of good will.

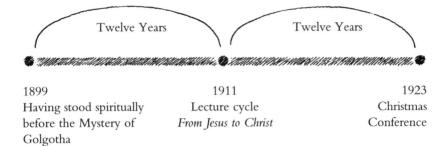

1899	1911	1923
Having stood spiritually before the Mystery of Golgotha	Lecture cycle *From Jesus to Christ*	Christmas Conference

This path that Rudolf Steiner chose to take can be detected in the sequence of the most important stages of the Christmas Conference. But if we wish to pursue this, it must be done in reverse sequence: First one becomes a member of the Anthroposophical Society, a purely exoteric institution recorded in the commercial register. Then comes a day when one begins to work with the Foundation Stone Meditation; then one continues on to its rhythms; and at last one reaches the point of laying the Foundation Stone into one's heart. With that one becomes a member of the true Christmas Conference Society as a purely esoteric institution (a spiritual foundation), whose members stand unshakeably on its supersensible Foundation Stone that is at its basis. This path of the Christmas Conference is open today to all people who have the will to work with the Foundation Stone, its meditation, and the rhythms, all of which in their totality form the spiritual centre of the Anthroposophical Society's esotericism.

	1	2	3	4
[Anthroposophical Society][87]	→ Foundation Stone Meditation	→ Rhythms	→ Foundation Stone	→ Anthroposophical Society of the Christmas Conference

The implanting of the Foundation Stone into one's own heart then leads to the inner experience of the resurrection-secret, meaning to the personal experience of which Rudolf Steiner spoke in the cycle *From Jesus to Christ*. Ultimately, this path can lead a person in the future to spiritually experiencing the Mystery of Golgotha that Rudolf Steiner wrote about in his autobiography.

★

Moreover, from all this the special relationship between Rudolf Steiner and Christian Rosenkreutz becomes clear, the two leading teachers of esoteric Christianity in the period of the consciousness soul. Both received a replica of the Christ-'I' into their 'I' at the culmination of their initiation: Christian Rosenkreutz in the sixteenth century[88] and Rudolf Steiner at the end of the nineteenth century in the year when Kali Yuga came to an end on Earth. This is why, as Rudolf Steiner explained to Ita Wegman, they stand together at a supersensible altar, and it can only be that altar upon which the sacred chalice glows that harbours the 'cosmic images' in which the 'secrets of Golgotha' live.[89] This means above all the secret of the connection between the resurrection body and the human 'I', as well as the secret that eventually Earth is to become a new sun and centre of the future Cosmos of Love.

But if work on the resurrection body was accessible in the Rosicrucian Mysteries only to the most advanced students within esoteric schools (schools that were strictly shielded from the outside world), in the new Mysteries founded at the Christmas Conference the connection with the forces of the Phantom (which leads to the introduction of a replica of the Christ-'I' into one's own 'I') is accessible to all who have the will today to enter upon this path.

Put differently, what Christian Rosenkreutz (the first within the esoteric schools established by him) accomplished was carried out by Rudolf Steiner for the whole of humanity inasmuch as he transformed the Philosopher's Stone—the centre of the Rosicrucian Mysteries—into the Stone of Love (or the hexagram into a pentagram). This was pointed out by Zeylmans van Emmichoven.[90] Rudolf Steiner accomplished this under the guidance and in the service of Michael, today's leading Time Spirit.

It is of significance here that Rudolf Steiner spoke of the secret of the Christ's Phantom and its connection with the human ego only two months prior to founding the independent esoteric group, 'Theosophical Ethos and Art' within the German section of the Theosophical Society. He intended to separate this group later on from himself and place it under the direct leadership of Christian Rosenkreutz.[91] The content of the cycle *From Jesus to Christ* is thus directly linked with the establishment of this group, as is Rudolf Steiner's mission with that of Christian Rosenkreutz.

In connection with the establishment of the esoteric group in the autumn of 1911, Rudolf Steiner spoke of three calls by the spiritual world to humanity. The first call issued forth in 1879 through Michael. And the response to it was the founding of Anthroposophy at the beginning of the twentieth century.[92] The second call happened along with the establishment of the esoteric group in 1911. It came from Christian Rosenkreutz, the leading Master of the 'White Lodge' of the Masters of Wisdom and Harmony of Feeling. The third call was the Christmas Conference.[93] This third call of the spiritual world was issued through Rudolf Steiner.

But if such a call were to go unheard for the third time, so Rudolf Steiner said as early as 1911, meaning if those to whom it is directed should pay no attention to it nor follow it, then mankind would have to wait a long time for the next suitable opportunity.[94]

Here we have a sequence of spiritual happenings, the basis of which is the event in Rudolf Steiner's life that he himself has described as 'spiritually having stood before the Mystery of Golgotha in most inward, most earnest joy of knowledge', meaning as the encounter with the Christ in Intuition. (GA 13)

1899	1900	→ 1911	→ 1923
Encounter with the Christ in *Intuition*	Call by Michael in *Inspiration*[95]	Call by Christian Rosenkreutz and response in *Imagination* (for that reason the group 'Ethos and Art')	Call by Rudolf Steiner and response to it in *comprehension* and will for collaboration

★

This makes it understandable why Rudolf Steiner, having formed the Foundation Stone in the morning of 25 December, forthwith handed it over to the members of the Anthroposophical Society. Not even for a moment did he keep it to himself but offered this, his greatest creation, at once to other human beings.[96] This corresponds to the nature of the Foundation Stone that was formed out of the substance of cosmic love and human love. In the lecture 'Love and Its Meaning in the World' (GA 143, 17 December 1912), Rudolf Steiner explained that during the creation of the world God merely held on to love, but for the sake of human freedom allotted wisdom and power correspondingly to Lucifer and Ahriman. Therefore, owing to its divine nature, from the very beginning only love has neither degrees nor levels—it either is or it is not. Wisdom and power on the other hand, require constant development in man, linked with the conscious effort to overcome Lucifer's and Ahriman's influence.

Nobody can therefore retain the fruits of true deeds of love, for love grows and bears fruit only if it is sacrificed to others. Here the principle of love cannot be separated from that of sacrifice. And this is why the 'Foundation Stone of *Love*', created as it had been out of the forces of Michael, could only belong to the General Anthroposophical Society, which means to a community of human beings who at this moment represented the whole of mankind before the countenance of the Time Spirit.

To all Christian initiates, the highest archetype of such service is the Christ who said of Himself: 'For the Son of Man also has not come to be served, but to serve and to give His life for the deliverance of many.' (Mk 10, 45)

In accordance with this commitment, Rudolf Steiner, the leading Christian initiate and present-day follower of the Christ, entrusted the Foundation Stone formed out of the highest forces of the macrocosm to the anthroposophists and united his karma with the karma of the Anthroposophical Society founded by him.[97]

★

In order to approach a true understanding of the esoteric nature of the Christmas Conference, it is necessary to realize that it is not enough merely to become aware of the one basic fact that Rudolf Steiner brought his students some new wisdom,[98] but above all, that he *created something completely new* in the spiritual world adjacent to the Earth. This was the first *creation* by a human being as representative of the tenth hierarchy who brought such a sacrifice in full *freedom* in order to create the *Stone of Love* in the spiritual world.

Just as the whole immeasurable sky is reflected in a little dewdrop in nature early in the morning, so the whole macrocosm is reflected in the microcosm. In this sense the deed by Rudolf Steiner at the Christmas Conference harbours within itself something of the Mystery of Golgotha and therefore represents a continuation of the latter. For the Mystery of Golgotha is not merely another source of wisdom bestowed on humanity. It is a completely new *act of creation* in the whole cosmos, the beginning of a *new creation*; the forming of a 'new' member of human nature 'out of the forces of freedom and love, out of the resurrection body as the foundation of the future Cosmos of Love'.[99]

It was not a matter of books or lectures at the Christmas Conference. Here Rudolf Steiner created something quite real in the spiritual world adjacent to the Earth. Only on this basis could he justifiably speak of this creation as the 'beginning of a cosmic turning-point of time'. (GA 260, 1 January 1924) This means he spoke of an event that is directly connected with the Mystery of Golgotha and therefore is a continuation of it on Earth, however not on the divine but human level. The deed that was accomplished out of *divine* freedom and love by the divine Word (Logos) descending out of spiritual heights was to form a foundation on which a human being, who has attained the stage of *human* freedom and love, might give a response to that deed in the direction from below to above on the path of the New Mysteries.

How was this possible? How could this be accomplished by Rudolf Steiner, the first human being to do so? Why was this path henceforth accessible to everybody? For this there are two explanations. A subjective one consists in the special, unique spiritual development of Rudolf Steiner; an objective one involves a certain spiritual event that occurred in the second half of the nineteenth century as communicated by Anthroposophy to us.

We are dealing here with the spiritual event which at that time took place in the spiritual world when Michael was completely engaged in the battle with the Spirits of Darkness. These are spirits who in their totality form the body of the ahrimanic dragon in the spiritual world; the dragon who, after thirty-eight years of conflict (1841–1879), Michael cast down from heaven to earth, out of the world of the gods into that of men.[100] This event is a repetition of the Mystery of Golgotha, but this time not on the Earth but in the spiritual world adjacent to Earth. Rudolf Steiner described it as follows:

'The seeds of earthly materialism, carried up since the sixteenth century in ever greater measure by souls crossing through the portal of death into the spiritual world (seeds that caused increasing darkness), formed the black sphere of materialism. In accordance with the Manichaean principle this black sphere was absorbed by the Christ into His nature so that it would be transformed. This caused "spiritual death by suffocation" in the angelic being in whom the Christ entity manifested since the Mystery of Golgotha. This sacrifice of the Christ in the nineteenth century is comparable to the sacrifice on the earthly plane in the Mystery of Golgotha, and can be designated as the second crucifixion of Christ on the etheric plane. This spiritual death by asphyxiation that brought about the cessation of consciousness in the angelic being is a repetition of the Mystery of Golgotha in the worlds lying directly behind our world so that a re-enlivening of the earlier concealed Christ consciousness in the souls of men on Earth can take place. This re-enlivening in the twentieth century turns into clairvoyant vision for humanity.

'In this way, the Christ consciousness can be united with the earthly consciousness of humanity beginning in the twentieth century, for the dying down of the Christ consciousness in the angelic sphere in the nineteenth century signifies the re-arising of the direct Christ consciousness in the Earth sphere. This means that, beginning in the twentieth century, the life of Christ will increasingly be felt in the souls of men as a direct personal experience ... Twice the Christ has already been crucified; once physically in the physical world at the beginning of our era, and a second time spiritually in the nineteenth century in the way described above. One could say that mankind experienced the resurrection of His body at that time. From the start of the twentieth century they will experience the resurrection of His *consciousness*.' (GA 152, 2 May 1913)

As a helper and 'mediator', Michael participates directly in this process of the gradual awakening of a new Christ consciousness in humanity. 'What I have been able to communicate merely in a few words will gradually penetrate into human souls and the mediator, the emissary, will be Michael who is now the messenger of the Christ. Just as he earlier guided the souls of men so that they could understand how His life was directed from heaven to earth, so Michael now prepares humanity to become capable of experiencing how the Christ consciousness is directed from the condition of unconsciousness to the state of consciousness.' (ibid.) The place where such an awakening of the new Christ consciousness can take place today under Michael's leadership is that of the New Mysteries inaugurated by Rudolf Steiner on Earth.

If therefore the first Mystery of Golgotha occurred on the level of physical *existence*, namely death and resurrection of the god in the physical body of a human being whereby all the relationships of the divine and human world were changed in the macrocosm, the second Mystery of Golgotha came to pass on the level of *consciousness* as extinction and 'revivification' of the Christ consciousness in a certain angelic being, who since the Mystery of Golgotha was the bearer of this consciousness. The effect of this supersensible Mystery of Golgotha is on the one hand the appearance of the Christ in etheric form starting in the twentieth century; on the other, during the course of the next three millennia, it is the gradual awakening of a new fully conscious clairvoyance among humankind, a clairvoyance capable of beholding the Etheric Christ.

As was shown in another work by the author,[101] this relationship of the original Mystery of Golgotha to the supersensible one clearly comes to the fore as a relationship of existence and consciousness in the New Mysteries. For they are linked to the second Mystery of Golgotha in the supersensible worlds in the same way as is Christendom (established on Earth) to the first Mystery. Just as Christianity could never have come into being without the death and resurrection of Christ on Golgotha, so the New Mysteries too could never have been founded, if the recurrence of the Mystery of Golgotha in the supersensible worlds had not preceded them.[102]

The key words of the Christmas Conference, 'the beginning of a world turning-point of time' (GA 260, 1 January 1924), point both to the connection of the New Mysteries with the original Mystery of Golgotha, as well as to their connection with the recurrence of the Mystery of Golgotha in the supersensible worlds.

The task of the New Mysteries in regard to the first Mystery of Golgotha is therefore a twofold one:

—to bring to humanity the new spiritual scientific insight concerning it and, with the help of this new insight,
—to bring about a conscious connection of man to the forces of the Phantom of the Christ.[103]

The twofold task is similar in regard to the second Mystery of Golgotha:

—to prepare humanity for the perception of the Etheric Christ, a subject to which Rudolf Steiner dedicated not merely a handful but hundreds of lectures (see Chap. 6)

And what is doubtlessly the main task of Anthroposophy in regard to the Etheric Christ, namely,

—that humanity becomes a new sheath for Him in the supersensible worlds.

At the conclusion of the Christmas lecture cycle in 1914, Rudolf Steiner openly pointed once to this central secret of Anthroposophy. He initially directed the attention of his listeners to the fact that the spiritual science he had inaugurated was as yet in its infancy, and that one could merely look with greatest humility to what would eventually originate from it. 'Today we really have in our newly begun spiritual science a child. Therefore the Christmas festival is truly our festival ...'. (GA 156, 26 December 1914). Still, although it is as yet a new-born infant, the most important central element in it is 'the new comprehension of the Mystery of Golgotha' and 'the new Christ-comprehension'. (ibid) Nonetheless, to the extent that this comprehension will develop and be disseminated in the world, there will occur what Rudolf Steiner, continuing on, calls 'the promise of a secure future' and harbours within itself the main task of Anthroposophy: 'Let us build up in our souls confidence in the fulfilment of this promise; the confidence we feel today for the child we want to adore—this child that is the new Christ comprehension—that it might grow, live, and before too long mature in such a way that, *in it, the etherically appearing Christ can incarnate*, even as the Christ could incarnate in the body of flesh at the time of the Mystery of Golgotha.' (ibid.)

Put differently, just as the Christ could incarnate during the Baptism in the Jordan in the sheaths of Jesus of Nazareth that were prepared for Him so, if Anthroposophy truly fulfils its task in the world in our age, the Etheric Christ will be able to 'incarnate' in the supersensible sheaths prepared by it. Then something shall come about in the spiritual world that can be compared with the Baptism in the Jordan, but this time not in earthly but in purely supersensible form; meaning not as a baptism with water but the baptism with spirit and fire as prophesied by John. (Lk 3, 6) Just as it had been a general human task for John the Baptist at the Turning-point of Time to carry out the Baptism and make it possible for the Christ to incarnate on Earth, so in our age it was the task of the founder of Anthroposophy, Rudolf Steiner, to create the possibility for the Etheric Christ, but now in higher worlds to incarnate in the sheaths that are fashioned for Him through the efforts of all earthly human beings who are connected with Anthroposophy.

This is moreover a further indication that Anthroposophy is not merely a teaching but an actual living being in the higher worlds, a being whom Rudolf Steiner called a 'supersensible' or 'invisible human being'. (See GA 231, 18 November 1923 and GA 258, 16 June 1923)

Furthermore, here the inner relationship between this loftiest goal of Anthroposophy and the founding of the Anthroposophical Society at the Christmas Conference becomes comprehensible. The latter was to become 'a true community of human beings for Anthroposophia', as Rudolf Steiner put it. (GA 260, 25 December 1923) We have here a certain sequence of events. Persons who of their own free will have joined together in the Anthroposophical Society are supposed to form a *soul-sheath* for the incarnation of the being Anthroposophia here on Earth. This is done by means of having embedded the Foundation Stone in their hearts, as well as by inner work on it, its meditations, and the rhythms; while on her part in the higher worlds Anthroposophia becomes the *spiritual* bearer of the Etheric Christ. That is the path on which the Etheric Christ can today enter into humanity.

—The General Anthroposophical Society becomes the bearer of the being Anthroposophia

—The being Anthroposophia becomes the bearer of the Etheric Christ.

This relationship can be deepened still more through the following words by Rudolf Steiner that he expressed immediately following the reference to the central task of Anthroposophy: 'Let us now be filled with the *light* that can illumine us through confidence in this promise to the deepest inner core of soul; let us be warmed with the *warmth* that can pulse through our heart [Gemüt].'[104] (GA 156 26 December 1914) These words correspond almost exactly to those he used when concluding the Christmas Conference at the end of the evening lecture on 1 January 1924. Now he added what was most important, something that nine years earlier had merely been confidence in 'the promise of a secure future', a future from which Anthroposophy was then 'no longer separated by such a long period of time'. (ibid.) This most important aspect consists in the Christ-Sun's lighting up in the New Mysteries:

> *Light Divine,*
> *Sun of Christ,*
> Warm Thou
> Our Hearts,
> Enlighten Thou
> Our Heads.

Thus in the course of the cultic Foundation Stone Laying, the light and warmth that henceforth shine forth in the etheric world from the Foundation Stone created by Rudolf Steiner, become reality in the present. Then this microcosmic light and microcosmic warmth of the Foundation Stone were connected with the macrocosmic light and macrocosmic warmth that the Christ bore at the Turning-point of Time into Earth evolution.[105] At the same time the threefold structure of the Foundation Stone was connected with the essential nature of Christ's etheric return. For the substance of the new revelation of the Christ is *Love*. The supersensible form of this revelation, on the other hand, consists of *Imaginations;* the light aura surrounding Him that makes visible this revelation in the spiritual world consists of the *thought-light* directed towards the spirit by human thoughts.[106]

With this, what in 1914 was still 'a promise of a secure future' was realized at the Christmas Conference, during which light and warmth found their concrete expression in the Foundation Stone as their spiritual fountainhead and then were filled by the macrocosmic light and macrocosmic warmth of the Christ which had entered into Earth evolution through the Mystery of Golgotha.[107] Owing to this, the 'embodiment' of the Etheric Christ into the being Anthroposophia could take place at the Christmas Conference. Moreover, the foundation could be created for participation in this process by all human beings who are intent on entering upon the path of the New Mysteries.

This important event that belongs among the esoteric foundations of the Anthroposophical Movement is thus a direct consequence of the repetition of the Mystery of Golgotha in the supersensible worlds; worlds that bestowed on humanity the possibility to develop the new Christ consciousness in their minds.

When we now become aware that the Foundation Stone Meditation is the most perfect and all-encompassing mantric expression of the being Anthroposophia (see Chap. 1) and that this meditation's rhythms in their sevenfold structure guide us directly into the nature of the ether world where the Etheric Christ is at work today, then we can view the work with the esoteric content of the Christmas Conference (an integral part of the New Mysteries) in all its central Christological significance.

Then the most important, one could also say, portentous question for the further development of the Anthroposophical Society will be: Will the above-mentioned supersensible processes merely form the content of the Anthroposophical Movement or will they likewise become the content and inner centre of the Anthroposophical Society, owing to the Society members' spiritual work that is aimed at actualizing the Christmas Conference's esotericism?

There is no theoretical answer to this question. The only possible practical reply can be given by means of the conscious efforts on the part of the members of the Anthroposophical Society for true comprehension and realization of the afore-mentioned ideal; in other words as a result of the fact that they pursue the esoteric path that the Christmas Conference unveiled for them:

| Foundation Stone | → Rhythms | → Foundation Stone Meditation | → Forming of General Anthroposophical Society out of forces of Foundation Stone |

All this furthermore leads to the conclusion that the union of the Christ with the being Anthroposophia at the Christmas Conference found its earthly reflection in the union of the Anthroposophical Movement with the Anthroposophical Society on Earth. For the Anthroposophical

Movement in the supersensible worlds is nothing else but the developmental process of Anthroposophia,[107a] who (being filled with the Christ Being) is spiritually able now to unite with the human *community* that is ready to work with her. Rudolf Steiner spoke about this possibility at the end of the cultic laying of the Foundation Stone, when he turned to all the members of the newly founded Anthroposophical Society with the words: 'Then will you found here a true community of human beings for Anthroposophia.' (GA 260, p. 62)

In this sense, Anthroposophia is a supersensible mediator in our age between the Etheric Christ and the human community that has received from her the task to prepare mankind for recognition of Him. A replica of this supersensible fact on Earth (and at the same time the paramount prerequisite for her activity as mediator) is the union of the Anthroposophical Movement with the Anthroposophical Society. This is something all members of the Anthroposophical Society can fulfil who place the Foundation Stone of the Christmas Conference into their heart and, based on it, do their anthroposophical work.

★

What now remains to be added is that, in the history of the Anthroposophical Movement, the above described process of *baptism* of the being Anthroposophia with fire and spirit (so that she can become the bearer of the Etheric Christ) has concrete significance. For her baptism with fire took place at New Year's Eve of 1922/23, when the First Goetheanum (the Johannes-Bau), representing her artistic-Imaginative appearance on Earth, passed across into the distances of the etheric world 'in which lived the Spirit', (GA 233a, 22 April 1924) the Spirit that then manifested at the Christmas Conference in the aura of the thought-light around the Foundation Stone.[108]

The baptism of Anthroposophia with fire and spirit is therefore that spiritual/historic reality which enables us today to recognize that at the Christmas Conference the Etheric Christ actually incarnated in her supersensible being. This signifies that the 'prediction', expressed by Rudolf Steiner at Christmas 1914, was in truth fulfilled. This supersensible fact belongs moreover to the inner substance of his words about the 'beginning of a world turning-point of time' whence the elemental spirits serving the Christ in the ether world call out to mankind: 'May human beings hear it!' Or put more directly: It was truly the Etheric Christ Himself who baptized the being Anthroposophia with the fire of the flaming Goetheanum and the Spirit that a year later appeared at the Christmas Conference.

From the standpoint of the inner development of Anthroposophia, this most important event in her 'spiritual biography' furthermore became possible due to her having reached at that time the twenty-first year in the course of her earthly evolution; the moment when the 'I'-principle awakened in her. This is why Rudolf Steiner spoke publicly for the first time in 1923, the year preceding the Christmas Conference, of her as a supersensible human being, and divided her development on Earth into three sequential seven-year periods, (see GA 257, 258) in the character-ization of which the three main elements of the future Foundation Stone can be discerned without difficulty:

First Seven-Year Period (1902–1909)	— Forming of Anthroposophy in thought (founding of spiritual science)	— Thinking (Science)	— Thinking as main instrument of spiritual insights
Second Seven-year Period (1909–1916)	— Imaginative forming of Anthroposophy (development of art)	— Feeling (Art)	— Imagination as basis for artistic activity
Third Seven-Year Period (1916–1923)	— Practical forming of Anthroposophy (the various initiatives)	— Willing (social activity)	— Love as a new creative force.[109]

Accordingly, since the Christmas Conference, the Etheric Christ is inseparably connected with the living supersensible being Anthro-posophia as her 'higher I'. Now it depends solely on human beings (the anthroposophists) to create such conditions on Earth that she is able to work through the Anthroposophical Society in the form Rudolf Steiner worded this at the conclusion of the cultic act of the Foundation Stone Laying.

★

On the basis of what has been presented in this chapter a supposition can be made concerning the possible substance of the Second and Third Class of the Michael School (the School of Spiritual Science) that was inaugurated by Rudolf Steiner directly out of the esoteric impulse of the Christmas Conference.

While in the First Class we mainly have revelations of the forces of Michael as representative of the higher hierarchies,[110] in the Second Class it is likely that because of its cultic forms[111] a relationship to the cosmic cultus of the eighteenth/nineteenth century was to be established. In this cultus the Anthroposophia Being assumed a central position, for the

Sophia-forces in the cosmos are connected with the Imaginative-cultic element (the 'royal art' of the Rosicrucians) due to their origin. The third or 'Master-Class' on the other hand, was probably supposed to bring about a direct relationship with the Etheric Christ. The possibility to inaugurate it was the most significant consequence of the 'incarnation' of the Etheric Christ in the Anthroposophia being at the Christmas Conference. This results in the following structure of the esoteric Michael School:

First Class   —*Michael*
Second Class —Michael-*Sophia*
Third Class   —Michael-Sophia-*Christ*

These three classes can then moreover be described as a process of ascent from Michael to Sophia and from her to the Christ, or from the Spirit of Strength to Heavenly Wisdom, and from her to Divine Love as the highest Creator Power in the universe.

A further aspect of the three classes of the School of Spiritual Science is that in them can be seen the step-by-step development of those spiritual forces that will be required in the course of the fifth, sixth, and seventh cultural period of the great Post-Atlantean Epoch (the fifth epoch). A reason for this conjecture ensues from Rudolf Steiner's indication that from the very beginning it has been Anthroposophy's task to make ready a small group of human beings who in the future can bring about the transition from the great Fifth to the great Sixth Epoch of humanity's evolution. (See Chap. 6 for this)

Since the main task of the fifth cultural period is the development of the individual 'I' through thinking, this means that what has been said above can be understood with the aid of Michael's Cosmic Intelligence, an intelligence that had once descended to man. The sixth cultural period, on the other hand, will have as its task the development of the social forces of humanity. (See GA 186, 7 December 1918) The inspirer of that period will be the heavenly Sophia. Ultimately, in the seventh cultural period that will outwardly be a time of the greatest moral decadence of mankind, the devastating 'War of All Against All' will reach its peak. Then, in order not to succumb to the evil that will rule the world but to fulfil their spiritual task and lay the ground for the Sixth Great Epoch, human beings in their battle with evil require the relationship to the Christ as their mightiest helper and bearer of those forces that alone are able to lead them into the future. All this was supposed to be prepared already in our time in the three classes of the esoteric Michael School.

On the other side, this development can also be seen as a conscious forming of the three sheaths for the Christ Impulse in humanity through the members of the Esoteric School. (GA 155, 30 May 1912) In this sense the First Class of the Michael School is chiefly linked with the development of the *forces of insight* or *knowledge*, something that is possible only on the basis of *awe* and *reverence* in regard to the spiritual world. (It is described at the beginning of the book, *Knowledge of the Higher Worlds and Its Attainment*.) In the Second Class, the development of the *social faculties* would then take centre-stage through new cultic forms. The fount of these new social faculties must be the awakening of the forces of *love and compassion* in man that are capable of extending even into karma itself in transforming ways, without which no social ideal can be realized (as for example the establishment of a new karma-community on Earth). In the final Third Class the unfolding of the *forces of conscience* in metamorphosed form (leading to the experiencing of the Christ as Lord of Karma) would likely have been the essential ideal. Such a 'seeing conscience' that is capable of clairvoyantly experiencing the consequences of deeds acted out in the past, something that is to begin in our time (see GA 116, 2 May, 1910) will be necessary for *co-operating with the Lord of Karma*. It will moreover be required in the future for the transition from the seventh cultural period into the Sixth Great Epoch of Earth evolution.[111a]

If we now become aware that the afore-mentioned faculties are intended to create the astral, etheric, and spiritual/physical sheath for the Christ Impulse on Earth so that the Christ as the highest 'I' of mankind might incarnate in human beings, a further goal of the Michael School becomes evident to us: the school that Michael himself leads as the 'sun-countenance' of the Christ and present-day Time Spirit.

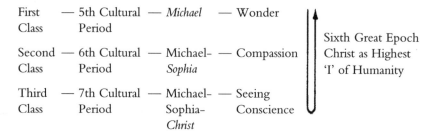

In order to forestall misconceptions, it must be added here that the founding of the Second and Third Class can only be carried out by Rudolf Steiner in his next incarnation or by another lofty initiate of his rank, meaning by one who likewise belongs to the circle of the Masters of the 'White Lodge' who manage the spiritual guidance of all mankind.

Moreover such an esoteric action cannot simply be carried out based on the wish of one or another person but only with the consent and determination of the spiritual world. Whether such a determination is made depends on the degree to which today's members of the Michael School will be in a position to actualize *all* the spiritual possibilities that were already given to anthroposophists along with the first part of the First Class. For it is only our relationship to the contents already given to us that can serve as the basis for a justified hope that Rudolf Steiner or another leading Master of the 'White Lodge' will one day continue with the extension of the Michael School on Earth.[112]

It is therefore not a matter of fruitless dreams concerning the establishment of the Second or Third Class, but active work for attaining the goals of the First Class-contents entrusted to us. That is the most urgent question of the present, and on its solution will depend the further destinies of the Michael School on Earth.[113] If presently incarnated anthroposophists do not accomplish this most important task, how can they hope that the spiritual world will guide them further and would permit those who have neglected the first stage to enter upon the second and third? The most secure and shortest path to the inauguration of the additional Classes of the Esoteric School consists therefore in occupying oneself in greatest possible earnestness with the already existing and active First Class and to take upon oneself all possible efforts to actualize its goals and tasks.

For the spiritual world, our attitude to the First Class is therefore the concrete expression of our true relationship to the spiritual beings who stand behind the modern Esoteric School—to Michael, Sophia, and Christ.

8. The Christmas Conference as a Path into the Temple of the New Mysteries

The inner connection of the First Goetheanum's foremost artistic structural elements with the general composition of the Foundation Stone has been cited repeatedly in anthroposophical literature. An essential aid for understanding these communal aspects can be Rudolf Steiner's indication that a visitor to the First Goetheanum receives three distinct impressions upon entering it which in turn correspondingly affect his thinking, feeling, and willing. Hence experiencing the pictorial contents, especially the colour scale of the paintings in the two cupolas, works in an enlivening and spiritualizing manner upon a person's *thinking*. Through moving one's glance from below to above along the columns, capitals, and architraves, they could then influence the sphere of *feeling* in a similar ordering and spiritualizing way. In so doing a special role was supposed to be played by viewing the glass windows with the initiation motifs and colour effects (the coloured light and shadows). From that followed the experience of the powerful metamorphoses of the capitals and architraves which in their movement and rhythmic sequence called forth a definite division of the building's inner space: Two rows of seven columns each in the great hall, and twelve columns in the small one. The overall inner space could thus work in a transforming, impulse-giving, way on the *will* as the visitor moved in the great hall from West to East, that is from the world of matter into the world of spirit.

This threefold effect of the inner configuration of the structure was once summed up by Rudolf Steiner as follows: 'Our structure thus expresses ... willing, feeling, and thinking, but in their evolution, in what *they are supposed to become* in the being of man, a being *that strives for a certain development of itself* ... If I walk from West to East in this building, I move the way the sphere of will moves in human beings. If I direct my glance from below to above and observe the forms of the columns and architraves, I concentrate on the secrets of the sphere of feeling in human nature. If I study what arches in the cupola-paintings on top of what we experience within the building, then we study the secrets of the sphere of human thinking.' (GA 287, 24 October 1914) What is striking in these words is that Rudolf Steiner speaks of the development of willing, feeling, and thinking in the identical sequence as will be presented later on in the Foundation Stone Meditation. Here the first part is devoted to the development of the will, of how it is supposed to evolve in the spiritual world. This is the reason why, instead of the word 'will' the word 'live' appears in the corresponding sentence of the Foundation Stone Meditation. For in the spiritual world, will becomes for humans the new life-element in which they then sojourn.[114] In the same way the second part of the meditation is devoted to the development and transformation of feeling, and the third to the spiritualization of thinking. The fact that in all three cases we deal with capabilities possessed by these soul forces already on *yonder side of the threshold* is borne out in the meditation by the word 'truly' as well as by the second line of the pairs:

And thou wilt *truly live*
In the All-World-Being of Man.

And thou wilt *truly feel*
'mid the weaving of the Soul of Man.

And thou wilt *truly think*
From the ground of the Spirit of Man.

The content of the large red window in the West attests to the fact that entry into the inner space of the Goetheanum was to turn into an artistic-occult crossing of the threshold, behind which a complete transformation of thinking, feeling, and willing has to occur. The centre of this window features the countenance of a human being who strives for self knowledge and has already attained to 'truth-filled' thinking, feeling and willing, and along with them the faculty to experience the 'All-World-Being', the 'weaving of soul' and the 'ground of the spirit' of his own being. At the right and left of his forehead two Angels are depicted who inspire the human being's thinking out of the spiritual forces of the Sun and Moon.[115] Below the Sun-Angel is the figure of a lion who represents the element of feeling; under the Moon-Angel a bull represents the will. In the vertical direction too, the red window has a threefold structure corresponding to thinking, feeling and willing. Thinking comes into view in the upper segment (on the forehead) through the two-petaled lotus flower, feeling through the sixteen-petaled one, and willing through the image of Michael who has engaged the dragon in the human heart in battle and has overcome it.

In this way the red window prepares a person on the verge of entering the Goetheanum's interior for what is then supposed to become an actual experience in him/her. It can furthermore be said in accordance with the Foundation Stone Meditation that on the red window appears the image of a human being who, at the threshold into the spiritual world, experiences the encounter with his higher 'I' in the figure of the Guardian of the Threshold. On the side-panels we see the depiction of the process of how thinking, feeling, and willing become 'truth-filled'. On the left side-panel appear the as yet not purified (not yet 'true') three soul forces in the form of three beasts who rise out of the abyss and threaten man who is striving consciously to cross over the threshold to the spiritual world. On the right side-panel, the overcoming of the beasts and the shining forth of the spiritual sun is depicted to the inner vision of the human being as the result of his thinking, feeling, and willing that have become 'truth-filled'.

The two halls, the large auditorium and the small hall in which the stage was located, correspond in the spiritual regard to the microcosm (the former one) and the macrocosm (the latter one).[116] The evolution of man through the seven planetary conditions formed the main theme of the architraves and columns of the big hall, whereas the twelve columns of the small hall represented the zodiac that surrounds and accompanies (inspires) man's sevenfold evolution. The connection of the big hall with the microcosm or evolution and the small one with the macrocosm or involution attests to the connection of the fourteen columns of the big hall with the twelve columns of the small one, just as the drawing by Daniel van Bemmelen[117] depicts it.

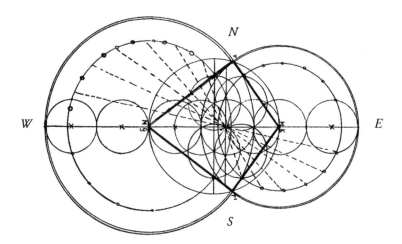

He himself explained this drawing as follows: 'If we draw directional lines from each column of the small cupola through the lectern, they will come to rest midway between the distance of two columns of the big cupola-hall.' In the spiritual sense, this means the *forms* of the capitals, columns, and bases (thrones) of the little hall connect with the intervals between the columns. If therefore the former seven are (physical) forms of the evolution of the universe, or Manvantaras, then the latter correspond to the spiritual intervals between these, namely the Pralayas. With that, the big hall points to the main evolutionary stages of the visible (earthly) cosmos, and the smaller to the spiritual world; the world out of which the material universe arises afresh again and again, in order then to reach the next higher stage of development.[118] The point of intersection by the twelve rays (or streams of forces out of the sphere of the zodiac) that proceed from the little hall and spiritually generate all the forms of the big hall therefore falls into the middle of the proscenium where, at the boundary of both halls (the intersection between microcosm and macrocosm), the lectern was supposed to stand from where anthroposophical lectures were to be given, meaning fruits of spiritual research that were to be communicated, above all by Rudolf Steiner in person. This location in the Goetheanum was to be the *fount of the Word* through which man in his capacity as the future tenth hierarchy was able to give answer to the gods who have created him and spoken to him through the forms of the building. Moreover, this is why Rudolf Steiner spoke of the fact that in their totality the forms and colours of the building were 'speech organs of the gods' through which they speak to human beings today and that the structure as a whole was 'the house of speech, the speaking house, the house that is alive in all its walls'. (GA 286, 17 June 1914)

In this capacity (in the new world epoch that has begun following the Mystery of Golgotha) the Goetheanum was supposed to renew the Mysteries of the Word out of the fountainhead of the Mystery of Golgotha; mysteries such as those nurtured long ago in the temple at Ephesus in Asia Minor that inspired John to write the prologue of his gospel. It was therefore no coincidence that the First Goetheanum had been called the 'Johannes-Bau' and that during the Christmas Conference on 31 December, the anniversary of the fire, Rudolf Steiner pointed directly to its connection with the fiery end of the temple at Ephesus: 'In this Goetheanum there was indeed, for those who had a feeling for it, a memory of the temple at Ephesus.' (GA 260, 31 December 1923)

★

All this makes the significance of the twelve thrones more comprehensible, the bases that form the lower end of the columns in the small hall. With their artistic-Imaginative shapes, they refer to the central secret of anthroposophical Christology, namely the circle of the twelve Bodhisattvas in the world of Providence (Buddhi) out of which the spiritual impulses descend into the earthly world, impulses that lead all of Earth evolution. This circle of the Bodhisattvas, which in its totality forms the body of the Holy Spirit as the 'personified omniscient wisdom of *our world*', (GA 113, 31 August 1909; emphasis by Rudolf Steiner) is grouped around a central fountainhead, a primal source that not only bestows on the Bodhisattvas the forces of wisdom but something infinitely more essential, namely omniscient life itself. And this sublime source is the Christ.

Rudolf Steiner once said about this: 'Twelve Bodhisattvas thus belong with the Christ who are to prepare and elaborate what He brought as the greatest impulse to our cultural development. We behold [in the world of Buddhi or Providence] the twelve and in their midst the thirteenth. With that we have ascended into the sphere of the Bodhisattvas and entered a circle of twelve stars—*and in their midst the Sun that illuminates and warms them*. From it they have that *fount of life* which they in turn have to carry down once again to Earth.' (GA 16, 25 October 1909) These words of the illuminating and warming Christ-Sun correspond precisely to the middle part of the meditation's fourth segment:

> Light Divine,
> Sun of Christ
> Warm Thou
> Our Hearts,
> Enlighten Thou
> Our Heads.

In the same lecture, Rudolf Steiner on that occasion continued to describe the service rendered by the Bodhisattvas to the Christ-Sun: 'Only when the last one of the Bodhisattvas belonging with the Christ will have completed his work, will mankind sense what the Christ is. Then shall *humanity be ensouled by a will in which the Christ Himself lives*. The Christ shall move into human nature *through thinking, feeling and willing*; and humanity shall be the outward expression of the Christ on Earth.' (ibid.) Here the reference to the three soul forces corresponds to the first three parts of the Foundation Stone Meditation in which the path is invoked that leads to their becoming 'truth-filled'; that makes them able to receive the Christ into themselves. And the word of the 'will ... in which the Christ Himself lives' corresponds exactly to the following two lines of the second or 'soul'-part of the meditation:

> 'For the Christ-Will in the encircling Round holds sway
> In the Rhythms of worlds, blessing the soul.'

In these rhythms in which the 'Christ-Will' sheds grace upon souls, the activity of the twelve Bodhisattvas out of the sphere of Providence is expressed throughout all of Earth evolution. The first six Bodhisattvas had the task of preparing the coming of Christ to the Earth; the other six to bring human beings the fruits of the Mystery of Golgotha.[119] All together the mission of the twelve Bodhisattvas encompasses the *totality* of Earth evolution. 'We cannot possibly speak of more than twelve, for when the twelve Bodhisattvas have accomplished their mission we have exhausted the duration of Earth existence.' (ibid)

In the Goetheanum, the compositional-rhythmic arrangement of the twelve columns in the small hall corresponds to this: Six on the left from the central Christ figure and six to the right of it. As mentioned above, there were twelve thrones in the place of bases on these columns. This in turn is in accord with Rudolf Steiner's indication: 'The twelve Bodhisattvas are *seated* in the sphere of Providence in the mighty spirit lodge around their centre; they are rapt in beholding the lofty entity who lets flow to them what they then have to carry as their mission into Earth evolution.'[120] (GA 114, 21 September 1919) It was this secret of the relation of the Christ and the twelve Bodhisattvas—the centre of esoteric Christianity—that Rudolf Steiner wished to bring to expression in the artistic-Imaginative configuration of the small hall.[121]

When we note that prior to the Mystery of Golgotha it was the task of mankind to overcome the luciferic forces that had penetrated into Earth development in the third pre-Christian millennium as a result of Lucifer's incarnation in China; and that since the Mystery of Golgotha the goal is to overcome the forces of Ahriman, whose incarnation on Earth will take place at the beginning of the third millennium in North America, meaning practically in our age,[122] we can better understand the deeper meaning of the placement of the sculpture-group in the eastern part of the small cupola. It is the group that represents the Christ as representative of humanity, or the higher 'I' of mankind, (GA 112, 24 June 1909) who subdues the forces of Lucifer who under His influence is cast into the abyss, and the forces of Ahriman who is restrained in the Earth's depths. In this sense the task of the first six Bodhisattvas was mainly to overcome Lucifer's forces in Earth evolution, and the mission of the six post-Christian Bodhisattvas will consist in the struggle with Ahriman and the gradual overcoming of his forces.

★

Viewed as a whole the structure of the First Goetheanum corresponds most precisely to the general composition of the Foundation Stone

Meditation that begins with a mighty call to the human soul (a soul striving for self-knowledge in the sense of the red window's theme on the western side of the building). Then follows entry into the big hall and the passage from West to East through the walkway in the middle (along the longitudinal axis). This forward movement, for which man makes use of his limb system in order to experience the configuration of the inner space, affects his will in a transforming sense. In a similar way the Foundation Stone Meditation's words work on his will, but now not on the Imaginative but Inspirational level. Here the content of the microcosmic part corresponds to the configuration of the big hall and the macrocosmic part to the small one (the stage). Furthermore, the Imaginatively experienced perception of the columns, capitals, and architraves, first of the big and then of the small cupola, has a transforming effect on feeling all the way to the rhythmic system of heart and lungs. In the Foundation Stone Meditation, the second segment of the meditation, which likewise consists of a microcosmic and a macrocosmic part, exerts a similar effect, but again in an Inspirative manner. Ultimately, beholding the paintings of both cupolas, something that works in a transforming way in thinking extending even into the forces of the head system, corresponds on the Inspirative level to the two parts of the third segment of the meditation.

As far as the fourth segment is concerned, it was spoken twice during the Christmas Conference, once on 25 December 1923 during the cultic Foundation Stone Laying and a second time on 1 January 1924 at the conclusion of the last lecture; and each time in a different relation to the three other segments of the meditation.[123] Comparing the two texts with the ground-plan of the First Goetheanum, the content of the first part of the fourth segment is in the first case to be equated with the place where the point of intersection of the two cupolas was located and where the lectern stood as the source of the *Word* in the building; in the second case to the place of the sculptural group in the eastern part of the stage.

A major difference, however, is that the adversary powers are not mentioned in the meditation since they were overcome to a certain degree in the two Mystery streams: Lucifer in the southern one whose representatives were the Shepherds at the Turning-point of Time, and Ahriman in the northern Mysteries whose representatives at the Turning-point of Time were the Kings. In regard to the first three segments of the meditation one can say that the Shepherds originally tended more to their microcosmic parts or to the path of self-knowledge, whereas the Kings originally tended to world-knowledge addressed in the macrocosmic parts. Under the influence of the Mystery of Golgotha, however, that united both types of Mysteries within itself, it became their task to acquire in each case the opposite characteristics. The Kings now have to take the path of self-knowledge and the Shepherds that of world-knowledge so that each group ultimately will unite both forms of insight in heart and mind, and so that through the light of the 'Christ-Sun' in the fourth part of the meditation each group becomes capable of linking up with the opposite.[124]

It is especially for the sake of this union that in modern Rosicrucian initiation we have today the growing together of both paths—of the path that through the encounter with the Lesser Guardian of the Threshold leads into the microcosm, and of the path that through the encounter with the Greater Guardian of the Threshold leads into the macrocosm. (See GA 124, 19 December 1910) Likewise in the book, *Knowledge of the Higher Worlds and Its Attainment*, *both* encounters are described; that with the Lesser as well as that with the Greater Guardian of the Threshold. Concerning the transition from one to the other it says, 'after some time'. (GA 10, p. 210) In the Foundation Stone Meditation, on the other hand, work with its microcosmic parts leads to the encounter with the Lesser Guardian of the Threshold, whereas work with its macrocosmic parts leads to the encounter with the Greater Guardian. For their union, the fourth segment was given.

★

All this can serve as preparation for a deeper comprehension of the Foundation Stone Meditation as a spiritual path, a path that leads the human being today into the Temple of the New Mysteries. (See Chap. 5) The following must however be heeded here. The transition from the First Goetheanum to the Foundation Stone Meditation did not take place in an unwavering development that merely concerns the physical plane, but as a mighty metamorphosis whose source must be sought primarily in the spiritual world. For due to its fiery demise, the Goetheanum with its Imaginative colours and forms passed over into the 'wide etheric world where the Spirit lives'; it lives 'in the Spirit-filled Wisdom of the world'. (GA 233a, 22 April 1924)

One can understand these words in the following way: In esoteric Christianity, the 'wisdom of the world that is [filled] by the Holy Spirit' was always revered as the divine Sophia who—in this case—works through the beings of the Third Hierarchy, the hierarchy of the Holy Spirit (third segment of the meditation). This signifies that in the 'wide etheric world' the forms and colours of the Goetheanum were received into the sphere of the Sophia and were filled by her cosmic wisdom.

Following this they returned as the spiritual Goetheanum, as what Rudolf Steiner called, at the end of the Christmas Conference, 'the good Spirit of the Goetheanum' in whose name and sign he carried out the Christmas Conference. (See GA 260, p. 272) Thus all this was a timely revelation of the divine Sophia for humanity out of the spiritual hierarchy standing nearest to mankind. This new revelation of the Sophia was then received by Rudolf Steiner and entrusted to human beings in the form of the Foundation Stone Meditation.[125] In his lecture on 22 April 1924 (GA 233a) Rudolf Steiner referred to this in the following words: 'Since the Christmas impulse anthroposophical activity is supposed to be imbued with an esoteric trend. This esoteric trend is present because through what had been an earthly event [the fire of the Goetheanum] there worked along in the physical blaze the astral light that rays out into cosmic space and in turn sends back its effects into the impulses of the Anthroposophical Movement, if only we are in a position to accept these impulses.' And the one who in the first place received these impulses out of the spiritual world was Rudolf Steiner himself, who formed the Foundation Stone Meditation out of them as the spiritual basis for the ensuing karma lectures and the Michael-School on Earth.

It follows from this that the meditation not only brings the artistic-Imaginative nature of the First Goetheanum (as a structure that once actually existed on the physical plane) to expression in words, but that in a deeper sense it is a concrete manifestation of the supersensible Temple of the New Mysteries. At the same time it is a path to this temple; a path on which the 'Spirit of the Goetheanum' brought the connection with this temple out of the 'wide etheric world' to Earth, for this Spirit is related to the temple from its very origin. This is why work with the meditation for reaching its objective, i.e. the connection with the supersensible Temple of the Mysteries, can be done as follows. Initially a student of the spirit tries to experience his work like an inner entry of the First Goetheanum, and in meditating imagines that he is standing before the red window and hears the call: 'Soul of Man!' Then follows the movement from West to East along the symmetrical axis of the large hall in the threefold course that consists of the will-driven grasp of the inner space (first segment of meditation); then comes the experience along with the metamorphoses of the architraves and capitals in feeling (second segment); next comes the viewing of the paintings of both cupolas with attentive thinking (third segment); and finally the encounter with the sculptural group in the eastern part of the little cupola in contemplation of the fourth segment. In so doing the images of the First Goetheanum should fill the soul in so lively and direct a manner as if one were actually seeing them.

After lengthy exercising in the just described direction, the following should be done: Gathering together all the forces of the soul, one must try to extinguish the images and colours of the Goetheanum in order to experience, for a moment, the whole tragedy of its fiery demise but all the while energetically continuing to meditate the words of the Foundation Stone. When describing the transition from the Imaginative to the Inspirational stage of insight, Rudolf Steiner refers in detail to such a process of extinguishing images, that up to then have carefully been built up in the soul. (see for instance GA 13) If after constant repetition this transition is actually achieved successfully, gradually quite new forms and colours begin to arise in the consciousness of the spirit disciple out of the Foundation Stone Meditation's own Inspirative character. These forms and colours do not now refer to the earthly Goetheanum but to its archetype in the higher worlds, the supersensible Temple of the New Mysteries that is mentioned in another work by the author.[126] On the path considered here, starting from the inner work with the Foundation Stone Meditation, one can indeed enter the Temple of the New Mysteries in the spiritual world adjacent to the Earth and in full consciousness experience its colours, forms, and inner configuration.

★

The necessity of finding access to this supersensible temple is one of the most important esoteric tasks of the Anthroposophical Society today, if it is to preserve its spiritual destiny that follows from the Mystery act of its founding at the Christmas Conference. It is only within this Temple of the New Mysteries that the relations of a human being with the spirits of the Third Hierarchy and Michael himself can become reality, something mentioned by Rudolf Steiner. (See Chap. 5)

This is likewise why the history of the Anthroposophical Society during the twentieth century can be understood as a path to this goal; all difficulties, conflicts, and mistakes of its members notwithstanding. Extensive literature exists that deals with the negative aspects of its development.[127] Here, following the exercise in positivism given by Rudolf Steiner, the positive aspect shall be considered.

During a conference at the Goetheanum in September 2000, Paul Mackay advanced an amazingly accurate comparison when he described the growth process of the School of Spiritual Science since its inauguration until today. This comparison deals with Parsifal who on the first occasion entered the temple of the Grail purely by grace of Providence, but not comprehending the significance of the situation at that time he did not pose the decisive question. Understanding only dawned on him when he found himself outside the walls of the castle. Then he resolved, whatever the cost, to search for the Grail once more and return to it, now based on his own efforts, meaning on the path of the—at that time—attainable initiation. This not only took him years but decades until, equipped with the soul-spiritual forces gained through suffering, ill fate, and trials, he was able to enter the Grail castle once more and lead the brotherhood of the Guardians of the Grail. In so doing he did not return alone but brought with him his brother Feirefiz.

This comparison can moreover be applied to the development of the esoteric impulse of the Christmas Conference during the past eighty years. One can say that at the Christmas Conference all the anthroposophists were given the possibility, without any special merit on their part, to enter the Temple of the New Mysteries. Moreover, in a sense they actually found themselves in it, at least from the moment when Rudolf Steiner laid the Foundation Stone on 25 December 1923 until his 'Last Address' on 28 September 1924. For it was out of this temple that Rudolf Steiner worked until his death. All his lectures, letters to members, articles and leading thoughts, and first and foremost the lessons of the esoteric school (either orally or in written form) were offered while standing before an invisible altar within an invisible ritual that was carried out in the supersensible world nearest the Earth 'in accordance with the order of Melchizedek'.[128]

As the subsequent developments made evident however, the members of the Anthroposophical Society did not understand this to a sufficient degree. The majority of them were unable to become aware that at that time they themselves had been within the temple in which Rudolf Steiner had then spoken and acted.[129]

Marie Steiner referred to this lack of understanding later on in the first preface to the shorthand notes of the Christmas Conference. 'To give a description of the Christmas Conference is perhaps one of the most difficult tasks one can set oneself. It is barely possible, with our limited insight, to gain an overall view of the impulse and power behind that event. It represents the most mighty endeavour of a teacher of mankind to lift his contemporaries out of their own small selves and awaken in them a conscious will to be allowed to become tools serving the wise guides of the universe. Yet at the same time this Christmas Conference is also bound up with something infinitely tragic. For we cannot but admit: We were called, but we were not chosen. We were incapable of responding to the call ...' (GA 260)

Another witness, Arvia Mackaye-Ege who, although still very young, participated at the Mystery of the Foundation Stone Laying, wrote in her memoirs of the Christmas Conference: 'From my seat in the background my heart cried out because I realized that something far beyond my power of comprehension was taking place; it seemed that my heart was threatening to break. Then something in me gave way and I drank in what followed like a great flood, knowing full well that I would only really understand in later incarnations what was happening right then'.[130]

Nonetheless, just as in Parsifal's case, the possibility of becoming aware in the course of time of this relationship with the temple, and thus of creating conditions on Earth for Rudolf Steiner's further work, depended on precisely this *understanding*. This is why when people were concerned about his declining physical energies, while at the same time he increased his activities following the Christmas Conference and somebody approached him with the plea to reduce at least the number of his lectures, Rudolf Steiner replied: 'These lectures do not exhaust me at all . . . On the contrary, they keep me well, . . . what tires me are the dead thoughts that one faces; it is the lack *of judgement, of understanding* on the part of people that debilitates one.'[131] Due to the untimely death of the teacher occurring soon afterwards, the Anthroposophical Society confronted the gates of the temple and henceforth had to seek its way to it independently. Thus the Society's fate depends on whether it will eventually be able once again to enter the temple in order to fulfil its spiritual task for humanity. As was shown in another work in detail, it is only through the forces of this supersensible temple that it will be possible to fulfil the tasks of the New Mysteries on Earth.[132]

This path to the spiritual temple, or 'temple of higher knowledge' as Rudolf Steiner called it in his book *Knowledge of the Higher Worlds and Its Attainment* (GA 10), lies at the basis of the spiritual-historical development of the Anthroposophical Society and bestows meaning on its existence to this day. Despite all the conflicts that shook up the Society in the course of the past decades—mistakes made by its members, the numerous problems unresolved even to this day—the fact that of the leading anthroposophists who knew Rudolf Steiner personally and worked with him almost none left the Anthroposophical Society voluntarily shows us that its members, some with full awareness (others less consciously), continued to perceive the spiritual reality standing behind it.[133]

In this sense one can compare the development of the Anthroposophical Society *after* the death of Rudolf Steiner with the passage through the three initiation trials of fire, water, and air; trials leading into the 'temple of higher knowledge', each lasting about thirty-three years. It goes without saying that the following is merely a comparison, yet something very real is concealed behind it. The events in the Anthroposophical Society that followed Rudolf Steiner's death can only be compared with a repeated fire, but now of the spiritual Goetheanum, meaning a 'fire-trial' in a quite actual sense of the word.

From 1925 until 1957 two big conflicts smouldered in the Anthroposophical Society that led to the splitting of the first Executive Council, the disconnection of two national societies (the Dutch and British society), and finally to the split almost of the whole Anthroposophical Society that separated into three karmic groups aligned either with Marie Steiner, Ita Wegman, or Albert Steffen.

Even though viewed from outside in the sense of the tasks posed to it at the Christmas Conference (namely the union of the various karmic streams), the Society had ceased to exist; still the majority of its members, regardless of which group they belonged to, remained unshakeably loyal to Anthroposophy and Rudolf Steiner, and worked for the realization of the Society's goals even when it was possible to say that everything had gone to ruin and that any further effort would be hopeless. What the members achieved during that period despite the two conflicts is simply astounding. Likewise the fact that they maintained their courage, steadfastness, and unshakeable confidence in themselves and their cause is equally astounding, notwithstanding the pain and suffering caused to the members by the deterioration of the Anthroposophical Society as well as the disappointments and failures of their intentions during the years of conflict.

For this very reason, the words by Rudolf Steiner can be applied particularly to this generation of anthroposophists in full measure; words with which he described the first, the 'trial by fire', as a *trial through life itself* on the path of the modern Christian-Rosicrucian path of initiation: 'For some people even ordinary life itself is a more or less unconscious process of initiation through the fire trial. These are the ones who pass through a wealth of experiences of such a kind that their self-confidence, courage, and steadfastness mature in a healthy way. And they learn to endure sorrows, disappointment, and failure in ventures with greatness of soul, and above all calm and unbroken strength. One who has passed through experiences of this kind is often an initiate without being clearly aware of it.' (GA 10) Many of those who were participants in the severe conflicts during this period possessed particularly these faculties of magnanimity, inner calm, and unbroken strength in withstanding sorrow and disappointment in connection with many frustrated hopes.

The destinies of Marie Steiner, Ita Wegman, and Albert Steffen, the three main participants in the Society's conflicts of that time, were particularly tragic during their last years of life. Since all three were esoteric students of Rudolf Steiner, and moreover his closest colleagues, later on each on his or her own, had to pass through a condition of great *power-lessness* caused by the impossibility of carrying out the task for which Rudolf Steiner had called them into the Executive Council, namely to lead the Anthroposophical Society *jointly* after his death. Nevertheless, each one of them, regardless of the enormity and predicament of this inability to act, remained faithful to Rudolf Steiner and the task they had been entrusted with, even after they had become aware of the impossibility of fulfilling it still in that lifetime.[134]

From the spiritual standpoint arises yet another quite different aspect concerning this tragic situation. For the soul force that a person must develop today for bearing up under such a condition of utter power-lessness is at the same time the force that prepares one for a conscious encounter with the Christ. (See GA 182, 16 October 1918) If we realize that such an encounter is above all one with the Etheric Christ, which can occur in the physical body as well as after death in the spiritual world, but in either case must be prepared on Earth, (see GA 131, 10 October 1911) it follows that the condition of greatest powerlessness that was experienced by the three closest colleagues of Rudolf Steiner (along with many other anthroposophists) prepared them, owing to their loyalty and courage, to meet the Etheric Christ after their death. This is possibly the most significant fruit of the 'fire trial'[135] that the Anthroposophical Society passed through in the 1930s and 1940s when the Etheric Christ began to move about among human beings.

The second trial that the Anthroposophical Society endured in the course of the following period of 33 years—from 1957 to 1990—was the 'water trial'. Rudolf Steiner describes that in this trial the spirit disciple is motivated to do something in which he is not led by outward events or interests or by his inclinations or wishes, sympathies, or antipathies, but by the directions he can perceive in 'deciphering the occult script' (GA 10) or those that manifest to him in 'the concealed speech'. (ibid.) This is 'because for one who has attained to the afore-mentioned stage of initiation there now exist duties for which there is no *outward* impetus'. (ibid., emphasis by Rudolf Steiner)

In the development of the Anthroposophical Society, something took place in this second period that can almost be called a miracle. For it is known from the centuries-old history of the most diverse spiritual communities that in the case of a rift they in fact never come back together again (and no 'ecumenical' movements or proclamations for outward tolerance can be of any help). The Anthroposophical Society represents a very rare exception in the long list of spiritual/social failures and catastrophes. The return of the Dutch society to the Goetheanum in the 1960s, and a little later that of the British Society; subsequently the surmounting of antagonistic relations between the three karmic groups[136] and as a consequence of that the revitalization of the General Anthroposophical Society—all this is an astounding example of such a reunification!

Particularly the decision by Willem Zeylmans van Emmichoven to unite the Dutch Society once again with the Goetheanum after a break of twenty-five years, a decision he made and carried out by turning directly to the individual who had once personally participated in his exclusion, is a sort of prototype for this process. In a conversation with Albert Steffen, Zeylmans explained his move with the one succinct sentence: 'Because we will to do it!', and in the circle of his closest friends he declared: 'In order to please Rudolf Steiner.'[137] To use a comparison, but one behind which stands something quite real in the spiritual sense, one can say Zeylmans actually 'read' the necessity to undertake this step in the 'occult script', for the outer circumstances rather favoured the opposite. The reconciliation was then truly mutual. Soon after the Dutch Society, the British one likewise reunited with the Goetheanum.

Many other leading anthroposophists likewise worked in those days in the same direction, among them Emil Bock, Klara Kreutzer, Fritz Götte, and others who, following the Second World War, strove for unification and consolidation of the Anthroposophical Society. They all acted out of the same occult impulse, for they were able to read the 'signs of the times' correctly.

Rudolf Steiner describes the 'water trial' like a trial through which the aspirant for initiation is led through life itself: 'If he were to combine with his actions even just a little of his own wishes, opinions, and so on—if only for an instant he would follow not the laws he has recognized as correct but his arbitrariness—something completely different would occur from what is supposed to happen.' (GA 10) Therefore the most important thing that was supposed to happen in the second period was the union of the Anthroposophical Society. And Rudolf Steiner continues: 'Through this trial a person has ample opportunity to develop his *self-control*.' (ibid., emphasis by Rudolf Steiner) Truly, how much 'self-control' was demanded of *both sides* in the hours and hours of conversations during many years between the leadership of the Goetheanum and the administrators of Rudolf Steiner's literary estate ultimately to reach a decision concerning, for example, the so-called 'book question' or the public distancing of the Executive Council from the 'Egger Brochure'! One can truly apply to these and also other situations the words that characterize the water trial: 'One who has acquired the capacity to follow lofty principles and ideals by putting aside personal capriciousness and arbitrariness; one who always understands how to fulfil his duty even when inclinations and sympathies would much prefer to divert him from this obligation; such a person is unconsciously an initiate in ordinary life.' (ibid) The love for Rudolf Steiner and devotion to Anthroposophy—as the highest obligation of every anthroposophist, that throughout the whole existence of the Anthroposophical Society rose above it like a kind of invisible 'hidden script'; this love for Rudolf Steiner thus attained an important victory over personal moods, inclinations, sympathies, wishes, and opinions of individual members; attitudes that so frequently formed the true causes for the various conflict-filled situations in the Society.

The third thirty-three-year period that began in 1990 has a completely different appearance. Above all it is characteristic of this period that now almost all the esoteric disciples and co-workers of Rudolf Steiner have departed from the physical plane. This signifies that those who during all the previous years had served as a link between the Anthroposophical Society and its founder have gone into the spiritual world. Comparable to the conscience of the Anthroposophical Society, they themselves had been a sort of 'hidden script' (to use a picture here) for those who came into the Society later on; a script that gave them the necessary orientation in line with the true intentions and goals of the Anthroposophical Movement.

When the author of this text visited Dornach for the first time at the end of 1981, one could still encounter many of Rudolf Steiner's personal students and speak with them, for example, Friedrich Hiebel, Edwin Fröböse, Madeleine van Deventer, Rudolf Grosse, Ilona Schubert, Karl von Baltz, Elena Zuccoli, Paul-Eugen Schiller. All these remarkable personalities were for me bearers of the 'hidden script' of our society; living witnesses of its founder, his words, and deeds. Many other anthroposophists too, who were still alive then and had known Rudolf Steiner personally, were representatives in the world as guardians and protectors of the unbroken connection with the teacher.

But how greatly the situation in Dornach has changed following their departure! Since then the third trial of the Anthroposophical Society—the 'air trial'—has truly begun! Now 'he who is being tested finds himself in a condition where nothing induces him to action. He has to find his way alone, relying only on his resources. Motivating circumstances or persons do not exist. Nothing and nobody can give him the strength he needs, only he himself. If he would not find this strength within himself he would soon be back where he had been before.' (GA 10) This danger particularly threatens the Anthroposophical Society at the present moment. For at this stage the spirit disciple must 'find his "higher self" in the truest sense of the word'. (ibid.) Especially now this signifies for the Anthroposophical Society as a whole to follow once more the central esoteric impulse of the Christmas Conference, relying on its own resources; meaning to find access to the Temple of the New Mysteries that are the Mysteries of man's 'higher self'.

Rudolf Steiner continued: 'Whatever is a deterrent from listening to the spirit must boldly be overcome. What matters is to demonstrate *presence of mind* [Ger.: '*Geistesgegenwart*,' literally 'spirit-presence'] in this situation.' (ibid.; emphasis by Rudolf Steiner) But in the context of everything that was stated above, the spirit whom the disciple must hear at this stage is the *Spirit of the Christmas Conference* who at the conclusion of the cultic Foundation Stone Laying manifested Itself in the thought-light of the dodecahedric Foundation Stone.[138] Here 'Geistesgegenwart' is to be understood *literally* as the presence of that concrete Spirit who is capable of leading us into the Temple of the New Mysteries.[139] Naturally to find this Spirit, in order with its help to enter the Temple of the New Mysteries (as Parsifal succeeded in doing, having initially lost the connection with the Grail but subsequently rediscovering it in full freedom after an arduous trial-filled journey), this is the actual task of the third 33-year-period. For 'if the disciple has passed this trial he may enter the "temple of higher insights".' (ibid.)

In his book, Rudolf Steiner communicates little about the sojourn in the temple. According to his words, the first concern is a certain 'pledge' that has to be made. At the Christmas Conference this 'pledge' appears as the 'promise' Rudolf Steiner mentions in his first lecture in Arnhem. (GA 240, 18 July 1924) It is a sort of archetype for what every disciple who enters the Temple of the New Mysteries today must be successful in doing. Not until he has offered up this 'pledge of fidelity' to the temple can he receive the two spiritual 'draughts' of forgetfulness and remembrance. In regard to the Christmas Conference, the first corresponds to the necessity of truly understanding that esoterically something completely new occurred at this Conference for which no analogy exists, neither in mankind's cultural life[140] nor in the earlier development even of Anthroposophy. 'Prior to the time of the Christmas Conference at the Goetheanum, I had to emphasize more than once that one would have to distinguish between the Anthroposophical Movement, which expresses a spiritual stream as reflected on Earth, and the Anthroposophical Society ... *Since Christmas the opposite must be stated*. No longer can the Anthroposophical Movement be distinguished from the Anthroposophical

Society. They are one and the same,' is the way Rudolf Steiner expressed it.

In other words, now something happened that was completely the opposite of what had taken place in the past. On this account, in this completely new situation, the past had to be 'forgotten', meaning that from now on the past was not allowed to disturb the proper understanding of the spiritual impulses of the present and future that would arise out of this wholly new situation. In his book *Knowledge of the Higher Worlds and Its Attainment*, Rudolf Steiner wrote concerning the characteristic of the 'draught of forgetfulness': 'If I judge what I encounter today according to what I have experienced yesterday, I am subject to many errors.' (GA 10) Naturally the past experience loses nothing of importance, for without it a person would never see the new. This notwithstanding, 'it is particularly for *seeing* the new, not for judging the new according to the old, that experience is supposed to serve'. (ibid., emphasis by Rudolf Steiner) These words can be directly applied to the Christmas Conference. It required Anthroposophy's whole twenty-one-year long development to make its esoteric nature 'visible' (which means, truly to make it a reality on Earth). But to judge it, meaning from a spiritual viewpoint to really *understand* what happened at that time and why this was *something completely new* in the Mystery development of humanity, for this the experience of anthroposophists that they had in the past is of no help.[141] On the contrary, just how much the experiences of the past and various habits acquired in twenty-one years could impede the right understanding of the new is proven through a whole series of statements by Rudolf Steiner himself in his struggles for bringing about an understanding of the Christmas Conference among the Society members.[142]

The constant recalling of the Christmas Conference's impulse coincides to the second draught. This can only be achieved by consistent inner work (practice) with the Foundation Stone Meditation that arose out of the 'Word of Worlds'. (GA 260)

Where Rudolf Steiner describes the effect of the 'draught of remembrance' in the spirit disciple, he emphasizes as its characteristic 'that through it ... the disciple [attains] to the faculty of always retaining higher secrets in his mind'. (GA 10) And he continues: 'One has to become completely one with the higher truths ... they must become practice, habit, inclination.' (ibid) The Foundation Stone Meditation too must work in the soul exactly in this way, a meditation that contains all 'higher secrets' of Anthroposophy. In this way, the Meditation's words must become completely one with the soul 'so that they cannot leave us'. (GA 260). This only becomes possible when its words 'flow through [the human being] like functions of life in his organism'. (GA 10)

Rudolf Steiner moreover spoke more than once about the esoteric content of the Christmas Conference as a whole, for example in a conversation with teachers of the first Waldorf School. 'The whole Dornach Conference only has real meaning if, in a manner of speaking, this meaning is *not* forgotten in all future times.' (GA 300/3, 5 February 1924) Expressed in the words of the book, *Knowledge of the Higher Worlds and Its Attainment*, it signifies that 'one not only must know [its spiritual content] but must independently *make use of it* in real live actions'. (ibid., emphasis by Rudolf Steiner) In other words, the Christmas Conference 'will be nothing if it finds no continuation, if it was [merely] a ceremony at which one experienced a little joy; afterwards one forgets the whole matter and lives on in the same old way'. (GA 260a, 6 February 1924) So that this might not happen, the members of the Anthroposophical Society must *remember* and work on the esoteric content of the Christmas Conference in such a form as if they had already received the 'draught of remembrance' in the supersensible temple.

★

An essential aid in practising *remembrance* of the Christmas Conference can be the work with its esoteric content in the rhythm of the year's course. In this connection its content can be compared with the four stages of a plant's life-cycle in the course of a year.

At Christmas, on 25 December, Rudolf Steiner created the Foundation Stone in the spiritual world adjoining the Earth in the form of an 'Imaginative structure of love'. Seen as a whole this Mystery act consisted of three stages. First, the secret of the threefold archetype of earthly man was placed before the members of the Anthroposophical Society who were present there. This insight was something Rudolf Steiner had worked on for many years. On a second, the most important stage, the Foundation Stone was created in a free spiritual creator-deed out of the highest forces of the cosmos. Ultimately on the third level, the Foundation Stone was presented to the Society members so that they might immerse it into the ground of their ether-heart. This final act is a sort of *spiritual repetition of the Last Supper* in which this Foundation Stone, augmented according to the laws of spiritual economy, was handed over to the members.[142a]

The macrocosmic deed that Christ Jesus accomplished at the Turning-point of Time on the physical plane was repeated by Rudolf

Steiner during the Christmas Conference in microcosmic form in the spiritual world nearest to the Earth. He thus gave anthroposophists the possibility to receive spiritual forces out of an ever-flowing fount in the form of the 'dodecahedric Stone of Love'. In the Grail Mysteries such a sacred meal was linked with the 'ganganda greida', the 'ongoing sustenance for the journey' or 'eventide meal', that gave all men the strength to serve the spirit everywhere in the world. (GA 149, 1 January 1914)

Comparable to the seed of an invisible spiritual plant, the Foundation Stone could in full freedom be immersed into the ground of the hearts of those attending the Christmas Conference.

During the following seven days Rudolf Steiner gave them the seven rhythms and in this way linked the Foundation Stone with the seven-fold ether cosmos. The forces that allow the spiritual seed in the human heart to develop and grow are concealed in these rhythms. On the last day of the Christmas Conference at the end of the evening lecture, Rudolf Steiner for the first time read the complete text of the Foundation Stone Meditation in the sequence in which it was published twelve days later in the *News Letter*. In this way the meditation was entrusted to all anthroposophists as the centre of their meditative work.

If the rhythms can be likened to a plant's process of growth out of the seed, the final form of the Foundation Stone Meditation can be compared with the blossom as the third stage of the metamorphosis. The concluding words of the Christmas Conference about the 'good star' whom, according to the will of the gods, anthroposophists are supposed to follow (even as the Magi from the East followed it at the Turning-point of Time[143]) represent the transition to the fourth stage. In the annual cycle of the plants, this corresponds to the forming of the fruits. In the light of the 'Christ-Sun' that warms the hearts (beginning of the Christmas Conference) and enlightens the heads (end of conference), referring to which Rudolf Steiner concluded the Christmas Conference, we have the power with the help of which the Foundation Stone can bear its fruits in the social life of human beings. The spiritual Goetheanum (the supersensible Temple of the New Mysteries) is supposed to become such a fruit that is meant to emerge out of all anthroposophical activities, individual and communal group-like ones, within the Anthroposophical Society as well as in the world outside. Rudolf Steiner described it as follows: 'Here we have laid the Foundation Stone. On this Foundation Stone shall be erected the building whose individual stones will be the work achieved in all our groups by individuals outside in the wide world.' (GA 260, 12 January 1924)

Foundation Stone	— Seed (physical body)	Winter	Christmas (Gabriel)
Rhythms	— Plant (etheric body)	Spring	Easter (Raphael)
Foundation Stone Meditation	— Blossom (astral body)	Summer	St John's Tide (Uriel)
New Social Community that was founded at the Christmas Conference	— Fruit ('I')	Autumn	Michaelmas (Michael)[144]

This new social community that is to emerge out of the Foundation Stone is described in detail in the chapter 'The Anthroposophical Society as the Temple of the New Mysteries' in the book *May Human Beings Hear It! The Mystery of the Christmas Conference*. Here it is important once more to point to the connection of the Foundation Stone with the third, the 'air trial', which the Anthroposophical Society confronts at the beginning of this new century. It is a trial the Society must endure if, despite all hindrances, it intends to come closer to its goal, namely to find the path into the 'Temple of the New Mysteries'. And it will pass this trial only if the above-described fourfold metamorphosis of seed-plant-blossom-fruit becomes reality in the soul; a metamorphosis that opens up to the soul the possibility of creating a new human community on Earth that maintains full public access in regard to the outer world, and at the same time bears within it the feasibility for esoteric deepening.

This is moreover the reason why a close connection exists between the Christmas Conference with its spiritual centre, namely the Foundation Stone, and the third and last trial. The significance of this relationship, particularly for our age, follows from the words that describe this trial: 'For only within himself can the spirit student find the *one firm point* to which he is able to cling.' (GA 10) This is why the third trial is called 'air trial' because he no longer feels any 'solid ground' whatsoever under his feet, not even in the form of the 'hidden script'. Here it is therefore a matter of the necessity, based on his own faculties, to create a new foundation, new ground or such support, that proceeding from it, he is able simultaneously to work in both the earthly and the spiritual world. As shown in Chapter 6, it is this that Michael expects from human beings particularly in our age, meaning he expects actions that emerge from unequivocal, absolute *confidence in the Spirit*. This is why Rudolf Steiner gave the members of the Anthroposophical Society at the Christmas

Conference his supersensible Foundation Stone which, when immersed in the human heart, can become spiritual ground (the firm foundation) in the heart. Standing on it, every anthroposophist and the Anthroposophical Society as a whole can achieve what Michael expects today.

So we can say that after the Anthroposophical Society had passed through the fire and water trial—and since the beginning of the 1990s has entered the sphere of the air trial—the real possibility exists that, once having passed this third trial, it finds out of its own resources a new, independent, and free relation to the *Spirit* of the Christmas Conference, a spirit who manifests in the thought light of the Foundation Stone. Now, when that occurs and the Anthroposophical Society under the guidance of the Spirit actually *enters upon the path that leads into the supersensible temple* in the new century, then the true nature of the esoteric content of the Christmas Conference will be revealed to it, connected as this conference is with the past as well as with the future. For just as the Mystery of Golgotha took place in the course of humanity's history almost 2000 years ago, but in the occult sense encompasses the *whole* of Earth evolution with its influence, so it is only from the standpoint of outer historical time that the Christmas Conference belongs to the past. After all, from the esoteric standpoint it unveils to us perspectives of spiritual development that encompass not centuries but millennia.[145]

From this it follows that all efforts at a judiciary renewal of the Society's constitution as well as endeavours to register the 'statutes' passed at the Christmas Conference in the trade register—as Rudolf Steiner had wished[146]—can only be given true meaning if the members of the Anthroposophical Society are fully aware that all this *serves only as the preparation* for the actual esoteric task of the Anthroposophical Society and its 'soul', the School of Spiritual Science. This task is to form the connecting link on Earth between contemporary humanity and the Temple of the New Mysteries. Once the Anthroposophical Society has recognized this task and begins with its realization, it will be able to become the bearer of the true ideal of Rosicrucian Christianity. In turn, this is the ideal that comes to expression in the image of the 'lost temple that once more is to be reconstructed'[147] (GA 98, 15 May 1905) and is prophetically depicted in Goethe's *Fairy Tale*.

When this essential Rosicrucian Imagination becomes reality one day in the Anthroposophical Society as the ultimate fruit of its tragic history during the twentieth century, it will doubtlessly exist rightfully. All its trials, crises and afflictions attain meaning and significance for Earth evolution through the activity of the Christ as Lord of Karma.

9. The Foundation Stone Meditation in Eurythmy and the Mystery of the Two Jesus Boys

The following deliberation presupposes familiarity with the corresponding chapter in the book, *May Human Beings Hear It! The Mystery of the Christmas Conference*, that deals with the Christological content of the Foundation Stone Meditation in eurythmy.[148] Here an important supplement to that chapter shall be brought forward.

If in the above-mentioned book the relationship of the Christ Impulse to the individual human being and to all mankind formed the main aspect, here the main focus shall be the actual Christological Mystery of the Turning-point of Time in the form Rudolf Steiner depicted it in the lectures about the *Fifth Gospel*—the Mystery in the centre of which stands the secret of the two Jesus boys.

Comparing these lectures with the prelude and postlude to the first three parts of the eurythmic movements of the meditation, it is possible to recognize that the individuality of Zarathustra or the Solomonic Jesus, whose origin is described in the Gospel of Matthew, plays the main role. If we consider that in the fourth part of the book *May Human Beings Hear It!* the connection of the eurythmic presentation of the meditation with the individuality of Christian Rosenkreutz was worked out, then (seen as a whole) both considerations can be viewed as a further testimony to the fact that these two leading masters of esoteric Christianity, the Master Jesus (Zarathustra) and Christian Rosenkreutz, were connected from the beginning with Rudolf Steiner's esoteric activity.

In the esoteric lesson of 1 June 1907 that Rudolf Steiner gave immediately following the separation of the 'western' esoteric school led by him from the 'eastern' esoteric school conducted by Annie Besant, he determinedly pointed to this fact: 'The Master Jesus and the Master Christian Rosenkreutz prepare two paths of initiation for us, the Christian-esoteric one and the Christian-Rosicrucian one ... At the head of our western school stand two masters: the Master Jesus and the Master Christian Rosenkreutz. They guide us on two paths, the Christian and the Christian-Rosicrucian path ... Their call goes out to all people in the West, asking whether they wish to join the guidance of the two masters of the West ... We need the wisdom of the future, the western schooling that is offered to us by both these masters ... What is given at the behest of the masters of the West through me moves along independently aside from what Mrs Besant teaches at the behest of the masters of the East.' (GA 264)[149] If we now consider the mission of the Master Jesus at the Turning-point of Time as described in Rudolf Steiner's spiritual research, the first thing to bear in mind is that the individuality of Zarathustra played the same role on the *esoteric level* in the Palestinian events as did the individuality of John the Baptist on the *exoteric level*. In the gospel, Jesus Christ spoke of John in the words of the prophet Malachi: 'See, my angel I send before you. He is to go before your countenance and prepare the way for you.' (Lk 7, 27 JM)

Just as John, inspired by an angelic being working on Earth out of the forces of the spirit-self, had the task to prepare the outer exoteric path of the Messiah,[150] so the individuality of Zarathustra was destined to prepare the way for Him from the inner esoteric side, and this not out of the impulse of the spirit self but out of the forces of the individual 'I'. Zarathustra prepared himself in the course of a number of incarnations for this mission at the Turning-point of Time. Moreover, the sacrifice he made in this, his most important incarnation, was the *third* in the course of his spiritual development. 'The Zarathustra-individuality, having sacrificed his astral body and etheric body in bygone times to Hermes and Moses, now offers up his physical body; meaning he leaves this sheath that is there with what it still contained as ether body and astral body.' (GA 123, 7 September 1910) Now this third and greatest sacrifice was a twofold one. First, at age twelve, Zarathustra left the physical body of the Solomon-Jesus, then, in the thirtieth year, he likewise left the physical body of Jesus of Nazareth.[151]

This individuality was destined to prepare all three sheaths of the Nathan-Jesus from within for the entry of the Christ. 'Zarathustra's "I", the most highly advanced human ego, could thus be foreordained to dwell for eighteen years in the sheaths that were then supposed to receive the Christ.' (GA 264) How vitally important this preparation was above all for Jesus of Nazareth himself was described by Rudolf Steiner as follows: 'Had the individuality of Zarathustra not permeated this corporeality up until its thirtieth year, its eyes would not have been able to tolerate the substance of the Christ from its thirtieth year until the Mystery of Golgotha. Its hands would have been incapable of being pervaded with the substance of the Christ in the thirtieth year. In order to make it possible to receive the Christ, this corporeality had to be prepared—expanded in a manner of speaking—through the individuality of Zarathustra.' (GA 131, 12 October 1911). Put differently, Jesus of Nazareth could never have fulfilled his chief task of becoming a true Christophorus, a Christ bearer *on Earth*, without this help by Zarathustra.

Now we must turn to the second Jesus boy or, putting it more precisely, to this unique being that incarnated at the Turning-point of Time in the figure of Jesus of Nazareth whose lineage is described in the Gospel of Luke. Based on his spiritual scientific research, Rudolf Steiner pointed out that until its incarnation at the Turning-point of Time this individuality had never before appeared in a physical body on Earth but that it had accompanied the development of human beings on Earth from the very beginning. Rudolf Steiner spoke of three deeds by the Christ through this special individuality—the so-called pre-stages of the Mystery of Golgotha in the higher worlds. Three times, Earth humanity was saved as a result of these three still completely cosmic deeds. At the end of the Lemurian age the physical body of man was saved; at the beginning and in the middle of the Atlantean age his ether and astral body respectively.[152] Describing the origin of this entity, Rudolf Steiner at one time called it 'the sister-soul of Adam', another time 'the true superman', (GA 142, 1 January 1913) and likewise 'the mother-soul of humanity', or 'the Adam-soul before the Fall', (GA 114, 18 September 1909). It was the soul who, because of its mission at the Turning-point of Time, was kept back and cared for in the higher worlds by the hierarchies.

We thus have two Adam entities who had originated from a common root: The earthly Adam who due to the Fall descended into the world of matter, and the celestial one who remained behind in the spiritual world in order to preserve the original properties of the paradisal human being. In the Bible the image of the two trees in Paradise points to this division: to the Tree of Knowledge—of which Adam eats so as to start on his path to the Earth that leads to knowledge of good and evil, and to the Tree of Life—of which it is said after the Fall that man may not eat of it. (Gen. 3, 22) Rudolf Steiner speaks about this biblical passage in the Bible as an Imaginative picture dealing with the separation of the paths of the earthly and heavenly Adam, where one descends to his earthly incarnation, and the other remains connected with the Tree of Life in higher worlds. (GA 114, 18 September 1909)

A second reference to the two evolutionary lines is contained in the biblical description of the dual nature of humanity's creation. In the translation from the Russian Bible it says: 'And God said: Let us create man after our [exact] image [Ger.: Ebenbild], after our [simile or] likeness [Gleichnis].' (Gen: 1,26; Luther: 'Let us make men, an image that may be like us').[Tr.1] In the tradition of eastern Christianity the two concepts, 'image' and 'likeness' are grasped as follows: Man succumbed to the Fall only in so far as he was the 'likeness' of God, not as His 'image'.[153] The latter was preserved by the divine powers in the spiritual world as a pledge to future humanity for a renewed union of God with man. In this distinction of the destinies of the two aspects of original man, we have a further indication of the same primal phenomenon. In the light of this primal phenomenon, the Nathan-Jesus is the bearer of man's 'image' that is preserved in the higher worlds and descended once into physical incarnation on Earth, taking along the whole abundance of paradisal being.[154]

Conversely, the path of all earthly initiates goes in the opposite direction. They do not strive for the descent of the human 'image' upon them from above to below, but for the ascent of the human 'likeness' from below to above. This means, they consciously seek to attain a new likeness of the Creator through ever higher stages of initiation. At the Turning-point of Time the main representative of this second path was the individuality of Zarathustra, the highest initiate who at that time worked openly on the Earth. When this individuality then parted from the sheaths of the Solomon-Jesus in the twelfth year and passed over into the Nathan-Jesus, for the first time since the 'expulsion from Paradise' the original 'image' became united with the 'likeness' in order together to form the human vessel which alone was capable of receiving the cosmic Christ Being into itself.

What is said above allows a better comprehension of how the principle of the Son of Man worked together with the Son of God at the Turning-point of Time. For we can best understand the Son of Man as a human being in whom both sides of his celestial creation, the 'image' and the 'likeness', have once more united as they had been during humanity's primal condition. It was only into *such* a being that the Son of God, the Christ, could then enter during the Baptism in the Jordan in order, in the course of three years, to live in this entity 'as true God and true Man'.

★

Here the following must be heeded: Rudolf Steiner spoke in many of his lectures about the Nathan-Jesus (the future Son of Man) as if he were a being consisting merely of three sheaths, so that the impression might arise in the reader that this Jesus had possessed no human ego at all. In reality it is a little more complicated. As Rudolf Steiner described it, the Nathan-Jesus did possess an 'I', the difference being that it was of quite another nature than the ego of all earthly humans, including the great initiates. For the main particularity of the ego of earthly humans results through the experiences it has gathered in the course of numerous earthly incarnations. Without these experiences the human 'I' would be like a vessel devoid of any content of its own. It was precisely so in the case of this virginal ego of the Nathan-Jesus that as yet was untouched by anything earthly. This is also why Rudolf Steiner spoke of it on most occasions not as an 'ego' but as a 'soul'—so radically different was his 'I' from what we normally connect with the concept of the human 'I'. Concerning this unique character of the Nathan-Jesus, Rudolf Steiner said, 'We can now imagine that a part of the substance of the Spirits of Form passed, in a manner of speaking, into human incarnations for the purpose of forming the human ego—occult research shows this. But at that time when the human being was handed over to its fleshly incarnations on Earth, something of what was to become "man" was held back. One ego-substance was in a sense kept back and not guided into the stream of fleshly incarnations . . . It was an "I", therefore, that continued to live *aside* from the rest of mankind, and until the time . . . when the events of Palestine were to take place, had never before been incarnated in a physical human body. It was an ego that was still in the same condition— if we now wish to speak in a biblical sense—as was the "I" of "Adam" *prior* to his first earthly, fleshly incarnation. Such an "I" always remained . . . This ego thereby had quite special peculiarities; it had the peculiarity of being untouched by what any human "I" had ever been able to learn on Earth at any time. It was therefore also untouched by all luciferic and ahrimanic influences; it was in fact something that in comparison to the other egos of human beings we can picture like an empty sphere; actually like something that was still virginal in regard to all Earth experiences; a nothing, a negative regarding all Earth experiences. This is why it appeared as if that Nathan-Jesus boy, whom the Gospel of Luke describes, had no human ego at all, as if he merely consisted of physical body, etheric body, and astral body.' (GA 131, 12 October 1911, emphasis by Rudolf Steiner)

Only when we can become aware of the diametrical difference of this youngest 'I' and one of the oldest and most highly developed ones, can we begin to approach an understanding of an astounding fact, the fact that this Jesus of Nazareth after his transformation at age twelve (in the Temple at Jerusalem), when he became filled in his mind with the wisdom and power of the Zarathustra-ego, nevertheless did not know until age thirty, meaning until the very end, that the ego of this lofty initiate lived in him during eighteen years. This is how alien all earthly influences, all experiences that result in the course of human lives, were to the heavenly 'I' of the Nathan-Jesus.

According to Rudolf Steiner's spiritual scientific communications, 'towards the end of his twenties' the Nathan-Jesus thought more than once 'how in his twelfth year a significant change, a revolution had occurred in his soul, something that had resulted from the crossing over of the Zarathustra-*soul* into his soul'. He had to think about how 'in the early times [after his twelfth year]' he had felt 'merely the infinite wealth of this Zarathustra-*soul* within himself'. Here and continuing further, Rudolf Steiner described this transition as a *soul* process. 'At the end of his twenties he did not yet know that he was the reincarnated Zarathustra; but he knew that a mighty change had taken place in his soul during his twelfth year.' (GA 148, 6 October 1913) And there is more: even during his last conversation with his mother that took place directly prior to the Baptism in the Jordan, when the Zarathustra-ego was already beginning to leave his sheaths, Jesus still did not know with full clarity of the long-lasting presence by the latter in his soul. The *Fifth Gospel* states about this: 'There shone forth something like a renewal of the ancient Zarathustra-teaching. *He did not yet clearly know* that he bore the Zarathustra-*soul* within himself [Rudolf Steiner once again used the word 'soul' here], but the Zarathustra-teaching, the Zarathustra-wisdom, the Zarathustra-impulse arose in him during the conversation. Together with his mother he experienced this great Zarathustra-impulse. All the beauty and greatness of the ancient Sun-teaching arose in his soul.' (GA 148, 6 October 1913)

This mighty experience of Jesus of Nazareth during his final conversation with his mother was a sort of farewell-gift by the Zarathustra-individuality, a gift that ultimately prepared him for his next step, for the reception of the highest spiritual being who originally, as Ahura Mazda, stood in the centre of the ancient Persian religion.

What remained, however, as a more or less unconscious experience for the Nathan-Jesus during those eighteen years, was lived through by the Zarathustra individuality (who was connected to him) in full consciousness. Yet Zarathustra could reach such a high stage of development only by uniting with his higher 'I' in the course of his initiation. For it was purely out of the forces of this 'I' (that exists and is active beyond the boundaries of birth and death) that he was able in his twelfth year to leave the sheaths of the Solomon-Jesus, and to pass over into the Nathan-Jesus; and then, prior to the Baptism in the Jordan, to leave the sheaths of the Nathan-Jesus also, and once again to pass over in full consciousness into the spiritual world adjacent to the Earth. (Concerning his subsequent paths see more below.)

It was, however, this lofty stage of consciousness of the Zarathustra-'I' that made it possible for him to experience in the above-mentioned processes a certain higher guidance; the guidance under which the Nathan-Jesus stood from the beginning, but that he was unaware of until the end. With this we have approached an answer to the question concerning the spiritual guidance of Jesus of Nazareth *prior* to the time the Christ descended into him. Now, however, we face the question: Who 'guided' and 'led' Zarathustra out of the spiritual world as he fulfilled his *esoteric* mission at the Turning-point of Time, just as John the Baptist had been sent and guided from out of the spiritual world in order to fulfil his *exoteric* task? That John the Baptist had such a higher guide was confirmed by him personally when he said: 'I did not know him, but He who sent me to baptize with water said to me: "He on whom you see the Spirit descend, so that it remains united with him, he it is who baptizes with the Holy Spirit".' (Jn: 1,33)

The question can likewise be formulated as follows: Who at the Turning-point of Time could possibly have said something concerning Zarathustra's 'I' that resembled what is stated in the gospels about John the Baptist? In regard to Zarathustra, such words could be: 'I send the "I" of my servant that is filled with the forces of my "I" so as to prepare my sheaths that "I" may dwell in them.'

An answer to this question is contained in the eurythmic *prelude* of the Foundation Stone Meditation where it comes to expression purely through eurythmic means without words.[155]

One can find an indication for this secret in lectures by Rudolf Steiner. Before offering a *eurythmic answer* to this question, we shall therefore first refer to one such passage dealing with the above. By refuting certain preconceived notions of traditional Christianity in regard to anthroposophical Christology, Rudolf Steiner hinted at this secret by posing a certain question and then answering it himself positively: 'It is quite correct to say that not until approximately the age of three can a human being begin to have memories. But does one say for this reason that what lives in man later [in his soul] was not in him earlier? When one speaks of the Christ's entry into Jesus, does one therefore deny *that the Christ was connected to Jesus starting from birth*? Just as little does one deny this as one denies that the soul is in the child prior to when the soul arises in a manner of speaking in this child during the course of the third year.' (GA 155, 13 July 1914)

Here the comparison with the child is especially important. It indicates that we deal here with the Nathan-Jesus who carried in himself the primal forces of childhood that average human beings can avail themselves of only until age three, meaning only to the point in their life they can remember under ordinary circumstances, namely that point to which consciousness of their earthly 'I' extends.[156] The Nathan-Jesus, on the other hand, had these original childhood forces at his disposal *during his whole earth life.* This indicates that starting from his birth until the Baptism in the Jordan he was under the direct guidance of the Christ, a guidance that still occurred *out of the spiritual world,* just as every child is under the guidance of the Christ until its third year of life. For according to Rudolf Steiner's spiritual scientific research, these original childhood forces are the forces of the Christ in every human being.[157]

In the sense of Rudolf Steiner's afore-mentioned words, we can therefore say that the Christ was *spiritually* connected with His future earthly bearer, Jesus of Nazareth (the Nathan soul) during his whole life on Earth starting with his birth. But it was only at the Baptism in the Jordan that He fully united with *the sheaths of the Nathan Soul.* Rudolf Steiner referred to this fact in an article in the following words: 'And this [spiritual] research finds that the Christ Spirit, who guided Jesus of Nazareth up to his thirtieth year, as if from outside, then moved into the innermost core of his being in that year [during the Baptism].' (GA 35) Even more radically, Rudolf Steiner described this set of facts in a lecture to members: 'Now, who transformed the body of Jesus of Nazareth in such a manner and finally brought it to a point where it could receive the Christ? *The Christ Himself has done that.* First He worked on it from outside and afterwards He could Himself move into the human being.' (GA 109/ 111, 3 June 1909)

Following his transition into the Nathan-Jesus, the Zarathustra-individuality likewise entered into this special stream of supersensible guidance by the Christ. But unlike the Jesus who experienced this guidance only unconsciously on the *soul* level, the Zarathustra-'I' perceived it in full consciousness on the *spiritual* level. (In eurythmy this fact comes to expression inasmuch as eurythmist No. V guides the activities of the four remaining ones from the beginning.)

Zarathustra prepared the sheaths of Jesus of Nazareth for the reception of the Christ during the eighteen years *under His direct guidance.* This process reached its culmination in the thirtieth year of Jesus with the mighty in-streaming of the Sun wisdom of the ancient Persian religion. It was the religion that Zarathustra had inaugurated under the guidance of Ahura Mazda, the revelation of the cosmic Christ. The whole Sun wisdom he had received through the Inspirations by the cosmic Christ, as well as the experiences he had gathered in his many incarnations in constant service to the Christ, were passed on by Zarathustra to Jesus of Nazareth during his last conversation with his mother. 'In the thirtieth year this Zarathustra individuality was in a position to pour everything that can come from such a lofty individuality into the threefold corporeality [of Jesus].' (GA 131, 12 October 1911) By doing so he could prepare Jesus of Nazareth for the reception of the Christ Entity once and for all.

Yet there was an additional special *karmic reason* for this powerful in-pouring of the Sun wisdom into Jesus of Nazareth. It means that this wisdom entered into his consciousness as a condition for him to receive the Christ into himself. This karmic reason consisted in the fact that the ancient Persian religion founded by Zarathustra moreover contained a reflection of the first cosmic deed by the Christ in the Lemurian epoch—a deed carried out through the future Jesus of Nazareth who in that age still remained in the spiritual worlds. 'Indeed this did continue; effects remained which had come about once in the old Lemurian time because the Christ Being had *ensouled* that entity who later became the Nathan-Jesus boy; the effects had remained, as it were, in the Sun activity. And Zarathustra's initiation consisted in his finding out that the Sun activity was *impregnated with these effects*.' (GA 149, 30 December 1913) This means, Zarathustra bore within himself the memory of the salvation of the *physical* human body through the Christ with the help of the Nathan-soul in the Lemurian epoch (first pre-stage of the Mystery of Golgotha). This recollection gave him the strength to establish the ancient Persian religion with its striving for illuminating physical matter with light, and to sacrifice his physical body twice at the Turning-point of Time.

This is why it was not only the Nathan-Jesus who received infinitely much through the fact that Zarathustra's ego remained in him for eighteen years. Conversely, Zarathustra likewise received infinitely much due to the fact that he sojourned in the sheaths of Jesus. And if the Nathan-Jesus could fulfil his actual mission on Earth—of becoming the bearer of the Christ—only due to Zarathustra's help, correspondingly Zarathustra could only begin with his future mission as Master Jesus (see further below) owing to the forces that he received from the Nathan-Jesus. 'Everything that Zarathustra as an individuality could acquire through these tools [the three bodies of the Nathan-Jesus] passes into the individuality of Zarathustra; goes on living with this individuality who now emerges out of the threefold corporeality [prior to the Baptism in the Jordan]. This indivi-duality benefits from that.' (GA 131, 12 October 1911) If we try to express this process of mutual fructification in biblical terms, we could say: Thanks to the connection of the two Jesus beings something of the original image ['Ebenbild'] of man passed over from Jesus of Nazareth into Zarathustra. And something that had been attained through the initiation of the 'likeness' [see Tr.1] by Zarathustra passed on its part over to Jesus. In both cases, under *the direct guidance of the Christ*, as we saw, the union of 'image' and 'likeness' of the human being was once more attained.[157a]

★

With this we have become prepared to look into the afore-mentioned events once more and to comprehend them in the particular form in which they make their appearance in the eurythmic presentation of the Foundation Stone Meditation. Thus, in the prelude to the first three segments of the meditation, a eurythmic depiction of the Mystery of the two Jesus boys and their union (the uniting of 'image' [Ebenbild] and 'likeness' [Gleichnis]) can be recognized, whereas the postlude deals with a eurythmic performance of the Mystery of the Baptism. In so doing the two Mysteries are pictured from the viewpoint of participation and activity by the individuality of Zarathustra as the greatest servant of the Christ.

Following the numbering given by Rudolf Steiner to the six eurythmists who join in the presentation of the meditation, the first four (I–IV) in their totality represent Jesus of Nazareth, or put more precisely, his three sheaths (physical body, etheric body, astral body) and his 'I'. As we saw, the latter is devoid of any earthly experience but filled with the special features described above. Eurythmist 'V' represents Zarathustra as the great initiate who participated in the events of the Turning-point of Time directly as the bearer of a fully developed higher 'I', and eurythmist 'VI' represents the Christ as the World-'I' and source of the true 'I' of man and humanity.[157b]

Even the order in which the eurythmists appear on the stage occurs in the sequence of the birth of the two Jesus boys. Historically the Jesus boy of the Matthew-gospel was born first. His birth took place at the beginning of the first year of the new era on 6 January. This is why eurythmist V enters first with the I(ee)-gesture that indicates the 'I' principle. This gesture is connected with the fact that it was Zarathustra's mission to develop the 'I' principle in order, proceeding from it, to work on the mission of the Earth. (See GA 264) Then the four other eurythmists appear, something that corresponds to the birth of the second Jesus boy that is described in the Gospel of Luke and occurred almost a year later on 25 December of the year 1.

Only then appears the main figure (VI) who from the start led the development and unfolding of the Nathan-Jesus out of the spiritual world. He likewise brought about the union of the two youths, when the 'I' of Zarathustra left the sheaths of the Solomonic Jesus in his twelfth year and passed over into the other boy, affirmed by the Temple scene depicted in the Luke Gospel. The words concluding this chapter, 'And Jesus progressed in wisdom, in maturity, and in grace in the sight of God and men' (Lk 2, 52 JM) therefore already refer to the two individualities. One increased more in wisdom (Zarathustra), the other more in love (the Nathan soul); henceforth however they worked through one and the same earthly body 'with increasing age'.

As we saw, during the eighteen years that the Zarathustra individuality dwelled in his sheaths, Jesus of Nazareth was only dimly aware of this fact. In a similar way he only obscurely sensed the guidance of his life through the Christ. Zarathustra on the other hand recognized this guidance with full awareness and followed it from his passing over into the sheaths of the Nathan-Jesus fully consciously. Thus we can say: What Jesus of Nazareth only *sensed dimly* was fully *known* to Zarathustra who indwelled him.

Seen as a whole, the appearance of the eurythmists on stage as well as the execution of the prelude can be described as a sequence of events that consists of five stages one after the other.

First Stage

Eurythmist V appears with the I(ee)-gesture that points to a lofty initiate who possesses a fully developed 'I'—the birth of the Solomonic Jesus on 6 January.

Second Stage

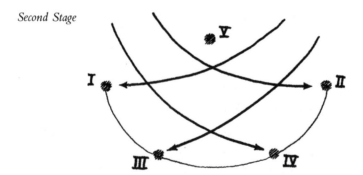

The other four eurythmists (I–IV) appear on stage with the gestures A and O that blend into each other. These gestures point to the soul-etheric content of the Nathan soul. The I(ee)-gesture is missing because it is a question of a being that as yet has no earth experiences as an individual 'I'. The four eurythmists shape the form of a *chalice* on stage that arises out of the triad IOA, the triad which brings to expression the nature of man *prior* to the Mystery of Golgotha. The birth of the Nathan-Jesus on 25 December.

Third Stage

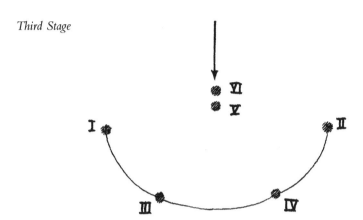

Eurythmist VI appears on stage with the I(ee)-gesture and positions himself *behind* eurythmist V who likewise stands there with the I(ee)-gesture (meaning that a spiritual impulse passes from 'I' to 'I'). At this moment both are still outside the chalice. The Christ as the true 'I' inspires Zarathustra's higher 'I' with His spiritual presence to pass from the one Jesus over into the other.

Fourth Stage

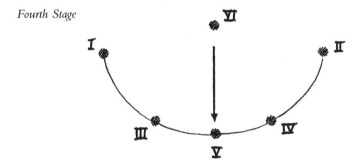

Eurythmist V descends into the chalice formed by the other four eurythmists, and steps through its inner space along the 'I'-axis and now becomes the support-bearing ground of the chalice. The union *of the two Jesus boys*. The Zarathustra-'I' passes over into the Nathan-Jesus. Scene of the twelve-year-old Jesus in the Temple of Jerusalem.

Fifth Stage

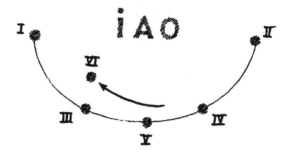

The chalice (the sheaths of the Nathan-Jesus) is filled with the substance IAO, in which Christ lives, preparing His incarnation on the Earth. This is why only eurythmist VI carries out this triad eurythmically. The remaining five eurythmists form its mirror image: OAI. The Zarathustra-'I' that forms the ground of the chalice participates fully consciously in this process, even though it first works merely on the level of *soul* in the Nathan boy.

Now the first three segments of the meditation are eurythmically performed.

★

After the presentation of the meditation text follows the postlude and the exit of the eurythmists from the stage. This process consists of seven stages.

First Stage

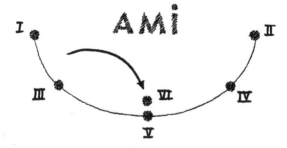

The chalice (the sheaths of the Nathan-Jesus) is filled with the substance AMI, but only eurythmist VI carries out this triad. The other five who present the form of the chalice, shape its mirror image: IMA. The Zarathustra-'I', still the ground of the chalice, participates in this process only on the *spiritual* level. For the transition from IAO to AMI, meaning the appearance of the *consonant* M in the triad, corresponds to the ascent from the soul level to that of the spirit, something that regarding the cosmological aspect corresponds to the transition from the Sun soul to the Sun spirit. This ascending probably takes place during the event at the pagan altar, when the soul of the Nathan-Jesus rises up into the Sun sphere and there, for the first time, hears the changed voice of the Bath-Kol who proclaims to this soul the macrocosmic Lord's Prayer. (See GA 148, 5 October 1913)[158]

The second stage begins when eurythmist VI takes his position with the I(ee)-gesture directly *behind* eurythmist V, who likewise eurythmizes the I(ee)-gesture (once again a spiritual impulse passes from 'I' to 'I'). Now both eurythmists (V and VI) find themselves at the base of the chalice. With His spiritual presence the Christ inspires the true higher 'I' of Zarathustra to leave the sheaths of Jesus of Nazareth this time, something which then occurs immediately prior to the Baptism.

Second Stage

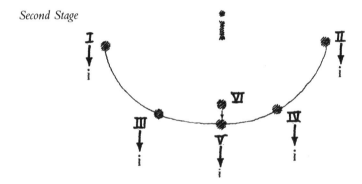

At the end of the second stage there follows a strong I(ee)-gesture, carried out simultaneously by all six eurythmists. But even though they all form this gesture together, it is still evident that the ether stream (the jointly formed I(ee)-gesture) proceeds initially from VI, passes over to V, and only then to the remaining four eurythmists.

One can therefore say that here the 'I'-impulse emanates from the Christ, passes over to the 'I' of Zarathustra and from it to the Nathan-Jesus. Putting it differently, the 'I'-stream passes through three stages in flowing down to Earth; from the true 'I' to the higher 'I', and from it to the earthly 'I'-consciousness of man. This moment corresponds in the earthly biography of Jesus to his last conversation with his mother that ultimately prepares him for receiving the Christ (the Baptism in the Jordan).

Thus, Zarathustra's ego first receives the impulse to move out of the sheaths of the Nathan Jesus from the Christ, who is on the [final] approach to His incarnation. Thereafter Zarathustra accomplishes his third and highest sacrifice. But while he leaves the sheaths of the Nathan-Jesus, he bestows on him at the same time a final and most powerful Inspiration from his Sun wisdom. As a result, for the first time in all the eighteen years, Jesus experienced the most intense presence of Zarathustra in his soul. According to the *Fifth Gospel*, this was at the end of the conversation between Jesus and his mother when Zarathustra's Sun-wisdom manifested to both their souls in all its splendour and greatness.

Third Stage

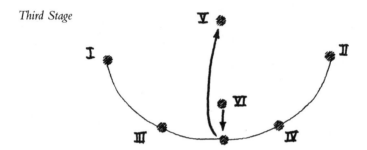

Eurythmist V leaves his locale to VI and moves out of the space of the chalice (the sheaths of Jesus of Nazareth) along the 'I'-axis. Eurythmist VI assumes his place and becomes the base of the chalice. *The Mystery of the Baptism in the Jordan*: The Zarathustra-'I' leaves the sheaths of Jesus of Nazareth and moves into the spiritual world adjacent to the Earth, and the Christ Being enters into the sheaths of Jesus of Nazareth as the true 'I' of man and humanity. This event is seen by the audience sitting in the hall as if they beheld it from John the Baptist's viewpoint who, as the representative of mankind, becomes the first witness of how a human being who is well known to him, namely Jesus of Nazareth, wades into the Jordan and after the baptism stands before him as a completely transformed personality—the human being who for the first time on Earth became a God-Man.[158a]

Here, the artistic and Christological accuracy of the eurythmic presentation is particularly impressive. First, eurythmist V moves backwards around VI and with that clears his own place for VI at the bottom of the chalice. Eurythmist VI then needs to take only one step to occupy the spot of V. With that the thirty-year-long process of the gradual union of the Christ Being with His earthly bearer, Jesus of Nazareth, reaches its culmination at the moment of the Baptism in the Jordan. Now it requires only 'one step' for the Christ to enter into the sheaths of Jesus. At that moment a new process begins, the process comprising the three years when the Son of God becomes the Son of Man.

Now, from the spiritual world adjacent to the earth (eurythmist V is outside the chalice), Zarathustra beholds the three years of the life of Christ in the earthly sheaths of Jesus of Nazareth and sees how the Christ gradually spiritualizes the three sheaths as well as the 'I' of Jesus (four eurythmists who form the chalice) until the culmination takes place in the Mystery of Golgotha. This is how, out of the spiritual world nearest to the Earth, the 'I' of Zarathustra experiences the Mystery of Golgotha as the overcoming of corporeal death through the Christ. The physical body of Christ disintegrates, only His 'I' remains that has vanquished death. At this moment, the four eurythmists (I–IV) leave the stage and only V and VI remain behind, standing on the 'I'-axis.

Fourth Stage

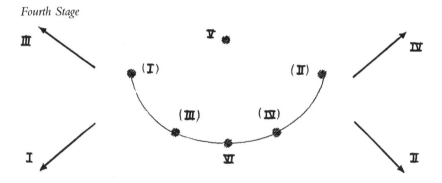

In order to understand the last three stages, attention must be paid to how Rudolf Steiner characterizes the further path taken by Zarathustra after he has made the third sacrifice and then has united in the spiritual world with the etheric body of the Solomonic Jesus. Now the Zarathustra-'I' was 'so mature that it did not require further passage through a devachan ... Thus, *for the very first time* that entity was then *born* which afterwards appeared again and again [on Earth]. Its manner of appearance was one where relatively brief spans of time elapsed between physical death and a new birth.' In this way this individuality 'could [become] the greatest helper for those who wished to understand the lofty Event of Palestine. As the so-called "Master Jesus", this individuality passes through the Turning-point of Time, so that, having reacquired his etheric body, Zarathustra, the Zarathustra-'I', began his spiritual calling as the "Master Jesus" throughout the evolution of humanity. Since then he lives again and again on our Earth for the direction and guidance of that spiritual stream that we call the Christian one ... He stands behind the great spiritual figures of Christendom, always teaching what the grand Event of Palestine does in fact signify.' (GA 114, 21 September 1909)

In the above-quoted words the most surprising thing is probably that Rudolf Steiner speaks here of the 'birth' of a new entity who 'for the first time' originated in Earth evolution. How this could take place becomes comprehensible if one becomes aware what the *macrocosmic* equivalence (meaning, its archetype) is in the life of Christ for the *microcosmic* 'birth'. Rudolf Steiner described this macrocosmic archetype only once in the cycle on the Gospel of Mark. When he explained the significance of the image of the 'unclad youth' who escaped the hands of the cohort (Mk 14,51–52) and is then seen on Easter morn next to the empty tomb, Rudolf Steiner spoke of the appearance of a 'new cosmic impulse in Earth evolution'. (GA 139, 23 September 1912)[159] Only inasmuch as the Zarathustra individuality took something of this new cosmic impulse into itself could it attain this transformation and become a new entity—the Master Jesus. This became possible because the new cosmic impulse is the beginning of the transformation of earth into a new sun. This in turn means that it represents a telluric and cosmic process that will be completed eventually with the union of Sun and Earth; something that always was the highest ideal and ultimate goal of the spiritual efforts by Zarathustra.

Now we shall turn once again to the eurythmic presentation of the postlude of the first three segments of the meditation and on this basis consider the last three stages.

Fifth Stage

Now eurythmist VI steps behind V and blesses him with the I(ee)-gesture for the new path. This signifies that, along with the I(ee)-gesture, the Christ entrusts to Zarathustra in the spiritual world something of the substance of His 'I', opening up for him access to the forces of the 'unclad youth who escapes arrest', meaning that he is filled with the 'new cosmic impulse'. The Zarathustra individuality experiences such a powerful transformation as a result, that Rudolf Steiner speaks in this connection of the 'birth' of a new being. Not until after the main figure (eurythmist VI) has passed everything on to his pupil (V) can he himself exit the stage.

Sixth Stage

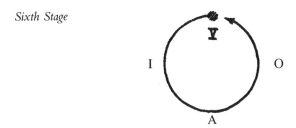

The large circle that eurythmist V forms on stage points to a profound secret that relates to the new activity by the Zarathustra individuality as the Master Jesus. Zarathustra could fulfil his new task in humanity only because, having left the sheaths of Jesus of Nazareth immediately prior to the Baptism in the Jordan, he united with the etheric body of the Solomonic Jesus that had been preserved in the spiritual world adjacent to the Earth. (See GA 114, 21 September 1909) This etheric body that Zarathustra had formed during the twelve years of his life in the Solomon-Jesus was to such great measure filled by cosmic wisdom that it could elude dissolution in the cosmic ether following the death of the youth. Only by uniting himself with it in the spiritual world could Zarathustra attain the faculty to incarnate in every century. In so doing he makes the sacrifice of foregoing a life in Devachan.

In nature and in spiritual science the form of the circle (more accurately the form of the sphere) indicates the activity of the etheric forces. With their help dew drops are formed for example. And in the macrocosm the Sun system appears to clairvoyant sight in the shape of ether spheres that are blended into each other. (See GA 136, 8 April 1912) This is why a sphere (globe) is the most perfect expression of the etheric principle. The human etheric body strives towards this form after death, something that leads to its gradual dissolution in the ether cosmos. The ether body of the Solomonic Jesus, on the other hand, was not only preserved in the spiritual world, but through the connection of the Zarathustra 'I' with it (the original I(ee)-gesture on the sixth level) was filled moreover with the IAO-substance (the sounds that the eurythmist forms while he moves in a circle). Concerning the esoteric significance of this triad, Rudolf Steiner said: 'Mood: IAO as name of the Christ. This is connected with the secret of how Christ works in the human being'. (GA 264) Only this ether body, filled as it was by the Christ-Impulse, could serve the Master Jesus as the basis for his new mission in humanity, and this is the mission that consists of the spiritualization of the Earth out of the forces of the 'new cosmic impulse', the impulse that has entered into Earth evolution through the Mystery of Golgotha.

In addition, this eurythmic circle points to the esoteric fact about which Rudolf Steiner states that, following the Mystery of Golgotha, the Master Jesus 'seeks out the location where the Mystery of Golgotha has occurred every year at Easter time'. (GA 130, 5 May 1912) This takes place in physical form 'during his earthly incarnations as well as in the purely spiritual sense. Then his esoteric disciples can receive the instructions concerning the spiritual events in Palestine. Regardless of whether [the Master] Jesus is physically incarnated or not, he seeks out this location annually. Then those of the disciples who have the maturity can have their union with him'. (ibid)[159a] The Master Jesus thus becomes 'the inspirer of those who wish to understand the living, evolving Christianity'. (GA 114, 21 September 1909)

Seventh Stage

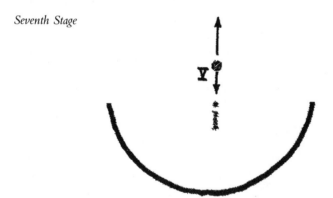

The last stage points to the nature of Zarathustra's new mission which he is obliged to fulfil henceforth in humanity as a result of the inner transformation called forth through his union with the Christ impulse. From this time on, as a completely new being, he bears the name 'Master Jesus' and since then incarnates in almost every century on Earth, *following the Christ in all his incarnations*. This is moreover why eurythmist V correspondingly moves offstage in the same direction as did VI, meaning on the 'I'-axis and also with the I(ee)-gesture. But before doing so, he on his part likewise blesses all mankind, now already as *Master Jesus*, and in this way adapts himself in his true 'I' to the activity of the cosmic 'I' of the Christ in the world. Since then he is one of the great masters who inspire and help those who have the task publicly to proclaim the wisdom of esoteric Christianity.

In comparing this last stage of the postlude (the exit of eurythmist V) with the first stage of the prelude (his entry on stage), one immediately notices a great difference. In the first case he still appears as one who is a 'receiver' of an 'I'-force; in the second case he is one who is a 'giver'. For Zarathustra this signifies the ascent from the higher 'I' to the true 'I'. In this manner it is pointed out at the end what the Mystery of Golgotha has brought into humanity's evolution. Into each human 'I' it places the ability for man to change from a receiving being into a giving being, and this signifies ascending from the level of the creature [a 'created one'] to the level of a creator.

★

If the secret of the union of the two Jesus boys as a *soul* event stands in the centre of the eurythmists' entrance on stage and the prelude to the meditation (an event that is therefore accompanied by the triad IAO), then the secret of the Baptism in the Jordan as a *spiritual* event that is therefore accompanied by the triad AMI stands in the centre of the conclusion and the eurythmists' exit from the stage. Furthermore, the two events as well as all the other stages considered by us (there are twelve of them) are depicted in eurythmy principally from the viewpoint of the participation by the Zarathustra 'I'.

As to the new mission of Zarathustra as the Master Jesus, it consists (aside from what has been mentioned above, see the quoted words by Rudolf Steiner) in preparing humanity for the transition from the fifth to the sixth cultural period. Rudolf Steiner depicted this as follows: 'John the Baptist proclaimed Christ Jesus ahead of time during the middle of the fourth sub-race [the Greco-Latin cultural period]. Now, however, it is the individuality of the Master Jesus who guides humanity from the fifth across into the sixth sub-race [from the present cultural period into the future Slavic one] once more toward John the Baptist, toward Aquarius.' (GA 264, 12 February 1906)

This signifies that the Master Jesus has the task in the course of the fifth cultural period—during which time the individual 'I' reaches its culmination in the consciousness soul of man—to prepare the transition from the previous period (that of John the Baptist, when it was only possible to receive the spirit-self-forces through initiation) to the sixth cultural period.

This will be the period when the spirit-self-forces will be accessible to all human beings. Then there will finally manifest in humanity the Mystery of the presence and effect of the Christ in man's 'I'. This is something that takes place in eurythmy inasmuch as the triad IAO is executed by eurythmist V during his passage through the circle, and then is brought to conclusion once more with the I(ee)-gesture. At the basis of this mission of the Master Jesus (the mission that has as its goal the preparation of the sixth cultural period), is the fact that this mission is a repetition (but now in new form and on a far higher level) of the second ancient Persian cultural period founded so long ago by Zarathustra. In this sense, the form of the circle is also the sign of the Sun (that is the cosmic origin of the human etheric body), or the new Sun sphere that gradually takes shape around the Earth as one of the consequences of the Mystery of Golgotha.

For Zarathustra himself, this stage becomes a kind of closure of a spiritual/historical circle of evolution that encompasses humanity's development from the second cultural period (when for the first time he showed earthly human beings a way to a conquest of the physical world) to the sixth cultural period. Then, a new ascent into the spiritual world is supposed to begin; an ascent not only of man but likewise of the Earth in the process of its transformation into the new sun as expressed in the sixth stage of the eurythmic presentation. But in the middle between the second and sixth cultural periods occurred the Mystery of Golgotha as a fount of transformation of the past impulses into impulses of the future, something that comes to expression in the individual fate of Zarathustra who became the Master Jesus.

★

A further aspect of the eurythmic presentation of the first three segments of the Foundation Stone Meditation is that (in a purely artistic form) in them is depicted the process of the development of the human 'I'-consciousness. This development began with its first awakening where it was only able to operate in a passive 'mirroring' manner. It continues on to its next stage, that of the present level of individualization all the way to a future spiritually creative stage of evolution that it is ultimately supposed to reach. In our age, this third stage of individual 'I'-consciousness is only attainable by great initiates like the Master Jesus, Christian Rosenkreutz, or Rudolf Steiner. Finally on the last, fourth, stage, the highest archetype of this development is revealed. It is the archetype on which Christian initiates orient themselves and which they follow.

We shall now consider these four stages in detail. The first stage is illustrated in the prelude and postlude of the first three segments. Here all five eurythmists form a chalice which is then filled by eurythmist VI with the IAO substance in the prelude, and later in the postlude with the AMI substance. In so doing only eurythmist VI walks in a space-form. The remaining five, standing still in their place, shape a mirror-image of his sound-gestures: at the start OAI, and then IMA. Here, this is therefore an 'I'-consciousness that is still linked directly with the divine primal fount, the fount that in the very beginning brought it forth. This consciousness is thus only capable of mirroring this fountainhead. That is mankind's original state of consciousness which the Nathan-soul brought along to Earth at the Turning-point of Time as a sort of primal memory of the source of the human 'I'.

> Practise Spirit-recollection
> In depths of soul
> Where in the wielding
> World-Creator-Being
> Thine own I
> Comes to being
> Within the I of God.

At the beginning of its earthly life, the Nathan-soul's consciousness had a more soul-like character (OAI), but in the end, prior to the Baptism in the Jordan, reached the spiritual level (IMA).

The second stage of human consciousness comes to expression in the eurythmic presentation and accompaniment of the first three parts of the meditation. Here it is already a matter of an independent development of the individual 'I'. This stage corresponds to the condition of the majority of human beings today. Eurythmically it is depicted through the four eurythmists (I - IV) who now move in a space-form but in such a way that two mirror-like forms arise, while all four walk in almost the same form: I mirroring II, and III mirroring IV. The four eurythmists repeat their forms several times and in this way exemplify the present (transitional) form of 'I'-consciousness which, by now separated completely from the divine primordial base, takes initial independent steps on the thorny path of individualization. Despite all this, human consciousness at this stage is still marked by a certain dependence; admittedly not on the spiritual world but by an influence exerted on it from the earthly world, particularly by other human beings. This influence is reflected in the individual consciousness, making it partially dependent on its earthly environment, even though this is generally not perceived.

The stage of individualization characterized here can be significantly deepened through work on oneself with the words, 'Practise Spirit-pondering / in balance of the soul', as the starting point (the balance comes to expression here through the two pairs of eurythmists who reflect one another). One who moves in this direction on the path of modern initiation can attain to a conscious encounter with the cosmic archetype of his/her 'I', and continuing on to an essential union of being with this archetype:

> Where the surging
> Deeds of the World's Becoming
> Do thine own I
> Unite
> Unto the I of the World.

And due to a conscious union of man's 'I' with the World-'I' in the sense of Paul's words, 'Not I but the Christ in me', it is possible to free oneself from all outer and inner influences and to reach the creative state of consciousness that is characteristic for all true initiates. This third stage is depicted by eurythmist V. While the text of the first three parts of the meditation is performed eurythmically, several times V repeats his own form in space on the stage, a form that is distinguished from the forms of the four other eurythmists and yet contains elements that connect their mirroring forms in a higher harmony. Here, eurythmist V clearly appears as the leader of the remaining four, because by now he has attained the faculty of 'Spirit-vision' and as a result can perceive in full consciousness what is contained in the words:

> Where the eternal aims of Gods
> World-Being's Light
> On thine own I
> Bestow
> For thy free Willing.

This is the level that only the leading Christian initiates occupy today, initiates who in their 'I' bear the substance of the World-'I' or Logos. One can moreover say that in the process of initiation their 'I' became like a 'micro-logos' and henceforth shares in the realization of the 'eternal aims of Gods' on Earth, and that means in the realization of the will of the Word of Worlds.

On the stage, it is eurythmist VI who represents this Word of Worlds or the 'Macro-Logos', the highest archetype and goal of the totality of 'I'-

evolution. This is why, from his first appearance on stage until his exit, he carries out a series of forms not repeated anywhere (all remaining eurythmists repeat their forms several times). By doing so he represents the universal world-principle of constant, never resting cosmic creation that alone is characteristic of the Logos (the Word). 'All things came into being through him and nothing of all this that has come into being was made except through Him'. (Jn. 1, 3)

These stages of consciousness can be summed up as follows:

First Stage: Primal consciousness of humanity (Nathan-Soul);
Second Stage: Consciousness of present-day human being;
Third Stage: Consciousness of the initiate who in the developmental process of the inner forces of his 'I' has reached the stage of the 'micro-logos', meaning one who has become the conscious 'servant of the Word' (Lk. 1, 2);
Fourth Stage: Super-Consciousness of the Word of Worlds.

In the Foundation Stone Meditation, the three main exercises of Anthroposophy correspond to the first three stages,

Practise Spirit-recollection,
Practise Spirit-pondering,
Practise Spirit-vision,

owing to which the individual 'I' develops. This 'I' development takes place while the 'I' passes through a threefold metamorphosis, which in the Foundation Stone Meditation to start with is depicted as the principle of the reflecting of the higher; then as the principle of union with the higher, and finally as the principle of free co-operation with it. This *moral* rising up of the individual 'I' takes place through the stages of 'comes to being' [Ger. erweset] to 'unite' [Ger. 'vereinen'] to 'bestow' [Ger. 'schenken'] (see first rhythm of the Christmas Conference). It corresponds to the transition from the unfree condition of the 'I' to the half free, where the free actions are mixed with the unfree ones, and finally to the condition of genuine spiritual freedom that is attainable today only for the true initiate.

Cosmologically, these three stages of 'I' development can be characterized as the *Moon stage* that is only able to reflect the outer light; as the *planetary stage* that aside from the ability of reflecting likewise avails itself of an inner life of its own; and the *Sun stage* on which exists the faculty for free creative activity.

Looking back to the eurythmic presentation of the three first parts of the Foundation Stone Meditation as a whole, one can say that in the centre of its prelude stands the secret of the union between the two Jesus boys. This in turn refers to the origin of the Son of Man out of the union of 'image' ['Ebenbild'] and 'likeness' ['Gleichnis'] in an earthly [human] being. Conversely, in the middle of the postlude stands the Mystery of the Baptism in the Jordan as the union of the Son of Man with the Son of God. And in the eurythmization of the meditation's first three parts, we have the artistic presentation of the spiritual process that takes place in the three systems of the Phantom—or the Resurrection Body that has risen out of the tomb on Golgotha.[159b]

★

We enter a completely different world when we turn to the eurythmic implementation of the fourth part of the Foundation Stone Meditation. Here we deal with the union of the two major Mystery streams of the past, the northern and the southern one, that were represented at the Turning-point of Time by the three Kings and the three Shepherds. In the spiritual-historical context, the first go to the birth place of the Solomon-Jesus (Zarathustra) and the others to the birth place of the Nathan-Jesus. In the fourth part of the meditation (just by the grouping of the eurythmists as they enter the stage), the beginning of the later process of union on the part of the two Jesus boys comes to expression, but here not only from the esoteric but likewise from the spiritual-historical standpoint.

Through the contrasting attire of the eurythmists, the affiliation of the two groups with either the Kings or Shepherds is readily perceptible. One group wears white garments and golden veils. This colour combination, according to Rudolf Steiner, is eurythmically linked with the gesture of knowledge [Ger. 'Erkenntnis'] and that means, it corresponds to the fundamental character of the Magi (Kings). Conversely, the second group in golden garments with white veils expresses more of the character of the Shepherds.

In the eurythmic performance, the 'Kings' develop the *beginning* of the fourth part as each eurythmist walks a personal form, and one following the other at that. Accordingly, the *individual* element holds sway here from the start. In the case of the 'Shepherds' on the other hand, who then perform the words of the fourth part eurythmically, the forms are partially the same (two of them are mirror images of the first) and they are performed simultaneously. This implies that the *social* element predominates between them. Moreover, comparing the eurythmic forms of both groups, it is immediately noticeable that the 'Shepherds' clearly are given the leading role (even though the whole fourth part is begun not by them but by the 'Kings'). The reason for this is that in the events of Palestine, the Solomonic Jesus (Zarathustra), whom the Kings welcomed, was the *preparer* of the Incarnation of the Christ on Earth, whereas, following the Baptism in the Jordan, the Nathan-Jesus was the *bearer* of the Christ. This is why the eurythmy configuration of the three 'Shepherds' is shaped so that two of them form a kind of chalice within which the third eurythmist moves in a form of his own.[160]

In this complete as well as complicated form, an image of the three systems of the physical body and the soul forces linked with them can be recognized in the sequence as they are depicted in the fourth part of the meditation. They are: The heart as representative of feeling, the head as bearer of thinking, and the will element that is connected with the bony system. As a whole they refer to the soul forces and corporeal organization of Jesus of Nazareth who, through the Baptism in the Jordan, was to receive the Christ into himself.

Now it is the triad IAO, eurythmically expressed throughout the entire fourth part of the meditation, that connects the two groups. (Each eurythmist forms this triad if he or she does not walk in any form.) One can therefore say that in the fourth part of the meditation the whole eurythmic space is constantly filled with the sounds IAO; something that, as we stated above, is an expression of how the Christ works in man. From this it follows that the presence of the Christ in man, as is the case after the Mystery of Golgotha, makes up the main eurythmic motif for the whole fourth part of the Meditation.

In the fourth part, the entrance as well as exit by the eurythmists from the stage takes place along with the gesture of the zodiacal sign of Libra ♎, something that points to the principle of the all-encompassing balance that came into the world through Christ's descent into the world. This is why Rudolf Steiner sometimes called the Christ Event the hypomochlion [or 'fulcrum'], meaning the principle of universal balance that brings harmony into contrasts:

- Head and heart
- Kings and Shepherds
- Northern and southern Mystery streams
- Zarathustra initiation and Buddha initiation
- Cain and Abel stream (Hiram and Solomon)
- Young and old souls
- Platonists and Aristotelians
- Spiritual research and spiritual revelation.

This principle of balance that is connected with the Christ Being was engraved by Rudolf Steiner in artistic-archetypal form into the Sculptural Group portraying the Christ as representative of humanity, who brings about the balance between the luciferic and ahrimanic powers. In the paintings of the eastern part of the small cupola of the First Goetheanum this same motif came to expression.

In the eurythmy of the fourth part of the meditation, the principle of balance and the higher synthesis is emphasized especially by the fact that the group of Kings exit the stage in the direction from where the Shepherds had come, and conversely the Shepherds exit to where the Kings had come from. This means that the Kings become Shepherds and the Shepherds become Kings, and in so doing each brings about the synthesis of the two principles in his own being. With this, the point is made in eurythmy that the Kings as well as the Shepherds have received the Christ Impulse into their being following the Mystery of Golgotha.

Moreover, prior to their exit from the stage, all six eurythmists carry out the sequence of the gestures from R–⌓–C, something that particularly emphasizes the principle of *balance*. For in eurythmy, the R-gesture that is made from behind—above to below—can take hold of the forces that are effective in matter, and shape them. And the C-gesture that is made from below to above represents the ascent into the spiritual world; the overcoming of the material element. In the earthly life of Christ Jesus, these two polarities correspond to the Baptism and the Resurrection; and the Mystery of Golgotha is their synthesis.

As was described in another work and briefly mentioned at the outset of this chapter, the sound sequence of C and R that is carried out by the eurythmists immediately after their entering the stage, and the opposite sequence R and C directly before their exit signifies:

‘Christian Rosenkreutz —at the beginning
rosae crucis   —at the end’   (GA K 23/1).

Considered esoterically on the other hand, the first points to the etheric body of Christian Rosenkreutz, who enables human beings, when it overshadows them beginning in the twentieth century, to behold the Etheric Christ. The second points to the repetition of the Mystery of Golgotha in the spiritual worlds at the end of the nineteenth century, the result of which was the etheric Second Coming. ‘The Rose Cross is the symbol for the second death of the Christ in the nineteenth century, for the death of the etheric body through the host of the materialists. The result of this is that the Christ can be beheld in the twentieth century in the way I have described it to you, namely in the ether body.' (GA 265, 8 February 1913)

Considering the depiction of the Foundation Stone Meditation in eurythmy from the viewpoint at the basis of this chapter, we can therefore say in summation: If (in the eurythmic presentation of the first three parts, in the esoteric sense) the central figure who follows the Christ is the *Master Jesus* (Zarathustra), then in the fourth part an equally central figure who follows the Christ is the individuality of *Christian Rosenkreutz*. Moreover, the two leading masters of esoteric Christendom are depicted in the eurythmic representation of the Foundation Stone Meditation together with the substance of their mission in humanity's evolution, which means together with what they are to accomplish in their service for the Christ Being in our time and in the future.

As we saw, the mission of each of these masters of esoteric Christendom is connected with the special character of their etheric bodies. One goes back to the initiation in the thirteenth century, the other to the events at the Turning-point of Time. These are two different yet equally significant etheric bodies. Beginning in our time, the etheric body of Christian Rosenkreutz has the effect of granting to those human beings whom it overshadows the distinction of beholding the Etheric Christ. The etheric body of the Master Jesus, on the other hand, that is completely filled with the Christ Impulse as the 'new cosmic impulse in Earth evolution', works in such a way that those who are overshadowed by it shall help the others to attain an awareness of the cosmic significance of the Christ and the Mystery of Golgotha.

At the conclusion of this consideration, we shall turn once more to the words by Rudolf Steiner that were quoted at the beginning of this chapter: 'At the head of our western school stand two masters, the Master Jesus and Master Christian Rosenkreutz ... Their call goes out to all people in the West, asking whether they wish to join the guidance of the two masters of the West ... We need the wisdom of the future, the western schooling that is offered to us by both these masters.' But what could be said in 1907 within the first esoteric school only in words, was affirmed once more seventeen years later in the New Mysteries through the performance of the Foundation Stone Meditation in the form of cultic eurythmy[161] as the most outstanding example of 'royal art' in our age.

10. The Foundation Stone Meditation as Esoteric Wellspring of the Constitution of the Anthroposophical Society

The four segments of the Foundation Stone Meditation contain the wellspring of the spiritual forces that are able to permeate the constitution of the Anthroposophical Society as the new 'esoteric impulse' mentioned over and over again by Rudolf Steiner in connection with the Christmas Conference.

Considered as a whole, the constitution of the Anthroposophical Society consists of three independent and at the same time inseparably interrelated institutions: The School of Spiritual Science as 'heart and soul' of the Anthroposophical Society (GA 260a); the world society or the 'Anthroposophical Society in the narrower sense' (ibid.) whose goal it is 'to nurture the life of the soul, both in the individual and in human society' (§1 of the Statutes); as well as the administration of the Goetheanum as the earthly place where both the School of Spiritual Science and the Anthroposophical Society are located.

In the spirit of the Christmas Conference, it is possible to summarize the above-mentioned three institutions by one name: the *General Anthroposophical Society*.

As was pointed out in another work by the author, these three institutions can be compared with the threefoldness of man's being.[162] The Goetheanum-Administration, whose main task is the management of the earthly affairs of the Goetheanum itself as well as the General Anthroposophical Society as a legal body, can be compared with the physical body of man, with the outer sheath of the human being. Just as a person is connected through his physical body with the whole surrounding earthly world, the Anthroposophical Society likewise enters through the judicial form of an association recorded in the commercial register into the judiciary realm. It thereby acquires the possibility to enter into relations with other judiciary bodies. This acquisition of a 'physical body' is therefore a process of complete and final embodiment of the Society on the Earth.

This is the reason Rudolf Steiner made every effort to secure such a judicial sheath for the Anthroposophical Society founded at the Christmas Conference.[163] For prior to the Christmas Conference, the Anthroposophical Society was merely 'an outer, exoteric, administrative location' for Anthroposophy (GA 260a), whereas subsequently it became a place where Anthroposophy was 'practised' (emphasis by Rudolf Steiner, GA 260a), even 'in all outward proceedings', (ibid.) meaning even including the administrative sphere, or in the words by Rudolf Steiner, where 'outward administration now has recourse to esotericism itself'. (ibid.)

It became archetypal for such anthroposophical working that Rudolf Steiner assumed chairmanship of the Society in person, and that implies even the responsibility for everything that took place in the administrative sphere of this society. It was a step that entailed a great 'risk' in regard to the further development of Anthroposophy on Earth. For henceforth its development (that originally followed purely spiritual laws) was inseparably tied up with 'outward guidance', the 'outward administration'. (ibid.) The result of this could have been that the spiritual powers that inspired Anthroposophy would not have accepted this step. The fact that this did not occur but that, following the Christmas Conference, the revelations by the entities linked with Michael became more and more abundant 'is', in Rudolf Steiner's words, 'an extraordinarily significant fact'. (ibid.) Thus this path of the Anthroposophical Society 'into matter' was from the beginning indicated through Rudolf Steiner and subsequently *sanctioned* by the spiritual world. It therefore belongs among the most important tasks of the Society, as well as of the Goetheanum as its earthly centre, to permeate the administrative realm with the new *spiritual impulse* which works within the Anthroposophical Movement since the Christmas Conference.

An initial step on this path was that Rudolf Steiner signed the twelve thousand membership cards in his own hand, something that took up many hours. He gave as the reason for this decision that he had the wish to lay eyes on the name of each member, even if only for a brief moment. Considered spiritually this can be understood as the desire of the initiate spiritually to bring to mind every person with whom, having assumed the chair of the Society, he linked up his own destiny.

Rudolf Steiner pointed this out particularly clearly the last time he spoke about the esoteric significance of the Christmas Conference to the members of the Society. In this lecture on 5 September 1924, he emphasized that in Anthroposophy 'the conscious force of conviction' must dwell 'that spirit is a concrete reality; that where (for outer human sense) matter exists, spirit not only penetrates and streams through this matter but ultimately all matter disappears for true human vision if it is capable of penetrating through things material to the spiritual'. (GA 260a) Then Rudolf Steiner spoke of the necessity to extend this fundamental 'view' to the Anthroposophical Society in the way it has developed through the Christmas Conference. For then 'the *spiritual archetype* of the Anthroposophical Movement (hovering) behind the Anthroposophical

Society' would be revealed to the members; an archetype 'that as a profound force of conviction must penetrate the heart of everyone who professes Anthroposophy. This must become reality in the activity and work of the Anthroposophical Society.' (ibid.)

Now the inner work on the Foundation Stone Meditation represents the path on which this 'spiritual archetype of the Anthroposophical Movement' can become reality in the Anthroposophical Society. This labour must attain such intensity in the souls of the members that they will furthermore be able to carry the Spirit-impulse even into the sphere of administrative activity within the Society (its 'physical body').

When Rudolf Steiner was striving to realize the judicial registration of the Anthroposophical Society, he hoped that the *Spirit Impulse* he had given at the Christmas Conference would prove to be strong enough to pervade all three spheres (institutions) and thus create a spiritual foundation for its 'uniform constitution'.

Rudolf Steiner expressed his intention very clearly to register the Society at the third extraordinary general meeting of the 'Goetheanum Association' on 29 June 1924: 'But then it will be necessary that out of *the whole spirit of the Anthroposophical Society*, the way it *now* exists [meaning following the Christmas Conference], this Anthroposophical Society functions as the actual association listed in the commercial register, meaning that it is that institution to the outside which has to represent everything here in Dornach.' (GA 260a) In this address, Rudolf Steiner likewise spoke of the necessity to bring about a so-called 'uniform constituting' in which the genuine 'Spirit of the Anthroposophical Society' (meaning of the Christmas Conference) should hold sway, a Spirit that is in a position to penetrate and unite all three institutions.

This is the *threefoldness striving towards unity* that Rudolf Steiner earlier pointed out during the cultic act of the Foundation Stone Laying, when he spoke of 'what can emerge out of the triune knowledge of man becoming harmonized into unity'. (GA 260, 25 December 1923)

School of Spiritual Science −

Anthroposophical Society and Foundation Stone −

Administration and Executive Council −

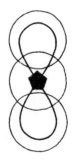

If we picture the 'uniform constituting' in the sense of a threefold organism that is permeated by the uniform spirit, the 'esoteric trend', and connect this organism to a higher unity,[164] we have the social structure that corresponds exactly to the four segments of the Foundation Stone Meditation.

★

The first segment of the meditation contains the main task of the third institution. This task consists in infusing the administrative sphere with spirit. For proceeding from the impulse of the Christmas Conference, the whole Anthroposophical Society must be filled by new living esotericism, even including its outer 'physical' sheath of the sphere of administration, including the Society's life of rights, and this within itself as well as in its relations to the outer world.

In the domain of rights, all members of the Anthroposophical Society who find themselves in a uniform area of rights (one beside the other) have the same rights. Yet the forming of this rights-sheath is not the goal in itself. On the contrary, it should help to attain those goals that emerge out of the *spiritual* life pervading and filling the Society in the sense of the words in the first part of the meditation concerning the limbs of the human being:

> Which bear thee through the world of Space
> Into the ocean-being of the Spirit.

Even as the limbs serve man in earthly life in the actualization of what he has recognized in the head and felt in the heart, so the rights activity as well as the administrative activity in the Society is only supposed to assume a subordinate character; one that serves its spiritual goals, hence in this way assuring more favourable conditions for its approach to the spiritual world or the 'ocean-being of the Spirit'. In this context the following words of the meditation,

> Thine own I
> Comes to being
> Within the I of God

can be taken as a reference to the original connection of spirit with matter, of the divine with the human element. This in turn signifies an indication that even in the domain of rights a connection is possible with the impulses coming directly out of the spiritual world in the way it comes to expression in the 'Statutes' of the Christmas Conference.

The consistent 'recollection' of the content of the 'Statutes', their spirit and wording, and as a result the activity of individual members and groups, is an obligation for each member of the Anthroposophical Society. The fulfilment of this task will lead to the attainment of the goal that Rudolf Steiner described in the following words:

> Then in the All-World-Being of Man
> Thou wilt truly *live*.

Here the expression, 'All-World-Being of Man' can be understood as a social-cosmic being; the social being on Earth and the cosmic one in the spiritual world.

In this sense, the 'Statutes' of the Anthroposophical Society are the spiritual-social instrument that enable the Anthroposophical Society to 'truly live' even in the domain of rights. Many anthroposophical authors have written about the relationship of the fourteen points of the 'Statutes' with the various spiritual-cosmic connections of the human being.[165]

Now, as to the permeation of the administrative sphere with spirit, the fount of the spiritual forces necessary for that can be found in the second macrocosmic segment of the first part of the meditation, where the Father-Spirit is mentioned who holds sway in the heights and begets life in depths of worlds. The Father-Spirit accomplishes this in order, through the mediation of the entities of the First Hierarchy, to imprint into the depths of worlds a replica of His Being, extending even all the way into matter:

> Let there ring out from the Heights
> What in the Depths is echoed.

More than once Rudolf Steiner pointed out that only the highest First Hierarchy can avail itself of the spiritual power to work in a transforming manner even into the foundations of the material world,[166] and this corresponds in the case of the Anthroposophical Society to its domain of rights and administration.

★

The second segment of the meditation is connected with the very life of the Anthroposophical Society, or in Rudolf Steiner's words, the 'Anthroposophical Society in the narrower sense'. For the latter, the words of the Christ, 'For where two or three are gathered in the name of my Being, there I myself am in the midst of them' (Mt. 18, 20 JM) must

become the most important social-formative force. In the meditation, the
words:

> For the Christ-Will in the encircling Round holds sway,
> In the Rhythms of Worlds, blessing the Soul

correspond to this fundamental social principle of every Christian community. Only when these lines of the meditation become reality in the
Anthroposophical Society will Rudolf Steiner's characterization of it
apply that was expressed in §1 of the 'Statutes': 'The Anthroposophical
Society is to be an association of people whose will it is to nurture the life
of the soul both in the individual and in human society, on the basis of a
true knowledge of the spiritual world.' (GA 260) For according to
Christian esotericism, such a 'nurturing of the life of the soul' consists in
making it possible for the 'Christ-Will', together with the human beings
belonging to Him, to work in the human community 'blessing souls'.

In order to attain this social ideal, it is necessary to pursue the direction
described in the microcosmic part of the second segment. This direction
begins with the consistent organizing of those measures in the Anthroposophical Society that are connected with the element of rhythm,
namely the weekly meeting in the branches, the celebration of the annual
festivals, and so on. For such *rhythmic* work can best promote the realization of §1 of the 'Statutes' ('to nurture the life of the soul').

In the meditation the following lines speak of this:

> Soul of Man!
> Thou livest in the beat of Heart and Lung
> Which leads thee through the rhythmic tides of Time
> Into the feeling of thine own Soul-being.

This 'feeling of one's own *soul* being' in regard to oneself as well as to
other human beings must be attained in the communal life of the
members of the Anthroposophical Society if this society is to realize its
social destiny.

Now the basis of such a nurturing of the rhythmic element in the
Anthroposophical Society comes about through the joint study of the
communications by spiritual science as represented in the books and
lectures by Rudolf Steiner. As the first level of modern initiation (see GA
13), such study signifies the start of actively practising 'spirit-pondering'.
But this stage of initiation can only be reached in the groups and branches
of the Anthroposophical Society if it becomes possible to overcome the

egoistic, subjective element in the souls of the participants, an element that is expressed above all in surging uncontrolled sympathies and antipathies. These emotions must be brought into full 'balance of the soul' during joint activity, even in the midst of the 'surging Deeds of the World's Becoming' which here can make their appearance as an unconscious expression of the communal karma.

Only in this way is it possible to reach the subsequent stage in the social life of the Anthroposophical Society that consists in 'uniting' one's 'own I' with the 'I of the World'. In this context these words can be understood as the process described by Rudolf Steiner as the Reverse Cultus. This process consists in a higher state of consciousness that awakens in man through 'the soul-spiritual of the other person'. (GA 257, 27 February 1923) Such an awakening in a higher sphere than the one in which ordinary day-consciousness exists results in an ascent into the angelic sphere during group work. Rudolf Steiner once described this process as follows: 'The Anthroposophical Society tries to lift human souls up into the supersensible world so that they might find themselves amongst the Angels.' (GA 257, 3 March 1923)

To thus 'sojourn amid Angels' is the first stage on the path to an actual union of our 'own I' with our 'higher I' that initially manifests from out of our surroundings through those who are karmically connected with us. This contact with the 'higher I'—the Angels are its representatives for human beings—turns into the first step for the union with the 'I of the World' which, as the Christ-'I', is moreover the new group-'I' of all humanity since the Mystery of Golgotha.

The path whose ultimate goal is the union with the 'World-I' thus leads to the actual soul-spiritual union of all Society-members who practise the Reverse Cultus,[167] something that at the same time promotes the actualization of §1 of the statutes of the Anthroposophical Society to a significant degree. The highest ideal of this paragraph speaks out of the words:

> Then 'mid the weaving of the Soul of Man
> Thou wilt truly *feel*.

Such an experience of one's own 'soul-working' in one's self as well as in others, through the mediation of 'truly feeling' a purified social insight (that has been transformed into a new organ), is the foundation of a human community that is capable of becoming the bearer of the impulse of the New Mysteries on Earth.

A further task of the Anthroposophical Society is indicated in the second segment of the Foundation Stone Meditation, this time in the macrocosmic part in the words:

> Let there be fired from the East
> What through the West is formed.

These two lines can be understood as a combination of total openness and true esotericism, the central task that Rudolf Steiner posed to the Anthroposophical Society at the Christmas Conference.[168] For according to occult comprehension 'East' signifies the spiritual or esoteric world, and 'West' the material or exoteric world perceived by the outer sense organs.

A profound connection of the main tasks of the Anthroposophical Society (the second segment of the 'uniform constitution') can in this way be recognized with the second segment of the Foundation Stone Meditation.

★

The third segment of the Foundation Stone Meditation is connected with the 'soul' of the Anthroposophical Society, the School of Spiritual Science, or the Michael-School on Earth.

Meditating the mantras of the First Class in the 'resting Head', a Michael-disciple can become acquainted with the experience of the 'Thoughts of Worlds' emerging out of the 'ground of the Eternal'. For the 'Thoughts of Worlds' which manifest to the Spirit-disciple of the Michael School truly come out of the 'ground of the Eternal'.

The following step consists in the transition from the meditative thought-imbued work with the mantras of the First Class to the '*Spirit vision*' of the spiritual reality standing behind them. This stage is reached when the flow of thoughts evoked through the meditation is brought to full rest and all soul capacities are concentrated on the force that produced this flow.

> Practise Spirit-vision
> In quietness of Thought.

This purely spiritual force is able to reveal to the human soul the true fount out of which the content of the First Class has emerged. The following lines of the meditation therefore accurately characterize what takes place spiritually in the Michael School when its participants receive its content into their souls:

Where the eternal aims of Gods
World–Being's Light
On thine own I
Bestow
For thy free Willing.

For the whole mantric contents of the First Class is nothing but the 'World-Being's Light' that shines in human souls and brings them recognition of the 'eternal aims of Gods' in the cosmos (the recognition of the divine-spiritual hierarchies). This enables the free human 'I' to participate in the realization of these aims, and that in turn means to achieve conscious co-operation and work with these hierarchies.

Thus the disciple of the New Mysteries can learn with the aid of his or her meditative activity

. . . truly [to] *think*
From the ground of the Spirit of Man.

Such 'true thinking' that advances even to grasping the very 'ground of the Spirit of Man', (meaning true thinking that leads to the point of grasping its own spiritual being) is the beginning of the 'redemption' process of the Cosmic Intelligence that had descended to Earth, and its being given back to Michael.

This process that forms the centre of the cosmic-telluric Michael Mysteries is mentioned in the second macrocosmic part of the third segment of the meditation. It begins with the reference to the present condition of the 'Spirit's Universal Thoughts', namely Michael's Cosmic Intelligence which, following the Mystery of Golgotha, came down to Earth and, starting with the eighth century, turned into the basis of man's individual intelligence. Since that time the cosmic thoughts, having become earthly, unceasingly beseech 'light' out of the depths of man's being in the hope of eventually being able, with man's help, to unite again with the kingdom of Michael from which they originally emerged.

When the spiritualization of earthly intelligence will have occurred and will have been carried by humans into the spiritual world, along with it they themselves will likewise have entered into that world. This will take place for the first time in all of mankind's history, in full consciousness. Then the words,

In the Spirit's Universal Thoughts, the Soul awakens

will have become reality in man's own inner experience. Then individual 'I'-consciousness awakens on yonder side of the Threshold and man can reach the goal to which the meditative path of the First Class leads. All this points to a profound inner affinity of the meditation's third segment with the contents and aims of the First Class of the School of Spiritual Science.

★

The same can moreover be said of the Rosicrucian words representing the centre of the three segments of the meditation, particularly in their translation into German through Rudolf Steiner. The concluding words of the third segment of the meditation,

> In the Spirit's Universal Thoughts, the Soul awakens

thus represent the goal of the School of Spiritual Science. The concluding words of the second segment,

> In Christ, Death becomes Life

should turn into the most significant inner impulse of the Anthroposophical Society which is destined to nurture 'the soul *life* . . . on the basis of a true knowledge of the spiritual world'. (GA 260) Now, the centre and goal of spiritual scientific knowledge is the Mystery of the living Christ in whom death becomes life. In Rudolf Steiner's words, 'the insight of the new initiation' has the 'Christ Mystery in its centre', (GA 13) and, as was shown in considering the second part of the meditation, in the Anthroposophical Society the Christ Impulse must penetrate even into its social life. For, 'in Anthroposophy, what matters are the *truths* that can become manifest through it in the Anthroposophical Society; what matters is the *life* that is cultivated in it'. (GA 260a, Third Letter to the Members; emphasis by Rudolf Steiner)

In this context it is striking how often Rudolf Steiner uses the word 'life' in the first three paragraphs of the 'Statutes' of the Anthroposophical Society (altogether seven times). Particularly two formulations are primarily significant here for its social life. They are words concerning the importance of what is cultivated in Anthroposophy that leads to '*brotherhood* in human relationships', (§2) and the words that these results can bring about 'a social *life* genuinely built on brotherly love'. (§3) In both instances, 'life' is linked with the principle of 'brotherhood' as the basis of a true human community.

Finally, the concluding statement of the first segment,

From God, Mankind has Being

speaks of the fact that all things visible have emerged out of the divine
protection of the Father-God as the foundation for the development of
humanity on Earth. And continuous 'recollection' of this fact can help
members of the Anthroposophical Society not to lose themselves in the
administrative activity necessary for their individual existence, but to keep
in mind that it too proceeds originally out of a divine source as does all
that is material in this world. This in turn signifies that such administrative
activity can at any moment be pervaded with the Spirit Impulse.

★

A further aspect linking the Foundation Stone Meditation with the
threefold constitution of the Anthroposophical Society is the trend of
activities on the part of the hierarchical forces in the meditation's three
segments. Thus in the first segment the macrocosmic activity of the
highest First Hierarchy is described as follows:

> Let there ring out from the Heights
> What in the Depths is echoed.

As we have seen, these lines correspond to what must steadfastly take
place in the administrative domain of a society such as the Anthroposophical Society. Particularly in this exoteric realm the spiritual principle must consciously be borne through the people active in it in the
direction from above to below, meaning out of the spiritual realm. And as
was considered above, the lines,

> Let there be fired from the East
> What through the West is formed,

are linked together with the work of the Anthroposophical Society itself,
not as a legal body but as a purely human community. The basis of the
latter are, however, not the 'equal rights' of the members but the inter-
human communication and freedom of spiritual initiatives rooted in the
soul life, thanks to which new spiritual impulses ('East') can again and
again assume concrete form for their appearance ('West').

Finally, the words in the second part of the third segment,

> Let there be prayed in the Depths
> What from the Heights is answered,

speak of the spiritual path that is open today to every spiritually striving human being in the New Mysteries and their centre, the First Class of the Michael School.

As a whole, this threefold constitution of the Anthroposophical Society as viewed in the light of the first three segments of the Foundation Stone Meditation is an earthly replica of the Cosmic Cross that is formed in the spiritual world by the totality of all (nine) hierarchies.

★

Even its Imaginative aspect can be added to this dynamic aspect of the Anthroposophical Society's constitution. If people enter the realm of esotericism, they always face the danger of changing esotericism into sectarian doings that only satisfy a person's own egoistic needs and an unconscious striving for escapism. To counteract this luciferic tendency, Rudolf Steiner placed the School of Spiritual Science with its various sections into the very midst of present-day life, a school comparable to an innovative modern university. This is why, early on in the 'Statutes' of the Anthroposophical Society, this esoteric school was mentioned, so that its existence, structure, and aims would be familiar to all people. (See paragraphs 5, 7, 8, and 9 of the Statutes)

The administrative sphere on the other hand, is always threatened by the danger of losing the connection to the actual human element and in this way to succumb to the ahrimanic influence, for it is a particularly difficult task to bring a spiritual impulse into this sphere. This is why Rudolf Steiner spoke of the risk he took when he decided to assume the presidency of the Anthroposophical Society, meaning, as a spirit-teacher to unite with it including even its administrative domain.

Finally, in the realm of the Anthroposophical Society that concerns the middle or heart sphere of its constitutional structure, where, according to §1 of the 'Statutes', the task is above all to nurture the 'soul life' in the individual human being as well as in human society, the connection with the Christ must be brought about on the social level. This is why the name of the Christ is mentioned only in the second of the first three segments of the meditation. For the Christ as 'Representative of Humanity' is not merely linked with the individual human being but moreover with the human community.

The threefold constitutional structure of the Anthroposophical Society can thus find its Imaginative archetype in Rudolf Steiner's 'Sculptural Group' that depicts Lucifer's banishment through the Christ out of the spiritual realm where He works in the social middle realm, and Ahriman's banishment who is active in the administrative realm.

Such an understanding of the constitutional structure of the Anthro-posophical Society allows us to recognize its task as the connecting link between heaven and earth, and in the constitutional regard between the modern esoteric school, as a purely spiritual institution that was inaugurated out of the spiritual world, and its exoteric leadership and administration.

★

The fourth segment of the Foundation Stone Meditation represents the key to the three preceding ones. Its centre, the 'Christ-Sun', fills the whole meditation with its substance. Its first three lines bear witness to this:

> At the Turning-point of Time
> The Spirit-Light of the World
> Entered the stream of Earthly Being.

This effect of the 'Spirit-Light of the World' in Earth existence, which began at the Turning-point of Time, lasts even to the present time and encompasses the whole future Earth evolution. In this sense there exists a connection of the words 'stream of Earthly Being' with the microcosmic parts of the first three segments of the meditation; the words 'Spirit-Light of the World', on the other hand, with the macrocosmic parts. Con-versely, thanks to the fourth segment—in the way it took place in the Mystery act of the Foundation Stone Laying on 25 December 1923[169]— the connection of the microcosmic and macrocosmic parts within the three segments characterizes the process of how the 'Spirit-Light of the World' entered the 'stream of Earthly Being'. Henceforth, this light can turn into the spiritual inspirer and fount of spiritualization for all three institutions that form the constitutional structure of the General Anthroposophical Society and—viewed as a whole—represent the body, soul, and spirit of its threefold organism:

– Administration of the Anthroposophical Society and the 'Goethe-anum';
– Anthroposophical Society in the narrower sense;
– School of Spiritual Science.

★

We shall now look more closely at the working of this 'Spirit-Light of the World' in the three institutions of the Society. When it enters into the domain of the administrative activity of the Society and there connects the microcosmic part with the macrocosmic one of the first segment of the meditation, then the possibility opens up to bestow the 'esoteric trend' on this physical realm of the Anthroposophical Society, a trend that since the Christmas Conference was supposed to be present in all the domains of work within the Society even including the administrative activity.

In a certain sense, the 'Spirit-Light of the World' is in itself the 'esoteric trend', for through it enter the forces of the 'Christ-Sun' into Earth existence. So we can say: In the first part of the meditation (when we consider it in its inner relationship with the fourth) we have the activity of the Christ Impulse (the 'Christ-Sun') through the sphere of the Father whence Earth existence originates. Out of this Father sphere the Christ manifests following the Mystery of Golgotha as the new Spirit of the Earth and Lord of the 'Divine Forces' on Earth.

As a result of the Christ's union with Earth evolution extending even into matter, the spiritualization of the administrative domain of the Society can occur based on the forces of part I of the meditation. For the Father forces, renewed as they are out of the fount of the Mystery of Golgotha, can take hold of matter (penetrate it with spirit) which in turn does include even the administrative activity of the Society. The very fact that at the Christmas Conference the Anthroposophical Society was united with the Anthroposophical Movement affirms that the Spirit Impulse can now be present in *all areas* of the Society's life, even including physical (material) aspects.

The next lines of part IV:

> Darkness of Night
> Had held its sway,
> Day-radiant Light
> Poured into the souls of men

point to the possibility of awakening individual 'I'-consciousness in this darkest (material) realm, whereby the spiritualization of the constitutional organism of the Society occurs in the first place.

Considered in its relation to part IV, part II of the meditation speaks of the Christ's activity out of the sphere of the Son, meaning out of His very own realm. And thus the name of the Christ is mentioned only twice in the Foundation Stone Meditation, in parts II and IV.

Working out of His own sphere, the Christ manifests to humanity as its new Group-'I', concerning which Rudolf Steiner once stated: 'Even as in each single human being the higher "I" is born, so, in Palestine, the higher "I" of all mankind, the Divine "I", is born.' (GA 112, 27 June 1909) Beginning with the twentieth century however, a new Christ revelation is taking place: The Christ becomes Lord of Karma and guides the process so that human beings can balance their individual karma in accordance with the spiritual goals of evolution of all humanity. Here the spiritual-social working of the Christ is unveiled to us. It is this to which the Imagination of the 'Christ-Sun' points; an imagination that forms the central point of the circle of the twelve constellations in the second part of the fourth segment. At the Turning-point of Time, an earthly replica of this cosmic primal archetype is the circle of the twelve Apostles around the Christ who perceive His social working and later on spread the 'glad tidings' (of the Resurrection) out of this fount.[170]

The lines directly after the reference to the 'Christ-Sun',

> Warm Thou
> Our Hearts,
> Enlighten Thou
> Our Heads,

likewise speak of the social aspect of the Christ activity. The field for its actualization today is supposed to be the Anthroposophical Society that received the knowledge of its common Michaelic karma from Rudolf Steiner[171] so as to form a new *karma community* on this basis for the first time in Earth evolution.

Within such a community, people must learn to work consciously on their karma and to develop the future of mankind in accordance with the Christ as Lord of Karma.[172] This is a further aspect of Christ's activity out of His own sphere (the sphere of the Son) that the words in the second segment of the meditation ('For the Christ-Will in the encircling Round holds sway') refer to; meaning, to His activity in the sphere of karma as well, a sphere that manifests above all to the human being out of his social environment.

Finally, the inner connection between part IV of the meditation with part III points to the working of the Christ out of the sphere of the Holy Spirit. Here the Christ Impulse enters directly into man's individual 'I' in the sense of Paul's words, 'Not I but the Christ in me'. (Gal. 2, 20) Rudolf Steiner, however, made it clear that the Christ can only enter into the human 'I' without extinguishing it with His power (the 'free willing' referred to in the third segment) when it occurs through the mediation of the Holy Spirit (see GA 214, 30 July 1922), for the Spirit always works in man individually. This is what is spoken of in the Whitsun Imagination where the fiery tongues are mentioned that descended *individually* on the head of each Apostle. (see Acts, 2,3)

The inner affinity between part III of the meditation, which is the spiritual fount of the School of Spiritual Science, and part IV is affirmed by the mention of the word 'aim' in both parts. In part III it is the 'World-Being's Light' proceeding from the 'eternal *aims* of Gods' with which a human being is entrusted through Michael in his esoteric school. And in part IV it is the striving to follow these aims independently proceeding from insight into them

> From our Heads direct with single purpose.
> (Also translated as: From our heads guide in true-*aimed* willing.)[Tr.2]

(In this case, the head represents the centre of the whole of the human activity of insight [Ger.: Erkenntnistätigkeit].) It is a matter of our conscious co-operation in the actualization of the eternal aims in Earth evolution, and that means above all participation in the present-day activity of Michael as Time Spirit.

In the entirety of the meditation's third and fourth parts, we thus have an expression of the present activity by the Christ through Michael, the Spirit of our age. This moreover allows a better understanding of Michael's role, who as the cosmic countenance of the Christ brings to mankind in our time the light of his spiritual scientific knowledge through general Anthroposophy as well as through the content of the First Class in particular. For in his first epoch of rule *after* the Mystery of Golgotha, Michael's task is chiefly to bring humanity the light of his knowledge in *renewed* form. 'Michael can give us new spiritual light that we can consider as a transformation of that light which was given through him at the time of the Mystery of Golgotha, and in our time human beings may place themselves into this light.' (GA 152, 2 May 1913)

At the Turning-point of Time, Michael's light inspired the Evangelist John to write the prologue to his gospel. In the twentieth century, his light inspired Rudolf Steiner in metamorphosed form to create the Foundation Stone Meditation.[173] But if the prologue of the Gospel of John describes the descent of the Logos to Earth, meaning the condition *prior* to the Mystery of Golgotha, the Foundation Stone Meditation characterizes the condition *following* it. This is why this 'metamorphosed light' of Michael now likewise contains the 'eternal aims of Gods', because for the gods the Mystery of Golgotha represents the highest fulfilment of their celestial religion.[174]

For this reason, of the *three* references to the macrocosmic principle of *Light* in the Foundation Stone Meditation, we find two in the fourth part and one in the third. This in turn signifies that in the first-mentioned two instances we have a movement out of the fourth part, one to the first and the other to the second; in the third case an opposite movement out of the third part to the fourth:

'The Spirit-Light of the World'— as Light of the Son
　　　　　　　　　　　　　　　with participation of the Father　(IV → I);
'Light Divine'　　　　　　　— as Light of the Son　　　　　　(IV → II);
'World-Being's Light'　　　　— as Light of the Holy Spirit　　　(IV ← III).

The fundamental difference between the first two kinds of Light is that they are connected with the sphere of the Father and that of the Son respectively, and they are effective in a manner independent of man. For the Coming-to-Earth of the Christ (the Baptism in the Jordan), in which the forces of the Divine Father still participated,[175] and the Mystery of Golgotha, are the results of a celestial decision by Christ Himself who was not dependent on anything but His own free will. ('But it was for this purpose that I came at this hour.' Jn. 12, 27) Conversely, beginning at the Whitsun event[176] or from the instant when the Holy Spirit descended upon the Apostles, there opened up the possibility for the human being consciously to co-operate on the divine plan of the Christ, the hierarchies serving Him, and essentially His sun–countenance, Michael.

This is why, in the last segment of part IV that begins with the words 'That good may become', the 'Light' is no longer mentioned. For it must be brought out of part III (where man's 'free willing' is mentioned) into the fourth one; the free willing that receives the 'World-Being's Light' from the 'eternal aims of Gods'. This connection with the 'aims of Gods' is necessary in order to carry the deeds of human beings into the world of True Goodness.

★

Viewed in this way, the Founding of the New Mysteries at the Christmas Conference with their spiritual centre, the School of Spiritual Science, can be considered as the beginning of the actualization of the 'reverse Whitsun' on Earth,[177] something that is connected with the Christ's activity through the Time Spirit Michael in the way it comes to expression in part III of the meditation. Here, the 'free willing' that in the New Mysteries is bestowed by the 'World–Being's Light' is addressed directly—the Light proceeding from the 'eternal aims of Gods'.

Thus in the New Mysteries, for the first time in Earth evolution the ground is prepared for the joint work of human beings with the gods. For beginning now '. . . human beings have to work together with the gods, with Michael himself'. (GA 240, 19 July 1924) It will become possible for this to happen when the individual consciousness of human beings begins to awaken beyond the threshold in the way this occurs in the teachings of the First Class; when the human 'I' becomes increasingly aware of its link with the Logos, the Logos that became 'flesh' at the Turning-point of Time, in Jesus of Nazareth who then passed through death and resurrection in the Mystery of Golgotha as referred to in the fourth part of the meditation. We can sum all this up as follows:

—Part I of the meditation depicts the Christ's working out of the forces of the Father. Here the Christ is experienced as the new Spirit of the Earth who works in a transforming manner even into the material sphere.
—Part II of the meditation refers to the working of the Christ out of the forces of the Son as the Lord of karma who forms the new karma among human beings.[178]
—Part III of the meditation describes the working of the Christ out of the forces of the Holy Spirit as the primal image of man's 'I' (the divine 'I Am') and the highest ideal of modern initiation.
—These three aspects are linked by part IV of the meditation into a unity. Here, the Christ-Sun is spoken of who encompasses all.

In the Foundation Stone Meditation lies the main fountainhead of the threefold constitution of the Anthroposophical Society. This is the reason why, through inner work with this meditation as the spiritual basis of the Anthroposophical Society, we can moreover permeate the Society's *whole* organism, including even the administrative domain, with the earlier-mentioned 'esoteric trend'.

In this way the ideal of the constitutional structure of the Anthroposophical Society can gradually be realized; a structure of which Rudolf Steiner said: 'The *whole* institution of the Society must bear an esoteric character. With that the Society will be able to receive the spiritual *life* that it needs.' (GA 260a)

11. The Preparation of Spiritual Communion in the Rosicrucian Stream and in the Grail Stream

In the last chapter of the book, *May Human Beings Hear It! The Mystery of the Christmas Conference*, the nature of spiritual communion which, like sacramental communion, consists of two elements, was described in detail. But what takes place in sacramental communion by means of earthly substances is attained in spiritual communion *directly* in a purely inner meditative way. In both instances, however, it is a matter of bringing about the spiritual connection to what Rudolf Steiner termed the Resurrection body or Phantom, and condensed etheric body of the Resurrected Christ.[179]

We can therefore say: the inner connection with the *flesh* of the Resurrected Christ takes place in spiritual communion due to receiving the forces of the Phantom, and the connection with the *blood* through receiving the forces of His condensed etheric body. The connection, however, between the etheric body of the Christ and His blood is based on the fact that the forces of the ether body are effective in all fluids of the human organism, and especially in the blood as the most important fluid.

Corresponding to these two elements of all true communion, Rudolf Steiner gave *two* basic meditative exercises in the New Mysteries established at the Christmas Conference, exercises that lead to spiritual communion. Thus, through the spiritual work with the Foundation Stone Meditation as described in detail in the above-mentioned book, a conscious connection can be attained with the Phantom of the Resurrected One; and through the inner work with the meditation's seven rhythms, a connection with His condensed ether body.

The sevenfold rhythm is at the basis of all etheric processes in the universe and the human etheric body. In the latter it is a result of the spiritual influences of the seven most significant planets of our solar system. Their forces were likewise effective in the inner configuration of the seven days during which the rhythms of the meditation were given for the first time at the Christmas Conference.[180]

As far as the Foundation Stone Meditation is concerned, it can be experienced as a mantric revelation of the temple of the physical body and its relationship with the whole macrocosm as described in the fifth chapter of this work. This relationship can be deepened even more if one notes that the cosmic communion is the content of the final lecture Rudolf

Steiner gave in the First Goetheanum. A few hours after this lecture the building along with the words about cosmic communion (words that had been inscribed into its aura) went up in the sea of flames to the widths of the ether-world. Out of that world they were later received in completely transformed shape by Rudolf Steiner as the words of the Foundation Stone. Put differently, the mantric words of the *cosmic communion* return in the form of mantric words of *spiritual communion* out of the cosmic widths. Thus the modern path to spiritual communion originated out of the tragic end of the First Goetheanum that is connected with the Mystery of the baptism with 'spirit and fire'.[181]

★

From all this it follows that for the first time in the history of Christianity the two elements of spiritual communion *were connected* on the esoteric level in the New Mysteries. We can grasp the significance of this deed by Rudolf Steiner when we note that the spiritual communion with the flesh of the Resurrected One, and with His etherized blood, only took place until then *separately* in the two forms of Mysteries. In a spiritual-historical sense, their guardians were on one side the Rosicrucians and on the other the knights of the Grail. We shall therefore consider these two esoteric streams more closely.

If we turn first to the Rosicrucian stream, we find in the centre of its Mysteries the efforts to create the so-called 'Philosopher's Stone'. 'This is what one calls the transformation of human substance into that substance the basis of which is actual carbon. It is the form of alchemy that leads the initiate to the point of building up his body in a way similar to how the plant does this today. One calls this the preparing of the 'Philosopher's Stone, and coal is the external symbol for it'. (GA 99, 6 June 1907) This is how Rudolf Steiner once described it.

These words point out that the transformation of man's earthly body is the aim of the work on the 'Philosopher's Stone'. This in turn is only possible based on the forces of the Resurrected One's Phantom. Concerning the Philosopher's Stone, Rudolf Steiner said: 'The term "Philosopher's Stone" refers to the body that is *transparent*, the one into which the other [new] organs are incorporated.' (GA 97, 30 November 1906) In another lecture he described the peculiar feature of the physical body that is transformed into the Philosopher's Stone: 'It will not be black coal but *transparent* carbon bright as water, when man's body will have become *star-like*.' (GA 97, 16 February 1907) Another lecture states: 'These are merely indications, but you will understand that behind the quest for the Philosopher's Stone something profound is concealed, something that relates to the transformation of all mankind. Man will become different from the way he is today—*he and the whole Earth*. So great and firm, morally great must the forces of the soul become that man even draws the flesh into the process of redemption.' (GA 97, 22 February 1907)

From the descriptions mentioned above, we can now gather the following basic characteristics of the 'Philosopher's Stone'.

This stone:

— corresponds to the transformed, spiritualized physical body that has integrated the new organs.

The work of the 'Philosopher's Stone':

— makes the physical body transparent,
— and star-like at the end of the process,
— something that brings about the transformation of the whole Earth.

These unusual characteristics of the physical body (that have been transformed into the Philosopher's Stone) correspond exactly to the way the forces of the resurrected Christ's Phantom work in the human being. For only this can transform a man's earthly body into a 'star-like' body and thus form a foundation for the gradual spiritualization of the Earth.

Along with that, the attainment of the Philosopher's Stone through spiritual-alchemistic work—in which the outer experiments are merely symbols—signifies gradually to permeate the earthly body with the forces of the Phantom of the Christ that has risen out of the tomb on Golgotha and is capable of working in transforming ways that even extend to the physical substances.

This transformation-process of human nature is depicted in detail in the book *The Chymical Wedding of Christian Rosenkreutz*. In it, the initiation that Christian Rosenkreutz went through in the year 1459 is presented in symbolic pictures. Rudolf Steiner described the spiritual stage of development that Christian Rosenkreutz reached in a lecture on 22 May 1907. 'In 1459 Christian Rosenkreutz was promoted within a strictly secluded spiritual brotherhood, the Fraternitas Rosaecrucis, to the rank of Eques Lapidis Aurei, Knight of the Golden Stone.' (GA 99)

Here a 'golden stone' is mentioned, meaning a stone that contains *sun-wisdom*, a wisdom capable of working even into earthly matter itself. As a result of this, such an initiate attains to what, in Christian occultism, is called 'life in one and the same body'. About this high stage of development that Christian Rosenkreutz attained in 1459 through his initiation, Rudolf Steiner related: 'What we undergo between birth and death is undergone by the initiate in such a way that when he dies he is soon born again as a child in a new body; but he experiences this path fully consciously. Consciousness remains present from one incarnation to the next. Even physical likeness remains in the initiate [who has reached this level] because the soul consciously builds up the new body based on the experiences of the previous incarnation. The highest leader of the Rosicrucian schooling [Christian Rosenkreutz] lives in this manner throughout centuries ... Since that time [following his initiation in the year 1459] this individuality of Christian Rosenkreutz has been present again and again as leader of the movement [of Rosicrucianism]. Throughout centuries he led a life "in the same body".' (GA 98, 15 December 1907)

The groundwork for being able to reach this high stage of initiation in the fifteenth century was Christian Rosenkreutz's initiation in the middle of the thirteenth century. This in turn was connected with his having taken the forces of the Phantom of the Christ into himself. (see Chap. 6) That came to expression in the fact that the physical body of Christian Rosenkreutz became 'quite transparent' meaning, to a large degree, that it became similar to the Philosopher's Stone. But at that time this took place outside his earthly 'I' consciousness, for he 'lay' there at that moment 'as if dead'. (GA 130, 27 September 1911) Having returned to his completely changed physical body, he did, however, receive the power in his next incarnation to establish the Rosicrucian stream on earth where, as far as its esoteric practice was concerned, work on the Philosopher's Stone was central. Christian Rosenkreutz continued to follow this esoteric path. In the thirteenth century the initiation process was conducted on him during his youth and he died shortly afterwards. But what had been attained by him at that time as a result of the event, which according to Rudolf Steiner 'could occur in history only once', (ibid.) he now had to undergo in full consciousness. This is what happened in the fifteenth century, during his initiation in 1459. This time the initiation did not take place at the beginning but the end of his life, when he was 81 years old.

Even though Christian Rosenkreutz experienced the conscious connection with the forces of the Phantom (the main fruit of the initiation in the thirteenth century), early on at the beginning of the next incarnation he completed the transformation of his physical body into the Philosopher's Stone through these forces only as a result of his initiation in the year 1459.

What Christian Rosenkreutz had attained in highest *archetypal* form, was realized in the ensuing period by many of his students, even though on a lower level. The path on which they strove to reach this goal was described by Rudolf Steiner in a lecture on 29 September 1911. (GA130) In the esoteric schools inaugurated by Christian Rosenkreutz and isolated from the outer world, many generations of Rosicrucians (through the experience of the three alchemistic processes of salinification, dissolution, and combustion) imbued the three systems of their physical body with the forces of the Christ's Phantom in this way:

through salinification (salt)	— system of the head and nerves,
through dissolution or etherization (mercury)	— system of heart and lungs,
through combustion (sulphur)	— the metabolic and limb system.

Here, through repeated experiences of these alchemistic processes, the connection with the Christ's Phantom was primarily brought about inasmuch as three soul qualities were attained that ultimately grew into great strength in the soul of a Rosicrucian. For as was said above, 'great and strong and solid, morally great must be the forces of the soul so that man can draw even the flesh into the process of redemption'. (GA 97, 22 February 1907)

These three soul faculties were: Out of experiencing the process of salinification, purity of thinking or selflessness of insight was to emanate from the soul of a Rosicrucian; through the process of dissolution, purity of feeling or the faculty of infinite compassion; and through the process of combustion, the purity of will or highest spirit of sacrifice.

In metamorphosed form, these three stages can furthermore be found in the Foundation Stone Meditation. In following the process of salinification, all expressions of egoism and lower passions were overcome by the Rosicrucians filling their thinking not with human thoughts but with thoughts of the gods. They experienced this purity and complete selflessness of thinking as the forming of spiritual or subjective copper. The nature of this process can also be expressed in the words:

> For the Spirit's Universal Thoughts hold sway
> In the Being of all Worlds, beseeching Light.

The medieval Rosicrucian alchemist furthermore reached perception of the gods' cosmic thoughts:

> In the Spirit's Universal Thoughts, the soul awakens.

This awakening of the soul in the sphere of the 'Spirit's universal thoughts' was a sign for the fact that the soul had become purified to a sufficient degree for receiving the forces of the Christ's Phantom. This is why one can call this first stage the *preparation*.

In contemplating the mercurial process of dissolution, human love and compassion are filled with the eternal creative love of the gods. Attainable in this manner, this 'higher love' was experienced by the Rosicrucians as the forming of spiritual or subjective silver. The nature of this second process can be put in the words:

> For the Christ-Will in the encircling Round holds sway
> In the Rhythms of Worlds, blessing the soul.

If only a spark of this 'higher love' is present—only once in the Mystery of Golgotha it shone forth on Earth in full measure—the physical body of a human being can be *penetrated* by the resurrected Christ's Phantom that is capable of overcoming the forces of death, even extending into earthly matter:

> In Christ, Death becomes Life.

The weaving of the new life forces awakened through divine love, where earlier merely death forces (of carbon dioxide that destroys all life) held sway in the human organism, proved to be the beginning of the transformation of the physical body out of the dead mineral into plant-like life forces. Rudolf Steiner described this in the following words: 'It [the alchemistic process leading to the development of the Philosopher's Stone] brings about the transformation of man into the bearer of a pure immaculate incarnation comparable to a plant.' (GA 97, 22 February 1907) As a result the physical body was felt by the Rosicrucians to be like a calyx that receives the effect of the impregnating forces of the Christ's Phantom in the form of a divine love-lance. (See GA 97, 16 February 1907) This second stage can therefore likewise be called the *union* with the Phantom of the Christ.

Finally, in considering the process of combustion, the soul of the Rosicrucian is filled with the will for 'sacrificial service', of being prepared to 'sacrifice oneself on the altar of the world'. (GA 130, 28 September 1911)

This highest stage of inner development is described at the conclusion of the book, *Knowledge of the Higher Worlds and Its Attainment*, where it says concerning the student of the spirit who consciously experiences the encounter with the Greater Guardian of the Threshold that henceforth 'he offers up . . . his gifts at the sacrificial altar of humanity'. (GA 10) The medieval Rosicrucian experienced this process as the forming of spiritual or subjective gold in his soul out of which the so-called 'golden stone' could then be shaped.

If therefore the Rosicrucian has received the forces of the Christ's Phantom into himself and, as a result of the transformation of his inner being, has begun in a new way to serve the Christ, he has attained the level of the 'Knight of the Golden Stone'. That can be coined in the words:

> For the Father-Spirit of the Heights hold sway,
> In Depths of Worlds, begetting Life.

On this level a Rosicrucian turns into a co-worker in the creation of a new cosmos ('of a new heaven and a new earth' Rev. 21, 1) in the 'Depths of Worlds', which is what our Earth represents from the standpoint of the macrocosm. For the transformation of the physical body, through the forces of the Phantom of the Christ, gradually leads to the spiritualization of the Earth, since all the kingdoms of nature are contained in it [the Phantom]. The highest level of spiritualization is thus connected with the revelation of the future Mysteries of the Father:[182]

> From God, Mankind has Being.

Such a conscious connection with the Divine Ground of the World affirms that a human being who has reached this stage of initiation can allow the forces of the Christ's Phantom he has taken into himself to stream outward into the whole of nature around him, and that is the beginning of earth's spiritualization. Such spiritualization, however, has become possible only through the mighty macrocosmic communion when on Good Friday the body of Jesus was taken down from the cross and laid into the tomb of the earth.[183]

This demonstrates that, due to the special nature of their initiation, Rosicrucians were fully aware of the occult fact that following the Mystery of Golgotha the Christ became the new Spirit of the Earth and highest guide of their further development. (See GA 103, 30 May 1908— II) This is why the connection with the forces of the Resurrection body was for them not merely the source of their own initiation, but likewise for the future of the Earth.

The three stages of the Rosicrucian-alchemistic initiation, that leads to the forming of the Philosophers' Stone in man, can be summed up as follows:

Salinification	— Purity	— *Preparation* for receiving the Phantom
Dissolution	— Love	— *Receiving* the Phantom
Combustion	— Willingness to sacrifice (Sacrificial service)	— *Issuing forth* of forces of the Phantom to *outside*

From the standpoint of ego development as depicted in the Foundation Stone Meditation, these three stages can also be characterized as follows:

Strengthening of 'I'-consciousness	— 'On thine own I Bestow For thy free Willing'	— Purification of physical body	— Preparation for receiving the Phantom
Awakening of forces of higher 'I'	— 'Do thine own I Unite Unto the I of the World'	— Spiritualization of physical body (Preparation of Philosopher's Stone)	— Receiving forces of the Phantom
Awakening of forces of true 'I'	— 'Thine own I Comes to Being Within the I of God'	— Magical (spiritualizing) effect on outer world	— Issuing forth of forces of the Phantom to outside

Just as the first three segments of the Foundation Stone Meditation consist in each case of two parts, a microcosmic and a macrocosmic one, the initiation-experiences of a medieval Rosicrucian likewise had a dual character. On the one hand he inwardly experienced the awakening of the higher faculties of purity, love, and willingness for sacrifice during the alchemistic experiments. Stating this in alchemistic terminology, he formed in his soul subjective copper, silver, and gold. At the same time, by observing the alchemistic processes that objectively ran their course on his laboratory counter, he learned clairvoyantly to behold in them the macrocosmic forces of the gods at work in nature surrounding him. He understood that in their forces the macrocosmic archetype was repre-sented in what he himself sought to develop microcosmically in his soul. The medieval Rosicrucian 'felt the connection with all the forces in the macrocosm' during these experiments. First of all, he experienced 'thoughts of the gods, secondly love by the gods, and thirdly sacrificial service by the gods.' (GA 130, 28 September 1911)

During his alchemistic experiments the medieval Rosicrucian did not merely try to experience the physical processes as actual symbols that reveal the nature of the alternate effects of the soul forces of man and the gods of the cosmos. In like manner he endeavoured to behold the most important objective of his initiation aside from the Philosophers' Stone. This was the so-called 'quintessence' or invisible 'fifth' substance forming the transition from sensible to supersensible (etheric) nature that is at the basis of the former.[184] In the European Mysteries, insight into this substance goes back to Aristotle's teaching concerning the 'first matter'. 'Here we have something'—as Rudolf Steiner put it—'that would not be comparable to any other physical substance, rather it is the essence of them all.' (GA 130, 27 September 1911)

Through strengthening the development of their moral soul forces, Rosicrucians prepared themselves to cognize this substance clairvoyantly, not only in the human being but in the world surrounding them (in the microcosm and macrocosm). But they attained this vision itself only after a long period of preparation due to their soul being overshadowed by the forces of Christian Rosenkreutz's etheric body that had originated as a result of his initiation in the thirteenth century.

In the Foundation Stone Meditation, this substance found between the physical and spiritual world corresponds to part IV. As to its content and nature, this part is as different from the first three as the metals copper, silver, and gold (the gods' thoughts, their love, and their sacrificial service) differ from the 'quintessence', a substance 'that is neither gold, nor silver ... nor copper', concerning which one can only say that 'nothing else in the world resembles it'. (GA 130, 27 September 1911)

When the inner work with the first three parts of the meditation therefore leads to the experience of the microcosmic and macrocosmic aspects of the forces that stand behind the alchemistic conceptions of copper, silver, and gold (the three kings of the 'Fairy Tale' by Goethe as symbols of power, beauty, and wisdom), then meditating on its fourth segment leads to a contemporary experience of the invisible substance or 'quintessence' permeating all earthly existence of the microcosm as well as the macrocosm. This substance, mentioned early on already by Aristotle based on Mystery tradition, then underwent a fundamental change through the Mystery of Golgotha. Following the Christ's union with the Earth sphere, it was permeated by His spiritual forces and thereby turned from a natural into a *moral substance* that is directly linked with the transformation process of Earth into a new

Spirit-Sun, something referred to in the fourth segment of the meditation.

Meditative work with the fourth segment as such can, however, only prepare a person to receive this new moral substance. Even in our time, beholding it directly requires the overshadowing by the etheric body of Christian Rosenkreutz. The link of this ether body with part IV of the meditation has been considered earlier in another work.[185]

When we note that the process of being overshadowed by Christian Rosenkreutz's etheric body likewise leads, beginning in the twentieth century, to the experience of the Etheric Christ as the spiritual Cosmic Sun, we discover in part IV of the meditation, which is linked with the Spiritual Cosmic Sun, the moral beholding of the 'quintessence' as well as the meditative path for experiencing the Etheric Christ. We discover the first in the reference to the active creation of the *Good,* 'that good may become...', and the second in the reference to the 'Christ-Sun'.[186]

We can thus interpret the general composition of the Foundation Stone Meditation in connection with the alchemistic activity of the Rosicrucians as follows:

Foundation Stone Meditation	Microcosmic Parts	Macrocosmic Parts	Mediator
Part I	— Sacrificial Service by Humans	Sacrificial Service by Gods	— Copper
Part II	— Love by Humans	Love by Gods	— Silver
Part III	— Thoughts by Humans	Thoughts by Gods	— Gold
Part IV	— the Good (Creative Deeds of the Good)	the Etheric 'Christ-Sun' as Source of the Divine Good	— 'The Essence of it all'

Now, what medieval Rosicrucians accomplished by still relying on external alchemistic experiments can be accomplished in the New Mysteries, whose nature comes to expression in most concentrated form in the Foundation Stone Meditation, by purely inward meditative means without having recourse to physical substances.

★

Turning once more to Christian Rosenkreutz's spiritual path we can say that during his spiritual development he underwent three initiations in two succeeding incarnations. During his initiation in the thirteenth century, finding himself *outside* his physical body, he lived through the encounter with the Christ and the imprinting of the forces of the Resurrected One's Phantom into his physical body.[186a] Yet the consequences of this first initiation emerged in full measure only in his next incarnation when, fully conscious, meaning now in his physical body, he repeated both fundamental experiences of the thirteenth century in the two subsequent initiations. The above-said was possible because in his next incarnation Christian Rosenkreutz was permeated by the forces of his etheric body that had been preserved in the higher worlds, the etheric body that in the previous century had originated as the 'fruit of the initiation of the Thirteenth One': 'In turn, this rare spiritual ether body illuminated and irradiated the new embodiment, the individuality out of the spiritual world in the fourteenth century. This is why he was motivated to experience the Event of Damascus once more.' (GA 130, 29 September 1911) The result was that Christian Rosenkreutz was now able to *recall* everything that had happened to him in the previous incarnation, and then with the aid of the spiritual forces of this ether body, *consciously* to repeat the spiritual experience of this preceding incarnation in the new embodiment.

In the fourteenth century he thus initially visited Damascus where— like Paul—he had a supersensible encounter with the Christ as the cosmic 'I-Am'. Then he travelled in the course of seven years throughout the then known world in order, on the basis of his 'Damascus experience', to bring about a synthesis of the wisdom gathered by him from all the religions by penetrating them with the Christ Impulse. The result of this comprehensive activity was the establishment of the Rosicrucian stream on earth. Later, at an advanced age, Christian Rosenkreutz then consciously experienced the second half of the initiation in the thirteenth century, namely how the forces of the Christ's Phantom imbued his physical body. That happened during his initiation in 1459, subsequently described by Valentin Andreae in his 'Chymical Wedding' and published for the first time in 1616. As a fruit of this new initiation, Christian Rosenkreutz was then able to establish the seven-fold path of initiation which alone is suitable for human beings in the Western world.[187]

According to Rudolf Steiner's testimony, in the ensuing period during his next incarnation in the sixteenth century (the first in the epoch of the consciousness soul that began in 1413),[188] Christian Rosenkreutz received a replica of the 'I' of Christ into his consciousness soul. This in turn was only possible because he had consciously received the forces of the Phantom in the previous incarnation into his physical body.[189]

Afterwards, at the end of the sixteenth century, Christian Rosenkreutz prepared one of his most important actions in the occult history of earthly mankind which he then carried out at the beginning of the seventeenth century. In the year 1604, he sent the individuality of the Gautama Buddha, 'his most intimate pupil and friend' (GA 139, 18 December 1912), from the Earth sphere to Mars. He could carry out this telluric/cosmic deed only as a result of having received the replica of the Christ-'I' into his consciousness soul.

His next incarnation occurred mostly in the eighteenth century, in the course of which he was active under the name Count S^t. Germain (1696?–1784?) in Europe. Finally the last of his known lives on earth was his incarnation during the second half of the nineteenth century. In this incarnation Christian Rosenkreutz was still active on earth at the beginning of the twentieth century. Concerning this one, Rudolf Steiner said concisely, 'Today Christian Rosenkreutz is reincarnated'. (GA 130, 27 September 1911) Moreover in this incarnation, his encounter with the young Rudolf Steiner took place.[190]

The last (seventh) incarnation of Christian Rosenkreutz in the above-mentioned sequence at the end of the twentieth and beginning of the twenty-first century is likewise his *first* incarnation during the epoch of the activity of the Etheric Christ within humanity, the epoch that began in the 1930s. (The beginning of the previous incarnation of Christian Rosenkreutz probably occurred before the middle of the nineteenth century.) It is from this incarnation onwards that Christian Rosenkreutz will become the greatest martyr among mankind in his service for the Etheric Christ. Concerning this stage of his Imitation of Christ, Rudolf Steiner stated: 'And those who know how it is with this individuality likewise know that Christian Rosenkreutz *shall be* the greatest martyr among men, aside from the Christ who suffered as a god.' (GA 133, 20 June 1912)

These words are found in a lecture given in 1912, meaning at a time when in all probability Christian Rosenkreutz was still incarnated on Earth, but they were uttered in the future tense. One can therefore assume that they refer to his next incarnation when he will follow the Etheric Christ in a quite new form. For only since the end of the twentieth century will the Etheric Christ, according to Rudolf Steiner's affirmation, become the Lord of Karma for all of humanity. And Christian Rosenkreutz's direct participation in this process will turn him into the 'greatest martyr among men' after Christ Himself.[191]

The co-operative work with the Christ in the field of karma will be the main task of Christian Rosenkreutz in this as well as in all subsequent incarnations.

Phys. Body	Ether Body 13th C.	Astral Body 14th/15th C.	'I' 16th/17th C.	(Spirit Self) 18th C.	(Life Spirit) 19th/20th C.	(Spirit Man) 20th/21st C.
1.........2		3	4	5	6	7
Participation in events of Turning-point of Time	Initiation in circle of Twelve (about 1250)	Experience before Damascus. Founding of Rosicrucian stream. Initiation to become 'Knight of Golden Stone' 1459. (1378–1484)	Receiving of replica of Christ-'I'. Sending of Buddha to Mars (1604)	Count Sᵗ. Germain	Encounter with Rudolf Steiner (around 1879)	First Incarnation in epoch of Christ as Lord of Karma

★

Here we must add that on the modern anthroposophical path of initiation, which is a metamorphosis of the Rosicrucian initiation path, the stage on which the spirit-pupil can begin conscious work for shaping the 'Philosophers' Stone' within himself is called the stage of Intuition (the fourth stage). On this level the process of insight reaches 'the character of being'[192] and the possibility arises for the initiate on the one hand to recognize the inner nature of other beings (their 'I'), and on the other to advance with his spiritual vision to the supersensible foundations of matter itself. This is why true perception of the Mystery of Golgotha as a free deed of Christ's World-'I' is only possible on this level.

At the end of the chapter on initiation in the book *Occult Science, an Outline*, Rudolf Steiner depicts these two aspects of Christ-knowledge in Intuition. One is linked with the experience of Christ in the figure of the Greater Guardian of the Threshold and simultaneously as the divine archetype of every human 'I'. The second is connected with insight into the Mystery of Golgotha in whose centre stands the genesis of the Resurrection body. (GA 13)

★

This, in general outline, is the spiritual-historical development of the Rosicrucian stream in whose womb the first element of spiritual communion was actualized. Its second component was evolved in the Grail stream. We must now turn to it. Two aspects of the Mysteries of the Holy Grail appear particularly significant in this context.

The first component concerns the connection of the content of the Grail Mysteries with the secrets of the etheric cosmos. (See GA 216, 1 October 1922) This relationship goes back all the way to the Mystery of

Golgotha. When on Good Friday the blood flowed to the ground from the wounds of Christ Jesus, it was received by the Earth. Having undergone an etherization process (see GA 130, 1 October 1911), this blood formed a 'new cosmic focal point' (GA 112, 6 July 1909) due to which Earth in the course of its further development can become the new sun in the universe. (ibid.)

This is the *macrocosmic* aspect of the Mystery connected with the continuing destiny of the Christ's etherized blood. Rudolf Steiner has described its *microcosmic* aspect in the lecture 'The Etherization of the Blood. The Entry of the Etheric Christ into the Evolution of the Earth'. (GA 130, 1 October 1911) Here he speaks of the fact that according to spiritual research a stream of the etherized blood of the Christ ascends since the Mystery of Golgotha in every human being from the direction of the heart to the head. If that is recognized, this can lead on the one hand to an experience of the Etheric Christ, and on the other to a recognition of the microcosmic Spirit-Sun in one's own heart, the seed of which was laid into the latter through the Mystery of Golgotha.

The fact that the Earth has received the blood of the Christ has not only caused the Earth to light up in the cosmos, but moreover signifies that the etheric body of human beings is being filled with the Christ-Light, meaning that the Spirit-Sun lights up in them: 'The Christ-Light flows into the etheric bodies of men', is the way Rudolf Steiner described it. (GA 112, 6 July 1909) Later on he depicted the future guidance of humans through the forces of the inner sun as follows: 'The sun-element that man throughout long periods of time only received out of the cosmos into himself will become radiant in the souls' interior. Man will learn to speak of an "inner sun". Even though this will not induce him to feel any less like an earthling during his life between birth and death, he will recognize his own being that moves about on Earth as being *led by the Sun*.' [Ger.: *sonnengeführt*] (GA 26; emphasis by Rudolf Steiner)

Then Rudolf Steiner pointed directly to the spiritual being who guides man to experience this inner sun: 'He [the human being] will learn to feel it to be a truth that in his inner being an entity places him in a light that, even though it shines upon Earth existence, is not enkindled in it.' (ibid.) This light that shines into Earth existence but does not derive its nature from it is the light that shines from the Mystery of Golgotha into the world, and the being who places man into this light is Michael.

In this way we have two interconnected spiritual processes that are evoked by the Mystery of Golgotha, a macrocosmic and a microcosmic one, which are the result of the etherization and further metamorphosis of

Christ's sacrificial blood in the spiritual aura of the Earth and the etheric body of man.

Both processes considered here represent the spiritual centre of the Grail Mysteries that make it possible through communion of the content of the Holy Vessel to behold the macrocosmic as well as the microcosmic aspect of the single etheric Mystery. Put differently, the participants of the Grail Mysteries acquire the faculty to behold how the Christ's etheric blood works in the Earth's aura and likewise in the human being. On the highest levels of their initiation they reach the point of perceiving the twofold Sun-process: The lighting up of the spiritual sun in the depths of the Earth and this sun's birth in the depths of the human heart.

Only through the union of these processes could the knights of the Grail receive into their souls the content of the Holy Vessel, the vessel that harbours within itself the single macrocosmic-microcosmic Mystery of the Christ's etherized *blood*.[193]

The second aspect of the Grail Mysteries represents their connection to the 'I' of man and all mankind. This aspect too is linked with the secret of the blood. For owing to its own element of warmth, in the human organism the blood is the physiological foundation of the human 'I'. This is moreover the reason why the content of the Holy Vessel is linked with the Mystery of the Christ 'I', which since its union with Earth evolution in the Mystery of Golgotha works in it [in this evolution] as the highest 'I' of all mankind. 'Just as the higher "I" is born in every individual human being, so in Palestine the higher "I" of all humanity, the Divine "I", is born.' (GA 112, 24 May 1909)

It was for this 'new-born' Christ-'I' that the knights of the Grail wanted to create three sheaths in mankind so that in time the Christ could become their new group 'I'. Rudolf Steiner described the development of these sheaths as the result of three moral faculties in the human being. The spiritual-physical sheath of the Christ will originate from the impulses of conscience; the etheric sheath out of impulses of compassion and love; the astral sheath out of the impulses of marvelling, devotion and faith. (See GA 155, 30 May 1912)

All three qualities can be clearly traced in Parsifal's Grail quest. Owing to the forces of conscience, knowledge of the Christ awakens in him and he enters upon the path leading to the Imitation of Him.[194] Due to his compassion he makes the decision to help the suffering Amfortas. His unshakeable faith and devotion (his wonderment) regarding the secret of the Grail ultimately permits him to become its new guardian.

These three virtues therefore form the foundation of every true Grail quest, in the past as well as in our time. In this sense we can likewise understand the '*golden* rule of the true spiritual sciences' that states: 'If you attempt to take *one* step forward in the perception of esoteric truths, take at the same time *three* in perfecting your character towards the Good.' (GA 10; emphasis by Rudolf Steiner) But as far as the Grail Mysteries are concerned the three steps in moral development correspond to the development of three virtues; conscience, compassion, and wonderment that lead to perception of the highest occult truth of Earth evolution, the truth that the Christ shall become the exalted group-ego of mankind.

Later, this part of the Grail Mysteries passed over into the secret schools of the Rosicrucians where it continued to survive until the beginning of our contemporary age. Rudolf Steiner summed up this transition in the words: 'He who is familiar with the secret of the Holy Grail knows that out of the wood of the cross emerges living, sprouting life, the immortal "I" that is symbolized by the roses on the black wood of the cross.' (GA 112, 24 June 1909)

In this way the truth lived on in the esoteric schools of the Rosicrucians (the truth that originally was the spiritual core of the Grail Mysteries) that Christ is the archetype of every human 'I' and since the Mystery of Golgotha the group-'I' of all humanity. But then this truth was once again revealed on a higher level out of the forces of today's Time Spirit Michael in renewed form in Anthroposophy so as to be accessible to *all* human beings of good will. 'This reborn [higher] human "I" continued on as a sacred secret; was preserved through the symbol of the Rose Cross, and is proclaimed today as the secret of the Holy Grail; as the secret of the Rose Cross.' (ibid.)

As we know, early on in the ninth century the Grail Mysteries left the physical level once and for all. From then on they were only accessible to human beings from the spiritual world adjacent to the Earth. There, only initiates living on earth and their disciples, likewise a few select individuals who were truly seeking the Holy Vessel, could fully consciously reach the Grail temple. Generally, however, the latter reached it only during sleep, and after waking up had a more or less clear memory of it.

That it happened to be the Rosicrucians who, due to their special initiation, frequently visited the supersensible Grail temple and as a result of that were actually the only heirs to its wisdom at the beginning of the modern age, is proven by the fact that Christian Rosenkreutz himself was the first to be granted the distinction to receive a replica of the Christ 'I' in the temple of the Grail.

After the Mystery of Golgotha, this replica of the Christ 'I' that had originated in the sheaths of Jesus of Nazareth was preserved in the Grail Vessel and later duplicated according to the laws of spiritual economy in the supersensible temple. It was there that Christian Rosenkreutz and likewise a few other initiated Rosicrucians received it.

Concerning the connection of the replica of the Christ-'I' with the Mysteries of the Holy Grail, as well as the task of spiritual science to prepare humanity gradually to receive a replica of the Christ-'I' into the individual 'I', Rudolf Steiner said in a lecture on 11 April 1909 (GA 109/111): 'There it is, this secret of the Christ-"I"—human beings should heed the call by spiritual science to understand this secret as a fact in order to receive the Christ-"I" in beholding the Holy Grail.' And this is only possible in the Grail's temple. In another lecture he pointed still more clearly to this central task of spiritual science in our age: 'It is part of the inner mission of the spiritual world-stream to prepare human beings to develop their soul substance so much that from now on an ever greater and greater number of human beings can receive into themselves a replica of the "I"-being of Christ-Jesus.' (GA 109/111, 7 March 1909)

Yet, what will remain for a long time a gift of grace from above for the majority of human beings, can be striven for on the path of modern initiation in full consciousness. For the initiate of today who has risen to the *stage of Intuition*, it is possible to have a direct perception of the Christ and to receive a replica of the Cosmic 'I' of the Christ. Rudolf Steiner himself achieved this at the end of the nineteenth century and later on referred to it as 'spiritually having stood before the Mystery of Golgotha'. (GA 28, Chap. XXVI). In *Occult Science, an Outline,* he described this experience as the encounter of the initiate with the Christ in Intuition, meaning in the intrinsic [Ger.: wesenhaft] union (communion) of two 'I'-beings.[195]

★

Summing all this up, the following can be ascertained. In Rosicrucianism, what was *originally* cultivated was the knowledge that the Christ became Earth's new spirit following the Mystery of Golgotha and the union of His physical body with the Earth. In the Grail Mysteries it was more the knowledge of the two Mystery-aspects of His blood that was cultivated.

This knowledge consisted of the fact that, due to the additional effects of His etherized blood in the macrocosmic and microcosmic regard, the Christ can become the new group 'I' of humanity, the group 'I' for which the above-mentioned three sheaths must be created.

As we saw above, the union of the Grail with the Rosicrucian stream took place initially on the esoteric level. And this means that it occurred only in the esoteric schools which were completely hidden from the outer world, and then only at the highest stages of initiation. This is because the union of the two streams presupposes the ability to seek out the Grail temple located in the spiritual world adjacent to the Earth.

The union of the two streams, not only in the supersensible world but likewise in the terrestrial one (meaning in the form that is accessible to *all* human beings), took place for the first time in Anthroposophy. The book *Occult Science, an Outline* attests to this. Just two-and-a-half months prior to his death, Rudolf Steiner wrote that this book '[contains] the outlines of Anthroposophy as a whole' and that what he presented in his books and lectures (1909–1925) was therefore only 'a further elaboration of the original outline'.[196]

More than once, Rudolf Steiner mentioned in his lectures and cycles given while working on *Occult Science, an Outline*, that as a spiritual scientific representation of the evolution of world and man (the centre of which is the knowledge of the Christ and the Mystery of Golgotha) the cosmogony depicted in this book could just as well be called 'the Theosophy of the Rosicrucian',[196a] and that the sevenfold path of initiation described in it is the Christian-Rosicrucian one. (ibid).[197]

Concerning the connection of *Occult Science, an Outline* with the Grail Mysteries, Rudolf Steiner wrote in the last chapter dealing with them that in *Occult Science* 'is contained the knowledge of the new initiation with the Christ Mystery in the centre'. For that reason, 'the initiates of the present time' (and Rudolf Steiner must be counted among them in first place) '... can likewise be called "initiates of the Grail".'[198] And 'the path which in its first stages was described in this book leads to the "knowledge of the Grail".' (GA 13)

What was initially linked on the level of *thought* in *Occult Science, an Outline* was then brought together on the level of *feeling* in the artistic Imaginative representations of the First Goetheanum. In it we have on the one hand the modern Grail temple on Earth,[199] and on the other the direct continuation of the temple tradition of the Rosicrucians.[200]

Finally at the Christmas Conference, we can recognize the third level of the metamorphosis. It is the return of the Goetheanum (which had gone up in flames) in purely spiritual form out of the widths of the etheric cosmos whose perception, as we saw above, represents an important part of the Mysteries of the Holy Grail. Out of this cosmic[201] Inspiration, at the Christmas Conference Rudolf Steiner formed its spiritual centre, the Foundation Stone as well as its meditation and rhythms, something through which he attained the third level of the Grail stream's union with the Rosicrucian stream on the level of *will*. This is likewise the reason he ended the text of the Foundation Stone

Meditation with the verb 'will' ['with single purpose' in the translation quoted in this book. Tr.].[202]

It was only on the basis of this threefold melding process of the Rosicrucian and the Grail stream that Rudolf Steiner for the first time could unite what amounted to the esoteric centre and highest goal of both streams: *the two elements of the spiritual communion*, the sharing in the Phantom of the Resurrected One, and His condensed etheric body. And Rudolf Steiner accomplished this not within an esoteric school sternly closed-off from the outer world, but publicly in front of all the people attending the Christmas Conference of 1923/24.

Since then, what had been in the past the property of a narrow circle of Christian initiates and their closest students is now accessible to *every* human being of good will who today wishes to enter upon the path, leading to *spiritual communion* as a promise of true Christianity, through the inner work with the Foundation Stone Meditation and its rhythms.

This is how we can understand the significance of Rudolf Steiner's words that 'the destiny of Anthroposophy would like to be that of Christianity'. (GA 226, 17 May 1923—II)

12. The Three Spiritual Sources of Anthroposophy

When we join together the text of the previous chapter with what was said in Chapter 6, we have a picture of the three spiritual streams before us; a picture out of which Anthroposophy emerged in the twentieth century. With that Anthroposophy has become heir to these streams and at the same time has reached the next stage of its own development. For the union of the Rosicrucian and Grail streams in Anthroposophy occurred in a completely *new* form, namely out of the Inspirations of the present Time Spirit, Michael. For Michael himself, his present guidance of humanity is the *first* in the world-epoch since the Mystery of Golgotha. This is why it is moreover impossible to form a judgement about Anthroposophy on the basis of the historical and traditional conceptions of the Rosicrucian and Grail streams. Based on the forces of the Michaelic Time Spirit both streams passed through a major metamorphosis in Anthroposophy. They emerged out of the remoteness of Mystery locations so as to become a property of all humanity.

In the Foundation Stone Meditation, the most complete and perfect expression of the spiritual nature of Anthroposophy (see Chap 1), we can discern the presence of all three streams. In the first part, the characteristics of the *Rosicrucian* stream are addressed. Mention is made here of the spiritualization of the *limb*s that contain the most solid mineral portions of the human body. Their spiritualization is only possible through the affiliation with the Phantom of the Resurrected Christ. A renewed connection of the limbs with the 'ocean-being of the Spirit' (out of which they emerged originally) is possible only with the help of the Phantom's forces.[203] Knowledge about this process now leads to the point of experiencing the original connection of man with the Father-God who once created his world. The words of the farewell talks by Christ Jesus with His disciples, as recounted in the Gospel of John, point to this relationship:[204] 'No one finds the way to the Father but through me ... He who has seen me has also seen the Father ... Believe me that my Self ["I"] lives in the Father and the Father lives in me.' (John 14: 6, 9, 11) This relationship, existing since eternities between the Son and the Father, can for us be an archetype of the relationship existing between the 'I' of every human being and the Father in the sense of the words in the Foundation Stone Meditation:

Where in the wielding
World-Creator-Being
Thine own I
Comes to being
Within the I of God.

That leads man to the goal:

And thou wilt truly *live*
In the All-World-Being of Man.

In His 'Farewell Talks', the Christ referred to this principle of the true or eternal *life* when He turned to the Father: '. . . since thou hast given him [the Son] power over all flesh, to give eternal life to all whom thou hast given him. And this is eternal life, that they know thee the only true God, and Jesus Christ whom thou hast sent.' (Jn. 17, 2-3, RSV)

By receiving into themselves the forces of the transformed flesh of the resurrected Christ, the Rosicrucians reached the source of death-vanquishing 'eternal life' and could thereby draw nearer to the sphere of the Father-God, meaning to the realization of the lofty ideal that comes to expression in the 'Farewell Talks': '. . . so that they may all be one; as you, Father, are in me and I in you, so they shall be one in us . . . I am in them, and you are in me . . .' (Jn. 17, 21/23, JM)

Such an experiencing of the Father-forces, that work by means of the highest First Hierarchy in the Phantom of the Christ which has re-arisen in its original form,[205] made it possible for the Rosicrucians in the process of 'Spirit-recollection' to attain to a perception of Ancient Saturn, the primordial fount of man's *physical* body. As we saw in the second chapter, the foundation for the physical body was created then through the spirits of the First Hierarchy, something that comes to expression in the words:

For the Father-Spirit of the Heights holds sway
In Depths of Worlds, begetting Being.
Seraphim, Cherubim, Thrones!
Let there ring out from the Heights
What in the Depths is echoed,
Speaking:
Ex Deo nascimur,

or as rendered into German by Rudolf Steiner:

'Aus dem Göttlichen weset die Menschheit'
(From God, Mankind has Being).

★

Whereas the Rosicrucians sought the path to the Father through the Son, and in so doing utilized various experiments with substances from nature, the knights of the Grail sought the connection with the entity of the Son. For that reason, their path was a purely inward one and the chalice with Christ's sacrifice-filled blood stood in the centre of their esotericism. In the Mysteries of the Grail, this chalice served as the fount of the forces of the Christ's Cosmic 'I', forces that since the Mystery of Golgotha are connected with every human 'I'.

This central secret of esoteric Christianity, which represents the essence of the Grail Mysteries, comes to expression in the second part of the Foundation Stone Meditation:

Where the surging
Deeds of the World's Becoming
Do thine own I
Unite
Unto the I of the World.

The union of the World-'I' with the individual 'I' of man that is expressed in these words, points to the secret of receiving the replica of the Christ-'I' into the consciousness soul (see Chap.11). The feeling of one's 'own soul-being' must however precede this reception, meaning an awareness of the *true nature* of the consciousness soul, the soul within the soul, (GA 9) must be attained, something that is only possible by developing the feeling of *devotion*.[206]

Then the human being receives a replica of the Christ-'I' out of the Grail's chalice into his consciousness soul and begins

... truly [to] *feel*
'Mid the weaving of the Soul of Man.

Now he knows based on his own experience that the true esoteric name of the Christ is the divine 'I Am'. Rudolf Steiner coined this in the words: 'The one true name of the Christ is "I Am"; he who does not know that and calls Him something else does not know anything about Him. "I Am" is His only name.' (GA 266/ I, 27 May 1909)

★

The second part of the Foundation Stone Meditation has a particularly profound relationship to the Christ-Mysteries of today through its reference to the rhythmic system which is based on a twofold rhythm: the rhythmic beating of the heart and the rhythm of breathing.

The first rhythm is connected with the Christ Being through the stream of His etherized blood that flows from the heart to the head. Insight into this occupies a central place in the Grail Mysteries. In the New Mysteries on the other hand, access to cognition of the ether-stream through transforming the heart into a new 'organ of perception' is revealed, something that was indicated during the cultic Laying of the Foundation Stone (on 25 December 1923). Then on a second level through immersion of the dual Foundation Stone into the ground of one's own heart, this stream of the etherized Christ-blood can be linked with the stream of the etherized blood of man, something that in our time leads to the beholding of the Etheric Christ.

In this way it is moreover possible to grasp the secrets of the Mystery of Golgotha Imaginatively. For this to happen it is necessary, utilizing the heart as a new organ of perception, to attain to the view of the 'Images of Worlds' [or 'cosmic Images'] in the way they are effective in one's own rhythmic system, Images that have a direct connection to the Grail Mystery. During the cultic act of the Foundation Stone Laying in the segment that relates to the second part of the meditation, it is said of these Images of the cosmos: Inasmuch as 'grasping this [that which is replicated in the rhythmic system of man as world rhythm] with a wisdom-filled heart that has become a *sense organ,* man can experience the God-given *universal Images* [Imaginations] as they actively reveal the cosmos out of themselves.' (GA 260) As we saw, on the one hand insight into the etheric (that is the *Imaginative*) cosmos was sought in the Grail Mysteries in connection with the Christ secret. On the other hand, the Grail chalice itself—and this is a further aspect of this Mystery—contains the *Cosmic Imaginations* that harbour the 'secret of Golgotha' within themselves. Rudolf Steiner wrote about this: 'Spirit beings harboured [in the chalice of the Grail] *Images of Worlds* [Ger.: 'Weltbilder'] in which lived the secrets of Golgotha.' In the epoch of the consciousness soul however, and since the beginning of Michael's period of rulership, these beings wish to pass these Images on to human beings so that the latter can 'develop a new, complete comprehension of the Mystery of Golgotha'. (GA 26)[207]

During the cultic Laying of the Foundation Stone Rudolf Steiner spoke moreover about the connection of the second rhythm in the human organism—the rhythm of breathing—with the Christ's activity in the Earth's airy sphere since the Mystery of Golgotha. He pointed to 'the

Christ force that is effective everywhere in the atmosphere, that moves with the breezes as it circles the Earth and works and lives in our breathing system'. (GA 260)

★

If we now turn once more to the 'Farewell Talks' by the Christ, His words, 'I am the way, the truth, and the life' (Jn. 14, 6) can in their whole pivotal importance open up a deeper understanding of the Foundation Stone Meditation. In the transition from the first to the second part, we have here the following process. To the *life* of the Father, that the Rosicrucians sought in the form of the 'quintessence' or 'primal matter' in their alchemistic experiments, is added the *truth* of the Son that is above all the truth of His greatest deed on Earth, the Mystery of Golgotha, the secret of which is contained in the Grail chalice. Then in the third part of the meditation, we have—as we shall see—the description of the *way* of modern initiation, the path that can be pursued in accordance with the Time Spirit ruling today in humanity.

Only through insight into this truth that has become accessible to mankind thanks to Anthroposophy as the modern 'science of the Grail' and also because the foundation stone of the New Mysteries is immersed into one's own heart, does it become possible to be admitted to the circle of today's knights as guardian of the sacred chalice. Eventually such a new knight can then consciously enter the supersensible temple of the Grail, where the 'Christ-Will' holds sway, so as to experience in that temple what is contained in the additional words of the meditation's second part:

> For the Christ-Will in the encircling Round holds sway
> In the Rhythms of Worlds, blessing the Soul.

These two lines describe how the knights of the Grail-brotherhood, who in the supersensible temple surround the Christ in spiritual worlds, receive his lofty 'blessing' into their purified souls ('And thou wilt truly *feel*') in order then to carry this blessing down to Earth[208] where, from East to West in connection with the forces of the Second Hierarchy (the Sun-hierarchy), it is supposed to be effective:

> Kyriotetes, Dynamis, Exusiai!
> Let there be fired from the East
> What through the West is formed.

In these words we moreover have a reference to the union of Christ's spirit-self (coming from the East, the historical location of the Mystery of

Golgotha) with His life spirit that is coming to meet the former from the West, a union that occurred in the year 869. A reflection of this super-sensible encounter is the coming together of the Mystery stream of King Arthur with the Grail stream on Earth. (see GA 240, 27 August 1924) Parsifal, who earlier had been initiated into the Mysteries of the Round Table and subsequently became royal guardian of the Holy Vessel, played a pivotal part in this process.

We thus discover in the New Mysteries the revelation of the threefold nature of the Christ in the way it was experienced in the course of centuries in the Grail Mysteries: His World-'I', His spirit-self, and His life-spirit. The 'I' of the Christ passed as the Son of Man through the Mystery of Golgotha; His spirit-self appeared as the 'youth' who left the Christ in the Garden of Gethsemane and then reunited with Him during the Resurrection,[209] and His life-spirit penetrated the whole Earth aura. In this threefold nature of the Christ, lies the source so that in the future the Earth can become like the Holy Grail that bears in itself the seed for the new sun. Its fount is the World-'I' of the Christ. This 'I' is connected with Earth since the Mystery of Golgotha, and its protective sheath is formed by the spirit-self, its radiant aura by the life-spirit.

After the Grail Mysteries have linked up with the Rosicrucian stream, the possibility will arise in the future for the [Rosicrucian] initiates not only to experience their lofty ideal in their own soul but moreover to participate in that ideal's actualization. This in turn implies to work consciously for the lofty goals of Earth evolution, and the transformation of humanity and earth into the starting point of the new creation, the future Cosmos of Love, the very essence of which will be the Christ.

★

The third part of the Foundation Stone Meditation is connected with the modern Michael-Mysteries that Rudolf Steiner described in detail in the Karma Lectures and *Leading Thoughts*.[210] In their centre stand the celestial and earthly destinies of the Cosmic Intelligence (the totality of the Creator-thoughts of all divine-spiritual hierarchies); an intelligence once governed by Michael in the spiritual world. But after the Christ had descended to Earth and had consummated the Mystery of Golgotha, it followed Him and thus gradually moved downward into humanity's domain. On Earth this intelligence became the foundation of individual thinking, something that made it possible for man to attain to freedom. According to what Rudolf Steiner said, this process began in the eighth century (see GA 240, 19 July 1924), and with the beginning of the consciousness soul-epoch (in the year 1413) encompassed all of 'civilized' mankind.

With the start of the new period or Michael's rule in the year 1879, his battle, waged for the ongoing destiny of human intelligence with the ahrimanic spirits in the spiritual world adjacent to the Earth, reached a decisive stage. In the centre of this battle stands man himself. This is why Rudolf Steiner stated: 'More than any other conflict this one is relegated to the human heart', meaning to the place into which the Foundation Stone of the New Michaelic Mysteries can be laid today. 'Therein this conflict is rooted, grounded since the last third of the nineteenth century.' (GA 249, 19 July 1924) Will man utilize the intelligence that is bestowed on him solely for comprehending the external material world or use it equally 'with good will' for an understanding of the higher worlds, and in that way return it to the Michael-sphere? It will be directly on this that Michael's present conflict with the dragon will depend.

In his opposition to Michael, Ahriman wishes more than anything else to usurp the Cosmic Intelligence that has descended upon human beings in order then to utilize it against Michael as the powerful weapon that— so he hopes—will bring him victory. But whether Ahriman will indeed attain this spiritual weapon depends above all on human beings who in our epoch are called upon to help Michael in his celestial struggle.

Rudolf Steiner gave yet another illustration to describe man's present-day relationship with Michael. He characterized how Michael, standing in the spiritual world, 'reaches down' to humanity with his hands in the expectation that, on their part, human beings stretch their spiritual hands up towards him—namely that their spiritualized intelligence is directed towards knowledge of the higher worlds. (See GA 219, 17 December 1922) The means to spiritualize earthly intelligence, so that it can be received by Michael in his sun-kingdom, is Anthroposophy. It is the sword, forged out of the spirit, with which Michael's struggle against the dragon can be won in favour of his impulse. 'It must become decisive what human hearts will do with this Michael-concern about the world in the course of the twentieth century. And in this course of the twentieth century, when the first century after the end of the Kali Yuga will have been concluded, mankind will either stand at the grave of all civilization or at the beginning of that era when, in the souls of men who in their hearts unite intelligence with spirituality, the Michael battle will be fought out in favour of the Michael impulse. (GA 240, 19 July 1924)

Concerning this secret of the Cosmic Intelligence of Michael, it says in the Foundation Stone Meditation:

For the Spirit's Universal Thoughts hold sway
In the Being of all Worlds, beseeching Light.

Here the reference is to the cosmic thoughts that were sent into the being of the world which from the viewpoint of the higher worlds is our earthly world. In it lives the being of man, above all its head system, as the centre-point of the death forces of its organism. Subjugated by abstract thinking and torn away from its 'Michaelic' homeland, the cosmic thoughts 'beseech' for 'light' in the human head, meaning they long for the possibility to return to the spiritual world.

But the possibility to spiritualize the human intellect depends on it being filled by the resurrection forces that emanate from the Mystery of Golgotha. Experiencing these forces in thinking in the sense of 'Per Spiritum Sanctum reviviscimus' or, amounting to the same thing, the awakening of the soul in the cosmic thoughts of the Spirit—that is the goal that man today can attain with the aid of Anthroposophy so as to become a comrade-in-arms with Michael.

Then the next lines of the meditation will be fulfilled:

Archai, Archangeloi, Angeloi,
Let there be prayed in the Depths
What from the Heights is answered.

Out of the depths of the being of humans, the spiritualized intelligence will then arise into the spiritual world, and its ascent will have been 'answered'. And that will be the start of that epoch when humans shall work together with spirits of the Third Hierarchy.[211]

In the meditation this future co-operation between gods and men is put in the words:

Where the eternal aims of Gods
World-Being's Light
On thine own I
Bestow
For thy free Willing.

This is how man learns 'to think truly' in his 'spirit-foundations'. This means not only to think human thoughts but moreover thoughts of the gods, something that is an unequivocal requirement for working together with them. In turn this signifies that henceforth the 'resting head' can open to the human being the world-thoughts from 'the ground of the Eternal', the cosmic thoughts that lead man to 'spirit-vision'. Now in our age, this signifies attaining the new 'intellectual clairvoyance' that lays open the vision of the Etheric Christ in the spiritual world adjacent to the Earth. (See GA 130, 18 November 1911)

The spiritualization-process of the Cosmic Intelligence, the process in which this intelligence is at the same time given back to Michael, moreover leads to a conscious entry into the spiritual world. This means that it is a modern path of initiation. To the two elements of the Christ-word, *life* and *truth*, the third element is added. It is a spiritual *path* that leads to the experience of the central point of the world-all; to the Christ-'I' that works in the spiritual worlds as Spirit-Sun mentioned in the fourth part of the meditation:

'*I am*—	*the path*—	*the truth*—	and *the life*'
Fourth part of the meditation	Third part of the meditation	Second part of the meditation	First part of the meditation

★

Among the spiritual scientific communications by Rudolf Steiner yet another reference can be found to Michael as the main inspirer of Anthroposophy. In several lectures during the year 1911, he spoke more than once of three cosmic calls within the spiritual-historical evolution of humanity in connection with its three great epochs, the epoch of the Father, of the Son, and of the Spirit.

In the first world-epoch, mankind was given the Ten Commandments of Moses. With that resounded the first call out of the spiritual world, the call of the epoch of the Father.

The second call resounded at the Turning-point of Time through John the Baptist. This call proclaimed to human beings something of the radical change of their faculties in regard to beholding and comprehending the world in connection with the coming of the second epoch, the epoch of the Son that began with the Baptism in the Jordan, meaning at the instant when the Christ reached the Earth. The start of this epoch is proclaimed in the prologue of the Gospel of John written by the 'beloved disciple' of the Christ: 'And the Word became flesh.' (1,14)

Finally, the third call resounded along with the founding of Anthroposophy on Earth at the beginning of the twentieth century. This signifies the beginning of the third epoch, the epoch of the Spirit. Rudolf Steiner said about this: 'He who knows how to read the *signs of the time* knows what it means to hear the third call by the living new revelation, or to let it pass by unheard.' (GA 127, 30 November 1911) As was depicted in another work, the expression 'signs of the time' refers in the language of Christian esotericism to the beginning of the present epoch of Michael's rulership,[212] the epoch in which Michael sends his new spirit revelation to mankind. (See further below)

In a lecture on 2 December 1911, Rudolf Steiner mentioned a relation between the three calls and the faculties of walking, speaking, and thinking acquired by man at an early age. (GA 130) On their part, these three faculties also have a direct connection to the first three parts of the Foundation Stone Meditation. Walking is based on the limb system; the faculty of speech emerges from the activity of the rhythmic system, particularly breathing; thinking is sustained by the head system.[213]

We can thus find the three calls in renewed form in the first three segments of the Foundation Stone Meditation, where each begins with the call 'Soul of Man!'

The renewal of the call that once resounded through Moses occurred in the first segment: the call to which, through the Ten Commandments, humanity owes the inner strength of moral uprightness out of the impulses of the Father-God.

In the second segment of the meditation the call by John the Baptist as well as that of John the Evangelist was renewed. Considered together, they proclaimed the start of the second epoch, that of the Son, the Christ, whose name is moreover mentioned in the second segment. As the Divine Word the Christ is the highest primal image of what stands as spiritual strength behind human language.

At the Turning-point of Time, the two Johns are the main witnesses of the most essential events: John the Baptist participated personally in the Baptism in the Jordan, and John the Evangelist was present at the Mystery of Golgotha.[214] Their working together can be recognized in the words of the Foundation Stone Meditation:

> Let there be fired from the East
> What through the West is formed.

Here John the Baptist represents the principle of *revelation* that comes out of the spiritual world, the way it took place during the Baptism in the Jordan. John the Evangelist on the other hand, represents the principle of *initiation* that comes from the West, here not meant in the geographical sense but in that of polarity and co-operation of two spiritual streams whose point of departure is on the one hand the world of the spirit (fire) and on the other the world of matter (form).[215]

Finally, in the third part of the meditation we do not have the renewal of a past call but a completely *new call* that sounds today out of the spiritual world and is addressed through Anthroposophy in our age to every human being of good will. This call, that in our present time proceeds from the supersensible temple of the New Mysteries,[216] comes to expression in the following lines of the third part of the meditation:

> Where the eternal aims of Gods
> World-Being's Light
> On thine own I
> Bestow
> For thy free Willing.

The actualization of these words in the New Mysteries will serve as the basis for the beginning of conscious co-operation with the Third Hierarchy.

The three faculties, standing erect, speaking, and thinking, develop in early childhood even before the 'I'-impulse awakens that only later lights up from this threefold basis. What occurs in every human being approximately in the third year of life as a first flashing up of individual ego-consciousness, took place for all mankind in the third year of Christ's life on earth through the Mystery of Golgotha. (See GA 112, 24 July 1909) At this moment the higher 'I' of all humanity was born on earth just as in the third year of life the child's 'I'-development begins.[217]

This is the reason why, after the first three parts of the Foundation Stone Meditation, the fourth part that summarizes them follows by necessity. In the centre of it, the Spirit-Sun of the 'I-Am' lights up which bestows immortality on every individual human 'I' as well as on all humanity.

And thus we can sum up:

Epoch of the Father	*Epoch of the Son*	*Epoch of the Spirit*
Call of Moses	Call of the two Johns	Call of Spiritual Science
★	★	★
First Part of the meditation	Second Part of the meditation	Third Part of the meditation
First Call 'Soul of Man!'	Second Call 'Soul of Man!'	Third Call 'Soul of Man!'

Limb System	System of Heart and Lung	Head System
Working of the Father-Spirit	Working of the Christ	Working of the Holy Spirit
★	★	★
Standing Erect	Speaking (the Word)	Thinking
★	★	★
LIFE	TRUTH	WAY

Fourth Part of the Meditation

★

Lighting up of Spirit-Sun
Birth of
I-AM
of Man and Mankind

All three calls that in renewed form are contained in the Foundation Stone Meditation have a direct connection to the activity of the Archangel Michael in humanity.

According to Rudolf Steiner's spiritual scientific research, Michael worked until the Mystery of Golgotha in the cosmos as the 'countenance of Yahweh'. This moreover implied that he served as mediator between Yahweh and the ancient Hebrew folk. This is why he was revered as the leading spirit by the people, for he was the one who influenced all their important representatives.[218]

Michael was linked in a particularly intimate manner with Moses who was capable in the most comprehensive way of showing the ancient Hebrew people their true spiritual-historic mission. Rudolf Steiner said of this connection: 'The folk spirit who united with Moses during his initiation and then indwelled him was Michael.' (GA 265, 15 April 1908).[219] From this it follows that the tablets with the Ten Commandments, and Genesis that tells of the Creation of world and man, issued from the Inspiration of the Archangel Michael, the mediator between Yahweh and the ancient Hebrew folk.

As a result of the Mystery of Golgotha that took place on Earth, a radical change occurred in the celestial destiny of Michael. Out of the 'Night spirit' he turned into a 'Day spirit' and out of the 'countenance of Yahweh' into the cosmic 'countenance of Christ'. (See GA 152, 2 May 1913 and GA 194, 22 November 1919.) Rudolf Steiner also spoke in this connection of two Michael-revelations *after* he had become the coun-

tenance of Christ. The first is contained in the proclamation of the prologue in the Gospel of John where it says that the divine Word had
become flesh at the Turning-point of Time and had dwelled among
humans to offer them the possibility of rising on their own in the future
and dwelling in the realm of the Word.

The possibility, however, to enter upon this path *consciously*, opened up
to mankind in the epoch of the Spirit, the beginning of which came with
the founding of spiritual science on earth. And this is connected with the
second Michael revelation. Rudolf Steiner said the following about this:
'The time must come when flesh becomes Word once more and learns to
dwell in the realm of the Word . . . so as to behold the divine secrets.' (GA
194, 22 November 1919)[220]

If we add to these two Michael revelations—the first from the realm of
the Son, 'And the Word became flesh', and the second out of the realm of
the Spirit, 'And the flesh shall become Word so as to dwell in the realm of
the Spirit'—the still older revelation from the realm of the Father which
was given by Moses, we have a sequence of three revelations. As to their
content they correspond to the three first segments of the Foundation
Stone Meditation:

1. Michael revelation out of the sphere of the Father	2. (I.) Michael revelation out of the sphere of the Son	3. (II.) Michael revelation out of the sphere of the Spirit
★	★	★
Genesis by Moses	Prologue of John's Gospel	Modern spiritual science
★	★	★
First part of the Foundation Stone Meditation	Second part of the Foundation Stone Meditation	Third part of the Foundation Stone Meditation

A further connection of the first and second Michael revelation results
from the fact that Rudolf Steiner began the Mystery act of the Foundation Stone Laying on 25 December 1923 with reference to the
necessity to renew 'out of the signs of the time' the ancient Mystery word
'Know thou thyself'. (GA 260) Here the expression 'signs of the time'
refers to the present rulership epoch by Michael (1879 to about 2400),[221]
whereas the Mystery-word, 'Know thyself!' that was once chiselled above
the entrance into the temple of the Delphi-Apollo Oracle, indicates his
previous epoch of rulership. That epoch extends from the birth of Greek
philosophy and its unfolding all the way to its full flowering. The first

Christians required its concepts to understand the Christ. For without the concepts of Greek philosophy such as the Logos or the Sophia that were derived out of the Michael Inspiration, the most profound of the four gospels, the Gospel of John, could never have been written.

Moreover, the fact that during the act of the Foundation Stone Laying Rudolf Steiner mentions the name of 'Apollo', points to a direct connection with Michael who manifested to the ancient Greeks through this Sun-god who was a patron of true self-knowledge as a basis for the development of individual ego-consciousness. With this we can determine the presence and influence of the Michael impulse in all three parts of the Foundation Stone Meditation. As far as the fourth part is concerned, the words below point to Michael as described by Zeylmans van Emmichoven:[222]

> Darkness of Night
> Had held its sway;
> Day-radiant Light
> Poured into the souls of men.

Here Michael appears as victor over the spirits of darkness who in their totality form the body of the ahrimanic dragon, whom the former cast from heaven down to earth, while he became the Time Spirit. (See GA 177, 14 October 1917) With that Michael opened up access for human souls to the new Spirit Light that leads contemporary humans to the perception of the Mystery of Golgotha.

Since Michael is the leading Sun-Archangel in the spiritual worlds he is by nature related to the Christ Entity and therefore filled by His Sun forces from the very beginning. As a result the words of the fourth part, 'Light Divine / Sun of Christ', refer not only to the Christ but likewise to Michael as His cosmic servant and Sun-'countenance'. For Michael 'can always be compared with a sun'. (Rudolf Steiner, GA 152, 2 May 1913)

We can thus discover the forces of Michael as the *Sun* Time Spirit and main inspirer of modern spiritual science[223] in all four parts of the Foundation Stone Meditation.

★

From all this it becomes obvious that the first three segments of the Foundation Stone Meditation contain the secrets of the three main streams of Christian esotericism: the Rosicrucian stream, the Grail stream, and the cosmic Michael stream. Naturally these three streams are connected with one another in esoteric life through a multitude of invisible threads. This constant working together is likewise reflected in the meditation. In the first segment, for example, the verb 'live' anticipates the second segment; in the second segment the word 'will' points to its connection with the first segment, and the word 'pondering' to its link with the third segment. In the same way the word 'eternity' in the third segment connects this segment with the first, and the word 'vision' [Erschauen] with the second segment, and so on.

Just as the first three parts of the meditation find their highest synthesis in the last, the fourth part in the all-encompassing creator-activity of the Christ-Sun, so too, the three streams of esoteric Christianity mentioned here, having united in Anthroposophy, will furthermore *serve the Christ* in the new form that alone corresponds to His etheric appearance as the Lord of Karma.

All true Rosicrucians, knights of the Grail, and Michaelites (to whom anthroposophists, Platonists, and Aristotelians, who have passed through the supersensible Michael school, belong in the first place), therefore have the same task in our time; a task that comes to expression in the last lines of the Foundation Stone Meditation out of the nature of the New Mysteries:

> That good may become
> What from our Hearts we would found
> And from our Heads direct
> With single purpose.

Addendum
The Three Forms of Communion
and the Foundation Stone Meditation

After the first edition of my book *May Human Beings Hear It! The Mystery of the Christmas Conference* had come out, a question was posed to me in reference to a description of the nature of communion and the relationship of sacramental to spiritual communion.[224] It regarded their connection with the ritual that Rudolf Steiner gave for the upper classes of the Waldorf School, known under the term 'Offering Service'.

This third ritual stands precisely in the middle between the sacramental cultus in which, through mediation of the ordained priest, the transubstantiation of the earthly substances of bread and wine takes place, and the spiritual communion where the connection with the body of the Resurrected One and His condensed etheric body is experienced in purely inner form on the altar of the soul. For in the ritual of the Offering Service communion takes place by means of the *Word* at the spiritual reality of the Resurrection.

The altar during the Offering Service, the participation of the 'congregation' and a 'conductor of the service' as mediator between it and the spiritual world, connects this ritual with sacramental communion. On the other hand, since no earthly substances are utilized and 'priestly ordination' is not required for conducting it, the Offering Service can be viewed as being in proximity to spiritual communion. But utilization of mantric (ritualistic) texts in the three forms of communion represents an element connecting them all. During sacramental communion the mantric word in the 'Act of Consecration of Man' evokes *transubstantiation* of the earthly substances on the altar and accompanies them. In the ritual of the Offering Service, the word that is spoken by the 'congregation' becomes bearer of the element of communion, whereas during spiritual communion the *meditation* that takes place in the soul's centre is assigned this task.[225]

Altogether we have three stages here that lead from without to within, from the substances that were taken from the outer (natural) world over to the power of the spoken mantric word to the meditation process experienced purely inwardly.

Even from the standpoint of the paradigm 'individual—social' one can recognize a sequence; due to its nature, spiritual communion can occur only in quite an individual manner in the depths of the soul to which none have access except man himself and the spiritual world. In the Offering Service the ritual is carried out by means of words and gestures that are addressed alternately to the spiritual world and the 'congregation' (those who are present). In so doing and as agreed upon, this ritual can on principle be conducted by *any* adult participant, which signifies that the difference between the one who conducts the service and the participants is not something absolute. In the sacramental ritual, on the other hand, where the one who conducts it has to be an ordained priest and where in the ritual itself physical substances are used, a higher degree of objectivity is reached (of course not so far as the effect of communion in the human being is concerned but in the sense of carrying out the ritual). Here, endowed with spiritual power, the priest appears before the altar while conducting the act of consecration as the representative of the spiritual world in reference to the congregation.

A third essential difference between the three kinds of communion is that the sacramental cultus of the Christian Community is essentially accessible to all human beings, whereas the Offering Service is directed merely to a limited (special) group of people, and the spiritual communion takes place in the inner sanctum of an actual human soul and therefore has an individual character.[226]

★

A further aspect of the three forms of communion that Rudolf Steiner gave to mankind out of the founts of the Christian Mysteries, consists of the following. The metamorphosis of spiritual forces active in early childhood in the human being that awaken in man the three main faculties preceding ego consciousness, namely upright posture, speaking, and thinking, can be traced in them [the above-mentioned three forms of communion]. In this process the development of these faculties is connected directly with the activity of the Christ Being by means of the true 'I' of man.[227] Viewed in this way, the spiritual force that causes man to be an upright being is related to the communion that plays a part in the process of transubstantiation on the altar, for both forces extend their effect to the physical body. The faculty of speech attains the highest point of its development in speaking mantric words. Thinking draws close to and enters the spiritual world by means of meditation.[228]

Furthermore, a connection of all three types of communion with the Foundation Stone Meditation can be ascertained, for all three emerge from the New Mysteries. Thus the first three parts of the meditation describe how the Christ Impulse (that is named in the fourth part) works out of the forces of the Trinity, meaning correspondingly out of the

sphere of the Father, the Son, and the Spirit. The Christ works out of the
sphere of the Father by means of the highest, the First Hierarchy, which
alone is capable of transforming matter (see GA 26, Leading Thoughts 71
and 76), something that stands in the centre of sacramental communion.
Out of the sphere of the Son, meaning out of His own sphere, the Christ
works primarily through His very own element, the Word, and the spirits
of the Second Hierarchy, the Sun Hierarchy, serve as mediators of it. This
revelation of the Word stands in the centre of the ritual of the Offering
Service. Finally, in meditative practice we have the basis of spiritual
communion. For meditative practice is connected with the transformation of human thinking and leads to the conscious experience of the
reality of resurrection; meaning (as affirmed by Rudolf Steiner) it leads to
'spiritually having stood before the Mystery of Golgotha in most inward,
most earnest joy of knowledge.' (GA 28)

One can likewise say that sacramental and spiritual communion
represent a kind of polarity, inasmuch as in the first communion the path
leads from the transformation of substances past the word to thoughts
(understanding),[229] and in the second conversely from thinking to the
inner word to the purely spiritual process of transforming the physical
body. The Offering Service on the other hand stands exactly in the
middle, inasmuch as communion takes place in it purely through the
word element.[230]

Taking note of the macrocosmic parts of the meditation we can
summarize:

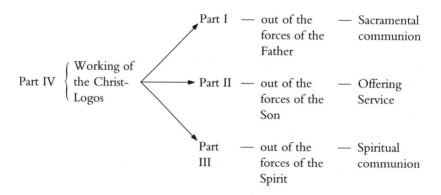

In part I of the meditation, the working of the highest, the First
Hierarchy or 'Spirits of Strength' is described: spirits who work in the
cosmos from above to below and bring about the transubstantiation of
substances in the sacrament on the altar:[231]

Let there ring out from the Heights
What in the Depths is echoed.

What takes place in the 'heights' of the cosmic midnight hour is likewise to have its reflection in the depths of matter which is to be transformed at the altar. In the course of communion this comes to expression inasmuch as the substances of bread and wine that originated from the 'world of space' as is mentioned in part I experience transubstantiation. Having been transformed through the forces of the First Hierarchy, these substances are received by the members of the congregation into their metabolic (and limb) system, in order, through the effects of these transformed substances, subsequently to form the basis in the physical organism of man for its spiritualization.

The Christ is present directly in this process, for His body and His blood (the Phantom and the condensed etheric body of the Resurrected One) participate in it. He works in this process through the forces of the Father-God 'in depths of worlds, begetting life', which means generating *new substance* or *being* during the transubstantiation at the altar.

The second part of the meditation mentions the ringing forth of the Sun-Word. Its cosmic sounding is linked with the movement of the Sun from East to West:

Let there be fired from the East
What through the West is formed.

These lines become audible through the Second Hierarchy, the Sun-Hierarchy or 'Spirits of Light' in the universe. Furthermore the activity of the Christ is indicated in the meditation which, similar to the activity of the Sun in the encircling round of the twelve parts of the zodiac, holds sway 'shedding grace upon souls' [or: blessing the Soul] even in the social environs (in the circle of the community):

For the Christ-Will in the encircling Round holds sway
In the Rhythms of Worlds, blessing the Soul.

These lines particularly clearly characterize the nature of the Offering Service where the Christ-Sun works exclusively through the Word shedding grace upon [or blessing] the souls of the participants.

In contrast to the sacramental communion that enters through the substances of bread and wine into the world of space, the Offering Service takes its course completely in the element of time. Just as the human word originates out of the confluence with the 'beat of heart and lung', the 'rhythmic tides of time' referred to in part II form the basis of the Offering Service. For the word works through its rhythms in the universe (' In the Rhythms of Worlds, blessing the soul.').

The lines of part III of the meditation:

> Let there be prayed in the Depths
> What from the Heights is answered,

point to the nature of spiritual communion which, like the modern path of initiation and the 'reverse' cultus,[232] is connected with the conscious ascent of man into the spiritual world; meaning above all with the ascent into the sphere of the Third Hierarchy or the 'spirits of soul'. This takes place in the direction of below to above. Rudolf Steiner said about this: 'One would like to say if one wishes to speak pictorially: The cultic gathering attempts to induce the Angels of heaven to come down into the cultic location so that they may be among humans. The anthroposophical congregation tries to lift human souls up into the supersensible world so that they may be among Angels. This is the community-building element in both.' (GA 257, 3 March 1923)

One could moreover say: Rising to the sphere of the Angels occurs here on the path that leads from earthly thoughts to the 'Spirit's Universal Thoughts', whose perceiving represents the first stage of spiritual communion. Rudolf Steiner described this as follows: 'Becoming aware of the idea in reality is the true communion of man'. (GA 1) This Imaginative stage of spiritual communion[233] is followed by its Inspirative[234] and then its highest Intuitive one that Rudolf Steiner attained at the end of the nineteenth century. He described the latter in the above-quoted words as 'spiritually having stood before the Mystery of Golgotha'.[235]

The path of inner communion that leads from spiritual perception of ideas to the supersensible experiencing of the Mystery of Golgotha furthermore stands in a direct relationship to the activity of the beings of the Third Hierarchy. In a lecture on 18 December 1913, (GA 148) Rudolf Steiner described the three main levels of spiritual research. The first is connected with the process where man experiences that he is thought by the Angels. On the second level, man observes that his life forces belong to the Archangels; and on the third one he becomes aware that spiritually he is 'consumed' and 'digested' by the Archai. These stages that Rudolf Steiner mentions in connection with his research on the Fifth Gospel—meaning, with the telluric-cosmic Christ-Mystery—are likewise three sequential states *of communion* with the consciousness of Angels, Archangels, and Archai that the human being experiences as a consequence of inner development on the Imaginative, Inspirative, and Intuitive level of higher knowledge.

Here, the communion that is attained through pure *thinking* (or supersensible 'perception of ideas') is a participation in the supersensible consciousness of the Angels; the perception of how one's own life takes part in the supersensible life of the Archangels leads to communion with their cosmic consciousness. Here the element of the *Word* gains special significance,[236] whose spiritual substance serves on this level as mediator for spiritual communion. Ultimately the highest form of communion, participation in the consciousness of the Archai, comes about when the initiate experiences the content of his soul as *nourishment* of these lofty spirits. Inasmuch as he participates in this supersensible 'process of digestion', the initiate reaches the highest Intuitive form, the way this is the case in sacramental communion, albeit in a different manner.[237]

In the Foundation Stone Meditation, Rudolf Steiner calls the spirits of the Third Hierarchy 'Spirits of Soul' and in so doing emphasizes their intimate affinity to the human soul.[238] The above points specifically to this relation. To the extent that the modern initiate becomes aware of this affinity, it turns for him into spiritual communion with these spirits' consciousness and thereby likewise with the cosmic consciousness of the Christ. For the spirits of the Third Hierarchy who participate in the process of spiritual communion are likewise those spirits who during the first, second, and third post-Atlantean cultural periods received the Christ into themselves and therefore serve today as mediators between Him and humanity.[239]

The comparison between the three forms of communion can furthermore be carried out by proceeding from the microcosmic segments of the meditation. Thus the sacramental communion, the foundation of which is represented by the transubstantiation of bread and wine, dates back spiritually and historically to the Last Supper at the Turning-point of Time and to the words by Christ: 'Do this in remembrance of me.' (Lk. 22, 19) In the Foundation Stone Meditation, this corresponds to the process of 'Practise Spirit-recollection'. This recollection guides the soul to experience the founts of the human 'I'; to its 'taking on being' out of God's 'I', the Creative Primal Foundation of the World.

> Where in the wielding
> World-Creator Being
> Thine own I
> Comes to being
> Within the I of God.

These words refer to the primal condition of World evolution when spiritual existence still had full power over material existence, something that in our time is the case only in the forming of human karma[240] and during transubstantiation. This is why, when receiving the transformed substances into his physical body, the communicant comes into contact with the primal condition of the world or with the 'Spirit's ocean-being' but now without losing his individual being in it.

The last words of this segment of the Foundation Stone Meditation point to that primal condition of the world that a human being can inwardly experience today:

> Then in the All-World Being of Man
> Thou wilt truly *live*.

And this 'living' as 'All-World Being' is what is revealed to man through true communion of the body and the blood of the Resurrected One.

In the ritual of the Offering Service where communion is carried out completely in the word-element without descending into the depths of matter, we have a kind of 'Spirit-pondering' of the spiritual world-being. This is why this ritual was given for young people between the ages of fifteen and eighteen in the Waldorf School, for they find themselves after puberty in a state of intense development of the intellectual thinking faculties, faculties that are supposed to be given the right direction through receiving the mantric words of this ritual.

Seen in this way the words of the meditation, 'Practise Spirit-pondering', can be viewed as referring to how the ritual of the Offering Service affects the soul, a ritual that arouses 'the feeling' of one's 'own Soul-being' in young people. It is a feeling that must be attained particularly at this age. If in addition one takes note that during this period the developmental process of the young person's 'I' (which is completed in the twenty-first year of life) is experienced with special intensity, the ensuing words of the meditation point quite clearly to the link of their second part to this ritual:

> Where the surging
> Deeds of the World's Becoming
> Do thine own I
> Unite
> Unto the I of the World.

These lines characterize the nature of the human ego's communion with the World-'I' of the Christ *through the Word,* the Word that fills the whole spiritual world with its creative sounds, and with that brings forth the 'surging Deeds of the World's Becoming' in that world. The young person, who at that age steps out into the world for the first time encounters the earthly replica of these 'surging Deeds' with full awareness, the very reason why just at this particular time he is in need of a strengthening of his own 'I' through the forces of the Christ's World-'I'. And when this takes place with the help of the ritual of the Offering Service he moves out into the world inwardly prepared for his task on Earth.

The Foundation Stone Meditation points to this ideal with the concluding words of the second part:

> Then 'mid the weaving of the Soul of Man
> Thou wilt truly *feel.*

This is what a young person between the ages of fifteen and twenty-one needs the most, and for that reason it is so important to participate in this Offering Service.

Now modern initiation leads to conscious 'Spirit-vision'. Here spiritual communion represents an inalienable part of such initiation.[241] In contrast to the other two forms of communion, it is by its very nature linked neither to space nor time. Taking place in the holiest of holy of the soul, it emerges 'out of eternal foundations'. Spiritual communion will therefore endure even when, due to the spiritualization of the whole cosmos, neither time nor space will any longer exist. (See GA 131, 13 October 1911)

The starting point of spiritual communion is the process of intense meditation to which the following words of the meditation point in the Foundation Stone:

> Practise Spirit-vision
> In quietness of Thought.

Such a meditation leads the spirit-disciple increasingly to a conscious perception of the '*eternal* aims of Gods' (meaning independently of space and time) and to co-operation with the gods in the realization of these aims.

> World-Being's Light
> On thine own I
> Bestow
> For thy free Willing.

In accordance with the Foundation Stone Meditation, the term 'gods' must be understood to refer chiefly to the beings of the Third Hierarchy and among them to Michael who works in our period as Time Spirit (Archē). Rudolf Steiner called him the 'spiritual champion of freedom', (GA 233a, 13 January 1924) because he is the one who (of all the entities of the Third Hierarchy) adjudicates full freedom to the human being, to the highest degree, which is why this key-word [free] is found in the third part. For the principle of freedom forms the unshakeable basis of the modern path of initiation, and this means, of the spiritual communion connected with it. The whole of this part of the meditation is summed up in the words:

> Then from the ground of the Spirit of Man
> Thou wilt truly *think*.

In this 'ground of the spirit' the true spiritual communion takes place that guides the human being to the 'eternal aims of Gods' whose archetype appeared in the Mystery of Golgotha on the Earth.

In a personal conversation with Marie Steiner, Rudolf Steiner once remarked that the Second (and according to another version likewise the Third) Class of the School of Spiritual Science were to have a ritual character.[242] In this case there would not only be three types of communion but moreover *three* forms with the rituals connected to them: The ritual of the Act of Consecration of Man, the ritual of the Offering Service, and the completely new ritual of the Michael School, which would lead the spirit-disciple to spiritual communion. Although the spiritual communion can be attained in a completely inner manner and with no contact whatever with the outer world, a ritual that has originated on such a basis could as a result of spiritual communion make possible a much more concentrated activity in the social life of men as well as in the spiritualization process of the forces of nature.

Rudolf Steiner could give mankind all three forms of the communion only owing to the fact that he himself reached this highest form of communion with the Christ Being in Intuition and as a result of it received into his 'I' a replica of the Christ 'I'.[243] But with that he likewise attained the ability to maintain his individual ego-consciousness during his spiritual researches on all levels of supersensible existence even to the cosmic midnight hour.

Accordingly, Rudolf Steiner was the *first* initiate who was in a position to trace the *entire* path of the soul through the spiritual world between two incarnations in *full consciousness*, which means, to the height of the cosmic midnight hour and from there back to the new life on Earth. Out of this fully aware experience of the forces of the cosmic midnight hour, Rudolf Steiner could then guide these forces to the Earth and with their aid establish the three forms of communion. For in true communion the forces of the cosmic midnight hour always hold sway. Without their presence communion would be impossible.

Making use of a comparison, one can say: Just as the first three parts of the Foundation Stone Meditation emerge according to their inner substance out of its fourth part in the centre of which radiates the spiritual Christ-Sun, so the three kinds of communion could be established on Earth by Rudolf Steiner only because his soul had united in its actual being [Ger.: wesenhaft] with the Christ-Sun. And this is something that opens up access to conscious experience and activity with the forces of the cosmic midnight hour.[244]

In conclusion it must be emphasized that each of the three parts of the meditation, whose common source is the fourth part, is connected with *all three* forms of communion. The only difference is that in sacramental communion those spiritual forces that are described in part I emerge more clearly because in their centre stands the transubstantiation of earthly substances. In the Offering Service, the spiritual forces described in part II hold sway inasmuch as communion forms its centre through the Word as the original creator principle of the Son or the Christ. And in spiritual communion, an inalienable segment of modern Christian initiation, the forces hold sway that are described in part III. This communion is attained on the path that leads from earthly thought to the 'Spirit's Thoughts of Worlds' that unveil to the human being the nature of the Mystery of Golgotha through spiritual participation in it 'in most inward, most earnest *joy of knowledge*'.

Foundation Stone Meditation

(I, 1)   Soul of Man!
Thou livest in the Limbs
Which bear thee through the world of Space
Into the ocean-being of the Spirit.
Practise *Spirit-recollection*
In depths of soul,
Where in the wielding
World-Creator-Being
Thine own I
Comes to being
Within the I of God
Then in the All-World-Being of Man
Thou wilt truly *live*.

(I, 2)   For the Father-Spirit of the Heights holds sway
In Depths of Worlds, begetting Being.
Seraphim, Cherubim, Thrones!
(Spirits of Strength!)
Let there ring out from the Heights
What in the Depths is echoed,
Speaking:
Ex Deo nascimur.
(From God, Mankind has Being.)
The Elemental Spirits hear it
In East and West and North and South:
May human beings hear it!

(II, 1)   Soul of man!
Thou livest in the beat of Heart and Lung
Which leads thee through the rhythmic tides of Time
Into the feeling of thine own Soul-being.
Practise *Spirit-pondering*
In balance of the soul,
Where the surging
Deeds of the World's Becoming
Do thine own I
Unite
Unto the I of the World.
Then 'mid the weaving of the Soul of Man
Thou wilt truly *feel*.

(*II, 2*)   For the Christ-Will in the encircling Round holds sway
In the Rhythms of Worlds, blessing the Soul.
Kyriotetes, Dynamis, Exusiai!
(Spirits of Light!)
Let there be fired from the East
What through the West is formed,
Speaking:
In Christo morimur.
(In Christ, Death becomes Life.)
The Elemental Spirits hear it
In East and West and North and South:
May human beings hear it!

(*III, 1*)   Soul of Man!
Thou livest in the resting Head
Which from the ground of the Eternal
Opens to thee the Thoughts of Worlds.
Practise *Spirit-vision*
In quietness of Thought,
Where the eternal aims of Gods
World-Being's Light
On thine own I
Bestow
For thy free Willing.
Then from the ground of the Spirit of Man
Thou wilt truly *think*.

(*III, 2*)   For the Spirit's Universal Thoughts hold sway
In the Being of all Worlds, beseeching Light.
Archai, Archangeloi, Angeloi!
(Spirits of Soul!)
Let there be prayed in the Depths
What from the Heights is answered,
Speaking:
Per Spiritum Sanctum reviviscimus.
(In the Spirit's Universal Thoughts, the Soul awakens.)
The Elemental Spirits hear it
In East and West and North and South:
May human beings hear it!

(*IV, 1*)   At the Turning-point of Time
The Spirit-Light of the World
Entered the stream of Earthly Being.
Darkness of Night

Had held its sway;
Day-radiant Light
Poured into the souls of men:
Light
That gives warmth
To simple Shepherds' Hearts,
Light
That enlightens
The wise Heads of Kings.

(*IV, 2*)   O Light Divine,
O Sun of Christ!
Warm Thou
Our Hearts,
Enlighten Thou
Our Heads,
That good may become
What from our Hearts we would found
And from our Heads direct
With single purpose.

Notes

Titles by Rudolf Steiner are here identified by GA number. See list following these Notes.

1 See more on this three-way metamorphosis that is at the basis of the whole development of Anthroposophy on earth in S. O. Prokofieff, *May Human Beings Hear It! The Mystery of the Christmas Conference,* Chapter 'The Philosophy of Freedom and the Christmas Conference'.

2 See also GA 103, 31 August 1908.

3 Inasmuch as Rudolf Steiner gave the fourth part of the meditation the form of a prayer, he likewise pointed to the beginning of the renewal of the religious domain.

4 The transmission of spiritual contents through art is an exception here.

5 See more details concerning this process in S. O. Prokofieff, *The Heavenly Sophia and the Living Being Anthroposophia,* Part I.

6 See GA 231, conclusion of the lecture on 18 November 1923.

7 See the description of the Foundation Stone Laying in *May Human Beings Hear It,* Chapter 'The Rhythms of the Christmas Conference'.

8 What is meant here is the physical world of the body, the soul world and the 'spirit land' as described in GA 9.

9 It goes without saying that the forces of the Trinity (as well as the entities of the various hierarchies ministering to them) are constantly working actively in man and the cosmos. Here, however, we are only considering *that aspect* of their activity that is depicted in the Foundation Stone Meditation.

10 Since there existed as yet no space in the contemporary sense on Ancient Saturn, what is being said here is merely an attempt to describe something in earthly language that by its very nature cannot be described in words.

11 When Rudolf Steiner employs the word 'spherical space' (i.e. 'Kugelraum') here, he emphasizes that we are not dealing with spatial, only spiritual processes.

12 Later on, to the First Hierarchy's activity is added that of the Second Hierarchy, of the Kyriotetes, Dynamis, and Exusiai, as well as that of the Spirits of Personality (Archai) who pass through their 'human stage' on Ancient Saturn. The *original impulse* that leads to the beginning of the new cosmic system does not originate from them, only from the spirits of the First Hierarchy. On the Ancient Sun, the Archangels join in this mutual activity of the hierarchies; on the Ancient Moon, the Angels.

13 In so doing, the first two categories of the spirits of the First Hierarchy, the Seraphim and Cherubim, participate in the new cosmic system's process of evolving in full freedom, for they do not require it for their own

development, whereas the Thrones follow the law of necessity in their creative actions, because it is only through their offering that they can reach the next-higher stage of evolution. (see GA 11) This difference likewise applies to the subsequent stages that are yet to be described.

14   During the transition from one planetary system to the next, one can likewise speak of the coming into being of a new solar system, since each condition of existence (Manvantara) is preceded by a purely spiritual condition (Pralaya).

15   See GA 102, 29 February 1908, and GA 13.

16   For in their totality they are creators of the Earth aeon.

17   See details of the cosmic path of the Christ to the Earth in S. O. Prokofieff, *The Twelve Holy Nights and the Spiritual Hierarchies,* Part I, Chapter. 2.

18   See more details in *The Heavenly Sophia and the Being Anthroposophia*, Part II.

19   See Note 18.

20   In GA 11, Part II, Chapter 3, Steiner describes that *five* cosmic conditions will still follow after Vulcan. Together with the preceding seven they will form a 'twelve-hood' of the World-cycle.

21   Details about the effects and working of the warmth and light of the 'Christ-Sun' see *May Human Beings Hear It!*, Chapters 'The Mystery Act of the Foundation Stone Laying on 25 December 1923, and '*The Philosophy of Freedom,* and the Christmas Conference'.

22   What a student of the spirit is able to experience today merely in quite elementary form is experienced by an initiate, who has reached the level of a Bodhisattva, in complete form. 'In linguistic usage of Mid-Eastern languages one would have said of an entity such as a Bodhisattva, who had incarnated on the Earth: This being is filled with the Holy Spirit.' (GA 114, 20 September 1909) (In the original German Rudolf Steiner uses the phrase 'vorder-asiatische Sprachen'. By this he is probably referring to the languages of the earliest Christian communities based around the Asiatic shores of the Mediterranean sea.)

23   The fact that the principle of Beauty is connected with the Sophia-entity is indicated already in the Old Testament where she is called an 'artist' beside God (Pr 8,30 according to the Russian Bible, or 'master workman' in English [RSV]) as well as in her iconography. In the Russian iconographic tradition, for example, she is frequently pictured in the form of an enthroned Angel with a fiery (red) countenance (in the Russian language 'beautiful' and 'red' have the same root), around her the star-strewn heavens as the image of *beauty* of the cosmic structure, and above her, blessing her, Christ within a solar disk of the Sun representing the highest leader of the Second Hierarchy.

24   That this primeval 'coming into being in the "I" of God' is followed by separation from Him—God bestows independence on His creation—is made clear through the corresponding lines of the meditation where

mention is made of the 'uniting' of man's own 'I' with the 'I of the World'—something that assumes a separation that preceded this union.

25 The German verb 'erwesen' ['coming into being'] is antiquated but was adopted anew by Rudolf Steiner and signifies something like 'to be present as a living force'.

26 Mk 10, 18; Lk 18, 19. Quoted as translated into German by Rudolf Steiner in GA 266/I, 30 August 1909.

27 See GA 239, 14 June 1924. This is why the first indication of awakening from sleep is an impulsive movement of the limbs. For this reason one was aware in the Middle Ages that the soul (astral body and 'I') departs the body after death through the mouth. See also Faust's death-scene in Goethe's *Faust*.

28 In GA 243, 13 August 1924, Rudolf Steiner mentioned that of all organs of man it is above all the heart that turns the human being in full measure into an earthly being. It was into this place that the Foundation Stone was laid.

29 See a more detailed description of this process in *May Human Beings Hear It!*, Chapter 'The Foundation Stone Meditation. Karma and Resurrection'.

30 In the course of the decline of the Mysteries in the era of ancient Greece and partly as early as in ancient Egypt, the perception of the Sun-entity of the Christ through the figure of Osiris or Apollo became increasingly weaker and indistinct. Only in the Zarathustra-Mysteries, the Christ was still experienced in all the radiance and purity of the Sun sphere.

31 See more details on this in the next chapter.

32 Concerning the appearance of this Spirit at the Christmas Conference in the light-aura of the Foundation Stone, see *May Human Beings Hear It!*, Chapter 'The Mystery Act of the Foundation Stone Laying on 25 December, 1923'.

33 This is moreover the reason why Goethe's *Fairy Tale*, into which (according to Rudolf Steiner's statement) something of the substance of the Imaginative cultus has flowed in 'miniature' pictures (GA 240, 19 July 1924), begins with the appearance of two elemental spirits (will-o'-the-wisps).

34 Among the events connected with this category of karma belong for instance, incurable diseases, accidents, and so on. But this is only the case when the karmic reasons for such events are based on an individual's own karma and not on the karma of the age or of other human beings with whom this person experiences a catastrophe of nature, for example.

35 Changes of karma are possible in this dimension only out of the forces of the First Hierarchy that work out of the heights of the Cosmic Midnight, meaning in so far as the physical world is concerned, out of the other side of world existence (see more on this in *May Human Beings Hear It!*, Chapter 'The Foundation Stone Meditation. Karma and Resurrection'.

36 See more on this process in S. O. Prokofieff *Eternal Individuality. Towards a*

Karmic Biography of Novalis, Chapter 'Representative of Humanity's Conscience'.

37   Concerning the past earth lives (the life between death and a new birth included) as basis of our *existence* during the present incarnation see, for example, GA 26, Chapter 'The Freedom of Man and the Michael Age'.

38   In this connection, Rudolf Steiner spoke of the human being who has reached the high point of his development as 'the religion of the gods' (hierarchies) in the supersensible world (see *May Human Beings Hear It!*, Chapter 'The Foundation Stone Meditation. Karma and Resurrection'; also further on in this work).

39   In the fate of Michael's Cosmic Intelligence that he originally guided out of the Sun sphere and which, following the Mystery of Golgotha, gradually turned into man's earthly intelligence and which must be given back to Michael by degrees with the beginning of his new epoch in the year 1879 in a transformed structure, we have a primal archetype of this process.

39a   In this connection, the Foundation Stone of the Christmas Conference whose light aura consists of 'cosmic-human-thoughts' assumes quite special importance. Implanted in the ground of the human heart, it can serve as mediator between human thoughts that have been spiritualized through the active interest in spiritual science and the cosmic thoughts of the hierarchies, meaning the cosmic thoughts living in the astral light.

40   See more in *May Human Beings Hear It!*, Chapter 'The Foundation Stone Meditation, Karma and Resurrection'.

41   In the lecture of 23 July 1922 (GA 214), Rudolf Steiner mentioned that such 'chosen living dead' are guardians of the Holy Grail in the spiritual world.

42   See for example the role of iron necessity or fate in the ancient Greek culture. The division into castes in ancient India, as well as the power of the Pharaohs and so on, comes from the same source.

42a   See more detail in *May Human Beings Hear It!*, Chapter 'The Foundation Stone Meditation in Eurythmy'.

43   See for example the lecture of 25 June 1908 (GA 104). This is moreover why Rudolf Steiner wrote in GA 13: 'The fifth and the sixth eras (cultural periods) are as it were the decisive ones.'

44   This refers to the Great Sixth Epoch. In 1904 Rudolf Steiner still employed the theosophical terminology that the majority of his listeners were accustomed to, but which he later discontinued in accordance with the ongoing development of Anthroposophy.

45   For the concrete form that the call of this Master in particular can assume, see for instance the lecture of 28 September 1911 (GA 130).

46   See more details on the path of the Christ to the Earth through the various spheres of the macrocosm in *The Twelve Holy Nights and the Spiritual Hierarchies*, Part I, Chapter 2.

47   In this connection, see GA 240, 19 July and 7 August 1924.

48   GA 99, 22 May, 1907. A still more obvious utterance by Rudolf Steiner is contained in a set of notes by Marie Steiner. There it says: '*The Fairy Tale* by Goethe represents the *alchemistic initiation* of the form inaugurated by Christian Rosenkreutz.' (GA 93, emphasis in the original) This is moreover why Rudolf Steiner in his first Mystery Drama, *The Portal of Initiation*, which was based on Goethe's *Fairy Tale*, gave it the subtitle 'A Rosicrucian Mystery'. (GA 14)

49   In GA 240, 19 July 1924, Rudolf Steiner spoke of the fact that something of the substance of the Imaginative cultus was represented in the Fairy Tale as if in 'miniature pictures'.

50   Concerning these two encounters, see more in *May Human Beings Hear It!*, Chapter 'Rudolf Steiner's Course of Life in the Light of the Christmas Conference', and in S. O. Prokofieff, *Rudolf Steiner and the Founding of the New Mysteries*, Chapters 1 and 2.

51   In the first esoteric lesson that was given soon after the separation of the two schools, Rudolf Steiner said: 'Our Western school is headed by two masters: the Master Jesus and the Master Christian Rosenkreutz.' (GA 266/I, 1 June 1907)

51a In this connection it is of particular significance that during Christian Rosenkreutz's initiation in the thirteenth century, the twelve sages who carried out this initiation entrusted to him the entirety of the Mystery wisdom of Atlantean and post-Atlantean times, a wisdom that was then supposed to serve in a form that was transmuted by the Christ as the foundation for the new Christianity. (see GA 130, 27 September 1911) Something comparable occurred later (but then in a cosmic sense) in Michael's supersensory school, when he initially revealed to his pupils the secret of the pre-Christian Mysteries of antiquity and subsequently made known to them the path of their transformation based on the Mystery of Golgotha so that the *new Christianity* might be established on earth. (see GA 240) This is how the two streams are prepared from two directions, the earthly and the cosmic one, for their union on earth in the New Mysteries.

52   The sequence of events speaks for itself. It was not until after the separation from the Eastern esoteric school that Rudolf Steiner spoke of the Michael Mystery during the esoteric lessons; and only after the separation from the Theosophical Society did he speak of it in lectures for the members.

53   This attempt was given up as a result of the betrayal by a member of the group. See more on this in GA 264.

54   The choice of London as the first location for a lecture on this theme had special significance since the easterly traditions of Theosophy were particularly strong there. It was here in London in the final years of her life that H. P. Blavatsky founded this school of eastern orientation (1888). It was called initially 'Esoteric School of Theosophy' and since 1889 'Eastern School of Theosophy'. Blavatsky died in London in 1891.

55   The beginning of its proclamation through Rudolf Steiner occurred in the year 1910. See in more detail at the end of the chapter.

56   See a description of these processes in GA 130, 28 September 1911 and their connection with the Foundation Stone Meditation in F. W. Zeylmans van Emmichoven, *The Foundation Stone*, Rudolf Steiner Press 1963, Chapter 'From the Stone of the Wise to the Stone of Love'.

57   For more details on this see *May Human Beings Hear It!*, Chapter 'The Mystery Act of the Foundation Stone Laying on 25 December 1923'.

57a If we consider that the Cosmic Intelligence has come out of Michael's Sun sphere to Earth in order to form the basis for a free and independent thinking in human souls (see also Chapter 10), so that a new comprehension of the Mystery of Golgotha becomes possible, one can say that the faculty for such a spiritual comprehension comes from Michael, whereas its [the Cosmic Intelligence's] turning towards a new understanding of the Mystery of Golgotha emerged out of the Rosicrucian stream. Here too, therefore, exists full and harmonious co-operation between these two streams within Anthroposophy.

58   In the early esoteric lessons (see for instance in GA 266/2), Rudolf Steiner referred more than once to the fact that the beginning of the union of the two Mystery streams (in which the initiates of the first one, Shepherds' path, sought the connection with the spiritual world through contemplation into the depths of their own soul, and the others, on the path of the Kings or Magi, through the union with the macrocosm) took place in Rosicrucianism. Concerning the Mystery streams of the Shepherds and Kings as the prototypes of the two main karmic groups within the Anthroposophical Society, see Hans-Peter van Manen, *Twin Roads to the New Millennium*, Rudolf Steiner Press, London 1988.

59   In the lecture on the etherization of the blood (GA 130, 1 October 1911) Rudolf Steiner spoke of *two* etherized blood streams of man: A microcosmic one streaming from the heart to the head and from there into the cosmos (in the context of this reflection we could call it the Rosicrucian one), and a macrocosmic one that enters man out of the cosmos and flows through the head into the heart (this one we could here call the Michaelic one).

60   In the course of the same month (September 1924) he points to the union of the two streams in the so-called 'Recapitulation Lessons' of the First Class of the Michael School with the cultic conclusion of these lessons.

60a At the end of the final lecture of the large karmic cycle consisting of 81 lectures, Rudolf Steiner spoke about a rounding off of those lectures. (GA 238, 23 September, 1924)

61   Their foundations had been worked out by Rudolf Steiner in the second spiritual section of his first esoteric school which existed from 1904 to 1914.

62   Rudolf Steiner touched for the last time on the theme of the union of the two streams in the article he wrote on 6 December 1924 under the title

'Hindrances and Advancements of the Michael Forces in the Upcoming Age of the Consciousness Soul'. (GA 26)

63   See more on the connection of the Foundation Stone and the Holy Grail in *Rudolf Steiner and the Founding of the New Mysteries*.

64   See more on this in F. W. Zeylmans van Emmichoven *The Foundation Stone*, op.cit., Chapter 'From the Stone of the Wise [Philosopher's Stone] to the Stone of Love'.

65   Margarete and Erich Kirchner-Bockholt *Rudolf Steiner's Mission and Ita Wegman*, Rudolf Steiner Press, London 1977.

65a In many earlier lectures, Rudolf Steiner kept pointing out that, in this book as well as later in *Occult Science, an Outline,* the modern form of the Rosicrucian path of initiation is being described (see for instance GA 97, 30 November 1906).

65b About this metamorphosis see Zeylmans van Emmichoven *The Foundation Stone*, Chapter 'From the Stone of the Wise [Philosopher's Stone] to the Stone of Love'; also *May Human Beings Hear It!*, Chapter 'The Mystery Act of the Foundation Stone Laying on 25 December 1923'. It is moreover no coincidence that in the lecture of 23 December 1923 in GA 232, just two days prior to the creation of the Foundation Stone, Rudolf Steiner spoke in detail of the Mysteries of the medieval Rosicrucians and the Philosopher's Stone.

66   See details in *May Human Beings Hear It!,* Chapter 'The Mystery Act of the Foundation Stone Laying on 25 December 1923'.

67   See more in *May Human Beings Hear It!,* Chapters 'The Mystery Act of the Foundation Stone Laying on 25 December 1923' and 'The Anthroposophical Society as the Temple of the New Mysteries', and also Chapter 7 of this work.

68   Concerning further aspects of Michael's relationship to the esoteric nature of the Christmas Conference, see *May Human Beings Hear It!*, Chapter 'The Mystery Act of the Foundation Stone Laying on 25 December 1923'.

69   The first Class Lesson of the School of Spiritual Science begins with the student's encounter of the Guardian of the Threshold who, starting from then on, becomes his or her spiritual guide.

70   In the esoteric schools of the Rosicrucians, a special place was assigned to the one actual example of reincarnation in the gospels, namely the reincarnation of the Prophet Elijah as John the Baptist. The Rosicrucians preserved this knowledge into later times. This is moreover why at times they were called 'Johannine Christians'. (GA 112, 24 June 1909) In artistic form this secret was referred to in the presentation of the first scene of the third Mystery Drama, *The Guardian of the Threshold*. (See GA 14) Furthermore, knowledge concerning reincarnation penetrated from the Rosicrucian Inspirations into middle-European culture of the eighteenth and nineteenth century. We encounter this thought in Lessing, Goethe, Novalis, Widenmann and Drossbach, as well as in many other central

European writers and thinkers (see GA 130, 27 September 1911), likewise in Emil Bock *Wiederholte Erdenleben. Der Gedanke der Wiederverkörperung in der deutschen Geistesgeschichte* (Repeated earth lives. The idea of reincarnation in German cultural history), Stuttgart 1996.

71   See more on the circle of the twelve Bodhisattvas in the sphere of Providence or the Buddhi in the lectures of 31 August 1909 (GA 113) and 25 October 1909 (GA 116).

72   That the Rosicrucians as the leading western occultists not only preserved the knowledge of reincarnation but likewise of karma is confirmed by the fact that when mentioning to anthroposophists that the Christ was becoming the Lord of Karma, Rudolf Steiner pointed out at the same time that this secret has been 'a common insight of occidental occultism for centuries' and that in our age has merely been 'confirmed once again' through spiritual scientific research. (GA 131, 7 October 1910)

73   See lectures in GA 237 and GA 240.

73a This is furthermore why the teaching of the Arabian philosophers is not wrong on principle, but only in the sense that they do not reckon with the new condition in the world that has arisen through the Mystery of Golgotha which they did not acknowledge. For without a relationship to the Mystery of Golgotha in after-death existence, there can only be two forms of consciousness: A supra-bright one that does not belong, however, to the human individuality (an experience known to Arabian philosophers and Eastern mystics who had reached the stage of Samadhi), or an individual 'I' consciousness in a merely shadowy form, the way the ancient Greeks experienced it.

74   See more in *May Human Beings Hear It!*, Chapter 'The Foundation Stone Meditation. Karma and Resurrection'.

75   See GA 224, 7 May 1923.

76   See more in *May Human Beings Hear It!*, Chapters 'The Mystery Act of the Foundation Stone Laying on 25 December 1923' and 'The Anthroposophical Society as the Temple of the New Mysteries'.

77   Rudolf Steiner once referred to this most important task of the modern spirit-stream (Anthroposophy) in the following words: 'It is part of the inner mission of the spiritual world-stream (Anthroposophy) to prepare mankind to cause their soul elements to mature to such an extent that ever greater numbers of human beings can receive a replica of the "I"-being of Christ Jesus into themselves.' (GA 109/111, 7 March 1909) And continuing: 'Those who understand the actual, true inner reality of the spiritual scientific world-stream (for this is its true inner spiritual reality), prepare themselves not merely for a knowledge but for an actual fact [the taking in of a replica of the Christ-"I"].' (ibid) From the standpoint of Rudolf Steiner's teaching concerning the threefold 'I'—the ordinary (or lower) 'I', the higher (or other) 'I' and, finally the true 'I'—(see for this GA 17), one can say that initiation bestows on man the possibility to become

fully conscious of his higher 'I', the 'I' that passes through all of his earth lives. On the other hand, the conscious experience of the true 'I', the source of the divine power in man, only becomes possible to the initiate by receiving the forces of the Christ's Phantom into himself. (See more details in *May Human Beings Hear It!*, Chapter 'The Foundation Stone Meditation in Eurythmy'.)

78   In the given context, the word 'will' points to the inner essence of the Phantom that in its original form was created as the basis for the later physical body of man on Ancient Saturn by the Spirits of Will out of their own being, meaning out of the spiritual substance of will.

79   See more in GA 112, 6 July 1909, as well as in S. O. Prokofieff *The Cycle of the Year as a Path of Initiation*.

80   See GA 233a, 13 January 1924.

81   In the opening lecture at the Christmas Conference Rudolf Steiner referred to this new Michael revelation: 'And with this I would like to call attention at the very beginning of our conference to the fact that it was indeed the last third of the nineteenth century when, on the one side, the waves of materialism rose up high and where, into this surge of materialism, there struck down from the other side of the world a magnificent revelation, a revelation of something spiritual that someone who has a receptive heart and mind can receive from powers of spirit-life. There opened up for humanity the revelation of a spiritual element.' (GA 260, 24 December 1923) This is why, from the beginning of his activity as a spiritual teacher, Rudolf Steiner spoke of the spiritual research-projects carried out by him (Rosicrucian principle) as well as the spiritual *revelations* received by him (Michaelic principle).

82   See more in *May Human Beings Hear It!*, Chapter 'The Rhythms of the Christmas Conference' in the passage on the sixth rhythm of the Foundation Stone Meditation.

83   In the lectures dealing with the etheric return of the Christ, Rudolf Steiner pointed out more than once that this, His *first* supersensible revelation, will spread among humankind in the course of the next three millennia. During that time two reigns of Michael will take place, the present one and one in the future. One can surmise from this: If the *beginning* of the Second Coming takes place in the present epoch, then up until the next epoch (approximately in the years 4100 to 4500) its *culmination* will have to be attained.

84   See more on this in *May Human Beings Hear It!*, Chapter 'The Anthroposophical Society as the Temple of the New Mysteries'.

Tr.1 Struggling to render the German translation of the Russian text as precisely as possible into English here and in Chapter 9 of this book, the German words 'Ebenbild' and 'Gleichnis' presented a problem. I researched German and English Bible translations that were available to me. Martin Luther's German version has neither *Ebenbild* nor *Gleichnis*, only *Bild* (image or picture) and *uns gleich*, (like us), hence translated literally in English: Let us make men, an *image* that may be *like us.*'

The Oxford Annotated Bible (Revised Standard Edition) has, 'And God said: 'Let us create man after our *image*, after our *likeness*'.'

King James Translation: 'Let us make man in our *image*, after our *likeness*.'

James Moffat Translation: 'Let us make man in our own *likeness*, to *resemble* us.'

The voluminous German/English Langenscheidt dictionary has *image* or *picture* for *Ebenbild literally* meaning 'image on same level' or 'exact image'. The second one, '*Gleichnis*', means 'simile', 'parable; or literally: 'the state of being alike'.Obviously the words *image* and *likeness* convey *two* slightly different meanings that have been obliterated through the millennia from what they originally were meant to convey. None of the conventional translations are wrong but all human languages have participated in the Fall. Since the text of *Genesis* first existed in Hebrew, I turned for clarification to the local Rabbi. The first word in Hebrew [translation of *image* or likeness] is *b'tzaumenu* and its root in Hebrew is *tzelem*; the second word in Hebrew [transl. *likeness* or, from the Russian, *parable*] is *kidmudome* and its root word is *domeh*, meaning *similar*. When I explained what the Russian Bible has in Gen 1, 26, the Rabbi agreed that *Ebenbild's* meaning in Hebrew is closer to 'exact image' than 'image', and that *Gleichnis* in Hebrew is not so much likeness, image, but *simile* or *allegory*. So the Russian *is indeed* closer to the original Hebrew, but the *precise* meaning of the two words can only be sensed when considered with the aid of spiritual science.

85   See more on this in *Rudolf Steiner and the Founding of the New Mysteries*, Chapter 'The Great Sun Period', and in *May Human Beings Hear It!* Chapter 'Rudolf Steiner's Course of Life in the Light of the Christmas Conference'.

86   See GA 109/111.

87   Formal joining of the Anthroposophical Society does not at once imply joining the Anthroposophical Society of the Christmas Conference. This is the case only when the inner work on the latter begins.

88   See Chapter 6.

89   Article 'Gnosis und Anthroposophie (Gnosticism and Anthroposophy)', GA 26.

90   See F. W. Zeylmans van Emmichoven *The Foundation Stone*.

91   See more detail about this in GA 264, 15 December 1911.

92   See the opening lecture of the Christmas Conference in GA 260, 24 December 1923.

93   See *May Human Beings Hear It!*, Supplement IX 'The Christmas Conference and the School of Spiritual Science'.

94   See GA 264.

95   In GA 15 (Chapter III) Rudolf Steiner mentions that the founding of

spiritual science resulted from the 'new Inspiration' received by him out of the spiritual worlds.

96   See more on this in *May Human Beings Hear It!*, Chapter 'The Mystery Act of the Foundation Stone Laying on 25 December 1923'.

97   See *May Human Beings Hear It!*, Chapter 'Rudolf Steiner and the Karma of the Anthroposophical Society'.

98   Naturally this likewise took place at the Christmas Conference, for example in the cycle of evening lectures that formed the start of the ensuing karma considerations.

99   See GA 131, 14 October 1911; also GA 13.

100   See GA 177, 14 October 1917.

101   See *May Human Beings Hear It!*, Chapter 'The Rhythms of the Christmas Conference'.

102   A further aspect of this relationship is contained in the contribution by S. O. Prokofieff, 'Das Erscheinen des Christus im Ätherischen und das Wesen des Grundsteins der Weihnachtstagung 1923/1924' (The appearance of the Christ in the etheric and the nature of the Foundation Stone of the Christmas Conference) in the volume of collected articles, *Wege zum Erleben des Christus* (Paths to experiencing the Christ,' Vol. III, Dornach 1991.

103   See in *May Human Beings Hear It!*, Chapter 'The Foundation Stone Meditation. Karma and Resurrection'.

104   In this connection the fact seems to be of significance that Rudolf Steiner originally intended to complete the construction of the Johannes-Bau (the First Goetheanum) by August 1914. If that had happened, its dedication and esoteric opening could have taken place at Christmas.

105   See *May Human Beings Hear It!*, Chapter 'The Mystery Act of the Foundation Stone Laying on 25 December 1923'.

106   See *May Human Beings Hear It!*, Chapter 'The Foundation Stone Meditation in Eurythmy'; also Note 102.

107   About the dedication of the Foundation Stone see *May Human Beings Hear It!*, Chapter 'The Mystery Act of the Foundation Stone Laying on 25 December 1923'.

107a   See more details about her process of development in *The Heavenly Sophia and the Being Anthroposophia*.

108   About the Goetheanum's fire-metamorphosis, see *May Human Beings Hear It!*, Chapters 'The Anthroposophical Society as the Temple of the New Mysteries', and '*The Philosophy of Freedom* and the Christmas Conference'. About the appearance of the Spirit at the Christmas Conference, see Chapter 'The Mystery Act of the Foundation Stone Laying on 25 December 1923'.

109   See details in *May Human Beings Hear It!*, Chapter 'The Anthroposophical Society as the Temple of the New Mysteries'.

110   This is also why Michael was called in Christian tradition the arch-strategist of the heavenly hierarchies.

111   See letter by Marie Steiner to Helga Geelmuyden of 8 February 1947 (GA 265).

111a The connection of the here mentioned three faculties with the three cultural epochs does not contradict the fact that these faculties must be developed consciously already today by human beings.

112   In a private conversation, for example, Rudolf Steiner pointed to the fact that the individuality of Manes/Parsifal could once again incarnate on earth in the twenty-first century. 'If the prerequisites are met, he will appear as a teacher of humanity and will assume guidance in the realms of art and religion.' (GA 264) Viewed esoterically, this can fully correspond with the Classes Two and Three of the Michael School. And further: 'He (Manes) will function with the power of the Grail Mysteries and will guide human beings on deciding about good and evil on their own.' Likewise this form of his activity can be understood in the sense of the continuation of the esoteric impulse of the Christmas Conference.

113   See also *May Human Beings Hear It!*, Supplement IX 'The Christmas Conference and the School of Spiritual Science'.

114   Besides, from the aspect of the path of initiation, the alternation from 'will' [verb form] to 'live' indicates that in the Rosicrucian initiation any form of direct effect on the will of a human being is excluded. For in this initiation, preserving individual freedom is an unalterable law. (see GA 131, 5 October 1911)

115   One can discover the image of a Sun- and Moon-Angel (oftentimes the Archangels Michael and Gabriel) on many Russian icons.

116   The Foundation Stone of the First Goetheanum, that was placed below where the lectern was to stand in the building, had the form of two inter-connected dodecahedrons of which the smaller was pointing to the large hall and the large one to the small hall.

117   Daniel van Bemmelen, *Das erste Goetheanum als Menschheitsbau* (The First Goetheanum as structure of humanity), Dornach 1975.

118   Here it is striking that World evolution is depicted in the seven capitals in such a way that the Earth-stage is divided into two parts; into the epoch of the Mars influence and that of the Mercury influence, in the middle of which occurred the Mystery of Golgotha. As a result, World evolution was depicted in the large hall merely up to the Venus-condition, not up to that of Vulcan. This is connected with a profound secret. For the epochs of the complete spiritualization (the Pralayas) to which the capitals of the small hall correspond, take place only between completed planetary conditions, not during the transition from Mars to Mercury, one that came about *within* the Earth aeon. With this, there occurred at this point of evolution something unique, namely not the regular spiritualization of the material cosmos for the purpose of ascension into the sphere of the Cosmic Midnight, but on the contrary, the descent of its spiritual forces into material existence, something that happened once only in the whole of

World evolution at the instant of the Resurrection of the Christ. (See more in *May Human Beings Hear It!*, Chapter 'The Foundation Stone Meditation. Karma and Resurrection'.

119   Viewed historically, the last of the first six Bodhisattvas was the Gautama Buddha and the first of the second six is the Bodhisattva Maitreya, who in the future (around AD 4500) will be the first Christian Buddha. (About him see GA 131, 14 October 1911)

120   It goes without saying that Rudolf Steiner's indication that the Bodhisattvas 'sit' in the sphere of Providence is merely an Imagination, but one behind which a concrete reality is concealed.

121   How seriously Rudolf Steiner took the significance of the thrones is borne out by the following episode. During a rehearsal on stage of the First Goetheanum, a eurythmist placed her purse on one of the thrones. Rudolf Steiner, who at that moment was present in the auditorium, immediately interrupted the rehearsal, asked that the purse be removed and then, turning to all the eurythmists, sternly forbade them to sit down on the thrones or to place anything on them.

122   Concerning the incarnation of Ahriman at the beginning of the third millennium, see GA 193; also S. O. Prokofieff, *The Encounter with Evil and Its Overcoming through Spiritual Science.*

123   The reference here is to the reading of the *whole* meditation that occurred twice, for the fourth segment is moreover addressed in the fifth and sixth rhythm. See GA 260 as well as *May Human Beings Hear It!*, Chapter 'The Rhythms of the Christmas Conference'.

124   See GA 202, 23 and 24 December 1920. The same task exists since the Christmas Conference for the two main karmic groups of the Anthroposophical Society, and since the end of the twentieth century for the Platonists and Aristotelians. For only in this way can the union of the two streams be successful. See also Hans Peter van Manen, *Twin Roads to the New Millennium*, op.cit.

125   See also Chapter 1 of this work. From a slightly different viewpoint, this aspect of the Christmas Conference is likewise presented in *The Heavenly Sophia and the Being Anthroposophia*, Part II.

126   See *May Human Beings Hear It!*, Chapter 'The Anthroposophical Society as Temple of the New Mysteries'.

127   See, for instance, Emanuel Zeylmans, *Wer war Ita Wegman?* (Who was Ita Wegman?) Vol. 3, Heidelberg 1992; *Marie Steiner, Briefe und Dokumente* (Letters and documents), Dornach 1981; Lili Kolisko, *Eugen Kolisko. Seine Lebensgeschichte* (Eugen Kolisko. His Biography), Stuttgart 1961; Fred Pöppig, *Rückblick auf Erlebnisse, Begegnungen und Persönlichkeiten in der anthroposophischen Bewegung. 1923–1963.* (Reflections on experiences, encounters, and personalities in the Anthroposophical Movement), Basle 1964.

128   Heb. 7, 17. In the Letter to the Hebrews (Chap.7), a clear distinction is

made between the priesthood of Levi and the succession of Aaron (verse 11) and the priesthood of the order of Melchizedek. Whereas the first is founded on outer tradition, and in the case of the Hebrew people is connected with the bloodstream (which through the generations is traced all the way back to Aaron), the sources of the second are situated directly in the spiritual world. This is why it is said of Melchizedek that 'he is without father, without mother, and without ancestors, without beginning of days or end of life: he is of similar nature as the Son of God and he is a bearer of priesthood for ever'. (Heb. 7, 3 JM) Such a characterization is possible only in the case of a supersensible being, or one who, while incarnated on earth, is in constant connection with the supersensible temple and in it conducts an everlasting service, gleaning from it the impulses for his actions. And it was in this very manner that Rudolf Steiner worked at the Christmas Conference and in the ensuing time. In that period he was in the true sense of this occult term a modern priest 'after the order of Melchizedek'. It must be added here that the tradition of the priesthood of the Roman Catholic church that goes back to the Apostle Peter and in this way bases the papal institution on outer succession, belongs to the priesthood of Aaron, while the founding of the Christian Community in September of 1922 in the *First Goetheanum* was carried out with the help of Rudolf Steiner without any outer tradition directly out of the spiritual world, meaning in accordance with the order of Melchizedek. In his address to the priests of the Christian Community, Rudolf Steiner did indeed express himself in this sense. (see GA 344, 19 September 1922)

129   As early as during the Christmas Conference when, during the deliberation of §2 of the 'Statutes' it was said that the Society members were gathering *in the Goetheanum*, Rudolf Steiner responded to the objection by van Leers that the Goetheanum had after all burned down a year earlier: 'Before our spiritual eye the Goetheanum stands here!' (GA 260a, 12 August 1924) (And later he reiterated: 'The Christmas Conference was in the Goetheanum.') (ibid.)

130   Arvia Mackaye-Ege, *The Experience of the Christmas Foundation Meeting 1923,* Hillsdale, New York 1981; see also S. O. Prokofieff (editor), *Die Grundsteinmeditation als Schulungsweg* (The Foundation Stone Meditation as a path of training), Dornach 2002.

131   Ita Wegman, *An die Freunde,* Arlesheim 1968. In 1924 Rudolf Steiner gave up to five lectures per day. See more about the last few months in Rudolf Steiner's life and activity in *May Human Beings Hear It!,* Chapter 'Rudolf Steiner's Course of Life in the Light of the Christmas Conference', and Supplement V 'The Tragedy of 1 January 1924'.

132   See *May Human Beings Hear It!,* Chapter 'The Anthroposophical Society as the Temple of the New Mysteries'.

133   The only exception is probably the resignation from the Anthroposophical Society of Count Polzer-Hoditz due to the tragedy of 1935. On the

contrary, of all the members who had been excluded from the Society, none returned his membership card. Even those who were excluded from the Executive Council, Ita Wegman and Elisabeth Vreede, did not leave the Society. The following lines from an open letter signed by twelve members of the British Society in answer to the publication of the minutes in the *Newsletter* of the annual meeting of 1935 bear witness to the frame of mind prevailing at that time among the circle of individuals who had been excluded: '*If* these motions should be approved by the General Assembly, they will not be taken into consideration by us. We will steadfastly continue on the basis of the freedom guaranteed to us by the founding Statutes to carry on with the tasks for the anthroposophical cause originating from Rudolf Steiner's life's work. We shall furthermore always consider the Goetheanum as the place "for all the members".' (Quoted from T. Meyer, *D. N. Dunlop. A Man of Our Time*, Temple Lodge, London 1992, (emphasis in the original). For the same reason Ita Wegman refused to participate in an initiative that could have led to the founding of a new society and was directed against Dornach. (See Emanuel Zeylmans van Emmichoven, *Who was Ita Wegman?* Vol. 2, op.cit.)

134   See more on this in *May Human Beings Hear It!*, Chapter 'The Esoteric Archetype of the Original Council', and in Supplement III 'Comments by the Members of the Original Executive Council on the Christmas Conference'.

135   Rudolf Steiner spoke of the fact that the etheric return [Second Coming] of the Christ is connected with the revelations of the fire trial in a lecture on 11 April 1909 (GA 109/111).

136   In her foreword to the first publication of the shorthand transcript of the Christmas Conference (1944), Marie Steiner wrote: 'The deepest esotericism could be to bring diverging earlier spiritual streams to a harmonious balance now in the persons of some of their present representatives.'

137   Emanuel Zeylmans, *Willem Zeylmans van Emmichoven*, Temple Lodge Publishing, 2002.

138   See *May Human Beings Hear It!*, Chapter 'The Mystery Act of the Foundation Stone Laying on 25 December 1923'.

139   See *May Human Beings Hear It!*, Chapter 'The Anthroposophical Society as the Temple of the New Mysteries'.

140   At the Christmas Conference, Rudolf Steiner himself broke the most important law of occultism that he had strictly followed during the previous years, a law to which he called his students' attention more than once. It is the law that requires that on the spiritual level the spirit-teacher may not be linked with the earthly forms of human society.

141   Concerning the fact that along with the Christmas Conference an entirely new creation occurred (a 'creation out of nothing'), see details in *May Human Beings Hear It!*, Chapter 'The *Philosophy of Freedom* and the Christmas Conference'.

142   An example are his words that the impulse of the Christmas Conference 'still does evoke reactions of dismay in the hearts of our dear anthroposophical friends.' (GA 260a, 24 August 1924) In another lecture he says: 'This Christmas Conference has indicated that if the Anthroposophical Society is in the future to unfold its activity correctly, it *must leave the paths* it pursued in the last ten years ... All in all it has to assume an esoteric character.' (GA 260a, 6 February 1924) And there are more such remarks.

142a In the lectures on spiritual economy (GA 109/111), Rudolf Steiner spoke of the necessity that higher hierarchical beings would have to participate in this process. In the case of the multiplication of the Foundation Stone, Michael was such a being into whose supersensible realm Rudolf Steiner carried up the Foundation Stone (see Chapter 6). During the Mystery act of the Foundation Stone Laying, this Stone's multiplication occurred in accordance with the laws of spiritual economy at the instant of the so-called 'consecration' of the Foundation Stone. See more in *May Human Beings Hear It!*, Chapter 'The Mystery Act of the Foundation Stone Laying on 25 December 1923'.

143   Viewed this way, the beginning of the Christmas Conference stands more under the sign of the Shepherds because here are more references to laying the Foundation Stone into the human heart, whereas its conclusion stands under the sign of Kings who follow the star.

144   In these connections the fact moreover comes to expression that of all four festivals only the date of Easter is movable. This is why the *rhythms* of the Foundation Stone Meditation correspond to Easter. This is at the same time an indication of a possible form of inner work with the substance of the Christmas Conference in connection with the cycle of the year.

145   See *May Human Beings Hear It!*, Chapter 'The Rhythms of the Christmas Conference'.

146   See GA 260a, 29 June 1924, as well as *May Human Beings Hear It!*, Supplement II 'On the Question of the "Constitution" of the Anthroposophical Society'.

147   An outwardly visible expression for such a 'finding of the temple' was the building of the First Goetheanum. Rudolf Steiner even referred to the trial model at Malsch that preceded it as the first Rosicrucian temple. The highest realization of this ideal is, however, the supersensible temple of the New Mysteries in the spiritual world adjacent to the Earth.

148   See *May Human Beings Hear It!*, Chapter 'The Foundation Stone Meditation in Eurythmy'.

149   See more in S. O. Prokofieff *The East in the Light of the West*, Part III 'The Birth of Christian Esotericism in the Twentieth Century and the Powers Opposing It'.

150   Rudolf Steiner spoke in a lecture on 12 December 1910 (GA 124) about the fact that John the Baptist received the Aquarius initiation, meaning the one of an Angel. Some time later on, he explained that the two words

'angel' and 'spirit-self' refer to one and the same reality. (GA 175, 20 February 1917).

151 It goes without saying that in both cases he left all three sheaths, i.e. also their ether and astral body.

152 See more on them in GA 149 and GA 152.

153 See the *Dobrotolyubie* or *Philokalia* Vol. 3, 'One-Hundred Ascetic Sayings' by the Blessed Diadochus; also S. O. Prokofieff: Author's report on the lecture, 'Esotericism in Eastern Christendom', in the Anthology *Esoterik der Weltreligionen* (Esotericism of World Religions), Dornach 2001.

154 The origin of the numerous legends and apocrypha connected with the childhood of Jesus is found here.

155 Previously, words by Rudolf Steiner were quoted to the effect that, in order to depict matters so profound that they cannot be expressed in earthly terms, he himself was in need of eurythmy; see in *May Human Beings Hear It!*, Chapter 'The Foundation Stone Meditation in Eurythmy'.

156 Ordinarily, a child learns to say 'I' to itself approximately at age three.

157 See for this GA 15, Chapter 1.

157a What occurred at the Turning-point of Time in macrocosmic manner on the world-historical level, meaning on the level of *existence*, is repeated in a genuine process of insight on the level of *consciousness* as described by Rudolf Steiner in GA 4. See Chapter 7 in S. O. Prokofieff *Anthroposophie und 'Die Philosophie der Freiheit'* (Anthroposophy and 'The Philosophy of Freedom'), Dornach 2006 (English edition in preparation).

157b See more detail concerning the three forms of the 'I', the ordinary (earthly), higher, and true 'I' in *May Human Beings Hear It!*, Chapter 'The Foundation Stone Meditation in Eurythmy'.

158 When Rudolf Steiner recited the macrocosmic Lord's Prayer for the first time on 20 September 1913 during the Foundation Stone Laying of the First Goetheanum, he began the prayer with the words, 'Aum, Amen' in which the consonant M assumes the central position.

158a See in *Eternal Individuality. Towards a Karmic Biography of Novalis*, Chapter 'Representative of Humanity's Conscience'.

159 In the lecture of 5 October 1913 (GA 148) Rudolf Steiner likewise spoke of the Mystery of Golgotha as of the 'birth' of the Christ in the Earth's sphere.

159a See more detail in *The Cycle of the Year As a Path of Initiation*, Chapter 'The Mission of the Master Jesus in the Year's Course'.

159b These processes are prepared early on in the physical body of Jesus of Nazareth during the three years of the Christ's sojourn in it. This is why the three parts of the Foundation Stone Meditation also reflect the nature of these three earthly years of Christ Jesus. About this see *May Human Beings Hear It!*, Chapter 'The Foundation Stone Meditation. Karma and Resurrection'.

160 See the reproduction of this eurythmic form in *May Human Beings Hear It!*, Chapter 'The Foundation Stone Meditation in Eurythmy'.

161   See more about cultic eurythmy in connection with the performance of the Foundation Stone in eurythmy in the article by S.O. Prokofieff: 'Eurythmie als christliche Kunst. Vom Ursprungsimpuls und Wesen des Eurythmischen' (Eurythmy as Christian art. On the primal impulse and nature of the eurythmic element). *Newsletter 23/24* of 8 June 2003.

162   Here, we deal with the human being's trichotomy consisting of spirit, soul, and body; not the threefoldness of the social organism. The relation of the latter to the Anthroposophical Society is not the subject of this chapter. See *May Human Beings Hear It!*, Supplement II 'On the Question of the Constitution of the Anthroposophical Society'.

163   This could only be realized during Rudolf Steiner's lifetime in an incomplete form by means of the 'Goetheanum Building Association', since it was not possible for the officials to record the 'Statutes' of the Anthroposophical Society in the Commercial Register in the form in which they had been passed at the Christmas Conference.

164   During the cultic act of the Foundation Stone Laying, Rudolf Steiner referred to the appearance of this Spirit in the radiant aura of the Foundation Stone. See *May Human Beings Hear It!*, Chapter 'The Mystery Act of the Foundation Stone Laying on 25 December 1923'.

165   See for instance, H. Witzenmann, *Die Prinzipien der Allgemeinen Anthroposophischen Gesellschaft* (The principles of the General Anthroposophical Society), Dornach 1984, and G. von Beckerath, *Die Michael-Prophetie Rudolf Steiners zur Jahrtausendwende im Spiegel unserer Seelen-Wege und Arbeitsweisen* (Rudolf Steiner's Michael-prophecy for the millennium in the perspective of our soul-directions and ways of working), Chapter 'Die Statuten der Weihnachtstagung als geistig-sozialeArbeitsweise' (The statutes of the Christmas Conference as a spiritual-social manner of working), Dornach 2000.

166   See GA 26, Leading Thought No. 71.

167   See more in *May Human Beings Hear It!*, Supplement VII 'The Reverse Cultus and the Nature of the Foundation Stone'.

168   See GA 260, 26 December 1923.

169   See *May Human Beings Hear It!*, Chapter 'The Mystery Act of the Foundation Stone Laying on 25 December 1923'.

170   The cosmic archetype is the circle of the twelve Bodhisattvas who in the sphere of Providence surround the spiritual Christ-Sun. (GA 113, 31 August 1909) Rudolf Steiner pointed out the connection with the circle of the twelve Apostles in a lecture on 28 August 1923. (GA 227)

171   See Rudolf Steiner's lectures on karma. (GA 235–240)

172   Rudolf Steiner spoke of the Moon karma as a karma connected with the past and of the Sun karma that points into the future. But the shaping of the latter, starting from our age, must take place together with the activity of the Christ-Sun in Earth evolution. (GA 240, 6 February 1924)

Tr. 2   The *two* references to 'aims' can easily be lost in English translations of the

Foundation Stone Meditation. The first is contained in Part III, 1, in the line, 'where the eternal *aims* of gods...' (The German term 'Ziele; is usually translated as 'aims'). The second reference occurs in the last line of Part IV, 2, as an adverb, '*zielvoll*' or '*aimfully*'. This line is usually translated as, 'with single purpose', or 'direct with single will'. Only Richard Seddon managed to include the word 'aim'. He translated this last line as 'guide in true-*aimed* willing'.

173   In this connection Rudolf Steiner spoke of two Michael-revelations, at the Turning-point of Time and in our time, which means in the epoch of Christ's life on the Earth in a physical body and in the present epoch of His etheric return. See GA 194, 22 February 1919; also *May Human Beings Hear It!*, Chapter 'The Foundation Stone Meditation. Karma and Resurrection'.

174   See more on this in *May Human Beings Hear It!*, Chapter 'The Foundation Stone Meditation. Karma and Resurrection'.

175   This is why, during the Baptism in the Jordan, the voice of the Father resounds: 'This is my beloved Son, today I have begotten him.' (Lk. 3, 22 in Rudolf Steiner's translation in GA 114, 21 September 1909) In the fourth segment too, it is said of this Light that it warms the Shepherds' hearts and enlightens the Kings' heads. This means that it was effective even before the Baptism in the Jordan and the Mystery of Golgotha.

176   Concerning the connection of Epiphany, Easter, and Pentecost with the first three segments of the Foundation Stone Meditation, see *The Cycle of the Year as a Path of Initiation*.

177   Concerning this aspect of the Christmas Conference, see *Rudolf Steiner and the Founding of the New Mysteries*, Part III, 'Anthroposophy: The Proclamation of World Pentecost'.

178   In the Gospel of John, this is indicated prophetically through the following words: 'For the Father judges no one, but has given all judgement to the Son.' (RSV 5, 22)

179   Rudolf Steiner spoke about the Resurrection Body (the Phantom) in a lecture on 11 October 1911 (GA 131), and about the condensed ether body on a lecture of 9 January 1912 (GA 130). See more about this in *May Human Beings Hear It!*, Chapter 'The Foundation Stone Meditation. Karma, and Resurrection'.

180   See more about this in *Rudolf Steiner and the Founding of the New Mysteries*, Chapter 'The Christmas Conference of 1923/1924'.

181   Rudolf Steiner spoke several times about the 'good Spirit of the Goetheanum' at the Christmas Conference. See GA 260.

182   In the lecture of 7 March 1907 (GA 97), Rudolf Steiner spoke of three kinds of Mysteries: the Mysteries of the Spirit relating to the past (they are the Mysteries of catharsis); the Mysteries of the Son that relate to the present; and the Mysteries of the Father that relate to the future. All three kinds of Mysteries are germinally contained in the Rosicrucians' path of initiation.

183   See GA 148, 2 October 1913) and also *May Human Beings Hear It!*, Chapter 'The Foundation Stone Meditation. Karma and Resurrection'.

184   This substance is called the 'fifth' because it comes after the four elements, earth, water, air, and fire.

185   See *May Human Beings Hear It!*, Chapter 'The Foundation Stone Meditation in Eurythmy'.

186   Concerning the 'Christ-Sun' and the Second Coming, see the description of the sixth rhythm in *May Human Beings Hear It!*, Chapter 'The Rhythms of the Christmas Conference'. This does not contradict the fact that the Imagination of the 'Christ-Sun' points above all to the Mystery of Golgotha, as a result of which Earth has begun to turn into a new sun. (see GA 112, 6 July 1909) This Imagination reveals to clairvoyant consciousness merely that aspect which it is capable of beholding at a specific level of the spiritual-historical evolution of humanity. Today it points to the *etheric sun* as the first consequence of the Mystery of Golgotha that is connected with the etheric appearance of the Christ. In the future it will point to the astral sun and still later on to the 'I'-Sun (Ich-Sonne), corresponding to the three supersensible revelations of the Christ (GA 130, 21 September 1911), of which each merely shows one of the aspects.

186a Between his incarnation at the Turning-point of Time and the one in the thirteenth century, the individuality of Christian Rosenkreutz passed through a number of interim-incarnations (Rudolf Steiner in a conversation with Friedrich Rittelmeyer). During these incarnations it had to absorb and work on the experiences of its participation in the events of the Turning-point of Time and prepare for its further mission in humanity.

187   In a lecture on 15 December 1907 (GA 98), Rudolf Steiner spoke of the fact that the establishment of this path of initiation was the result of Christian Rosenkreutz's initiation in the year 1459.

188   In his earlier incarnation, Christian Rosenkreutz was born in the year 1378, meaning prior to the end of the epoch of the intellectual or rational soul.

189   See more on this process in Chapter 6.

190   See in connection with this *Rudolf Steiner and the Founding of the New Mysteries,* Chapter 1.

191   GA 131, 7 October 1911. See more about the reasons for the martyrdom of Christian Rosenkreutz in *May Human Beings Hear It!*, Chapter 'Rudolf Steiner and the Karma of the Anthroposophical Society'.

192   In the Book of Revelation this stage of initiation is indicated when John was supposed not only to read but to eat the Book of Wisdom (10, 9 and 10). See also the fourth apocalyptic seal in GA 104.

193   This moreover explains the plight of Amfortas who was forced to Grail service with an unchastened soul. The result was that each time during the Grail service his wound opened and his blood, filled as it was by cravings and egoistic desires, began to flow from it, causing him great agony. For as

a bearer of unchastened blood, he could not approach the chalice without the former beginning to flow.

194 Rudolf Steiner spoke about conscience as the organ for the perception of the Christ Being on 2 May 1910 (GA 116).

195 See here *May Human Beings Hear It!*, Chapter 'Rudolf Steiner's Course of Life in the Light of the Christmas Conference'.

196 Preface to the 16th to 20th edition, written on 10 January 1925 (GA 13).

196a This is likewise the title of the lecture cycle in 1907 (GA 99) which has approximately the same content as *Occult Science, an Outline* (GA 13).

197 See more about the development of the Rosicrucian impulse in Anthroposophy in Chapter 6. Rudolf Steiner expressed himself in a particularly determined way about the connection of Anthroposophy with the 'new esotericism' (that goes back to the initiation of Christian Rosenkreutz in the middle of the thirteenth century) in the third chapter of GA 15.

198 Concerning the connection of Rudolf Steiner with the Grail Mysteries and his place in the spiritual/ historical chain of guardians see *Rudolf Steiner and the Founding of the New Mysteries*, Chapter 'The Michael Age and the New Grail Event'.

199 Concerning the connection of the First Goetheanum with the Grail temple see *May Human Beings Hear It!*, Chapters 'Rudolf Steiner's Course of Life in the Light of the Christmas Conference' and 'The Anthroposophical Society as the Temple of the New Mysteries'.

200 The 'Model Structure' at Malsch, erected according to specifications by Rudolf Steiner and called by him a Rosicrucian temple, was an architectural and spiritual precursor of the First Goetheanum.

201 Concerning the threefold metamorphosis '*Occult Science, an Outline*—First Goetheanum—Christmas Conference' in the connection with the Grail Mysteries, see Note 198.

202 Rudolf Steiner concluded §1 of the 'Statutes' of the Anthroposophical Society founded at the Christmas Conference with the same verb.

203 According to the spiritual research by Rudolf Steiner, the limbs of a human being are created prior to an incarnation on earth through the hierarchies out of the spiritual world, whereas man's head itself is not a new structure but a metamorphosis of the limbs in the past life.

204 Concerning the connection of the Apostle and Evangelist John with Christian Rosenkreutz, see GA 264.

205 These original Father-forces were corrupted in the physical body of man as a result of the 'Fall into Sin'. In the Resurrection of the Christ, they were restored in their original splendour. (see GA 131, 10/11 October 1911)

206 See GA 59, 28 October 1909. In an address to young anthroposophists, Rudolf Steiner pointed out that anthroposophical meditating—meaning meditating in the consciousness soul—consists of transforming spiritual scientific insight into devotion: 'Indeed, meditating means to transform what one knows into devotion, particularly each single detail'. (GA 260a)

207   See also the words from GA 13 quoted above in the eleventh chapter concerning the Grail.

208   The cosmic archetype of this circle of the twelve Grail knights is the circle of the twelve Bodhisattvas around the Christ in the sphere of Providence (Buddhi). See on this *Rudolf Steiner and the Founding of the New Mysteries*, Chapter 'The Foundation Stone Meditation'.

209   This is the unknown 'youth' who, according to the Gospel by Mark, eluded the soldiers in the Garden of Gethsemane but then showed himself once again on Easter morning at the tomb of the Resurrected One. (GA 139, 23 September 1912)

210   See for instance the Arnhem lectures in GA 240, 18–20 July 1924, and GA 26.

211   Rudolf Steiner spoke in a lecture on 26 October 1918 (GA 185) about this co-operation between the human being with the spirits of the Third Hierarchy. This [co-operation] must be attained by the sixth cultural epoch.

212   See on this *May Human Beings Hear It!*, Chapter 'The Mystery Act of the Foundation Stone Laying on 25 December 1923'.

213   See more on this in the article by Ernst Katz: 'Gedanken über die Grundsteinmeditation (Thoughts on the Foundation Stone Meditation) published in the anthology, *Die Grundsteinmeditation als Schulungsweg* (The Foundation Stone Meditation as a path of schooling), Dornach 2002.

214   Rudolf Steiner spoke about the special relation between the two Johns at the Turning-point of Time in his explanations regarding the 'Last Address' (28 September 1924) in GA 238, edition of 1981.

215   Here, John the Baptist represents the Abel stream, and John the Evangelist the Cain stream. (see GA 264)

216   See more about this temple in *May Human Beings Hear It!*, Chapter 'The Anthroposophical Society as the Temple of the New Mysteries'; also Chapter 8 in this work.

217   See details about this connection in GA 15, Chapter 1.

218   The Prophet Daniel spoke about Michael as the folk spirit of the Hebrews. (Dan., Chapter 10)

219   An Old-Testament-Apocryphon refers to Michael's special relation to Moses, where it speaks of Michael's struggle with Satan concerning the corpse of Moses.

220   Concerning these two Michael revelations and their relation to the Foundation Stone Meditation, see also *May Human Beings Hear It!*, Chapter 'The Foundation Stone Meditation. Karma and Resurrection'.

221   See more detail on this in *May Human Beings Hear It!*, Chapter 'The Mystery Act of the Foundation Stone Laying on 25 December 1923'.

222   See F. W. Zeylmans van Emmichoven, *The Foundation Stone*, op.cit.

223   In the lecture on 2 May 1913 (GA 152), Rudolf Steiner called the spiritual science which he had founded 'a gift from Michael'.

224 See *May Human Beings Hear It!*, Chapter 'The Foundation Stone Meditation. Karma and Resurrection' as well as Supplement VIII, 'The Spiritual and the Sacramental Communion'. These form the basis of the present Addendum.

225 In this case the Foundation Stone Meditation and its rhythms. See Note 224.

226 A more detailed consideration of the 'Offering Service' and its relation to sacramental and spiritual communion requires an independent examination outside the framework of this book.

227 Concerning the activity of the Christ in the course of the awakening of the afore-mentioned faculties, see GA 15, Chapter 1. Regarding the true 'I' as the 'site' of the Christ's presence in man, see *May Human Beings Hear It!*, Chapter 'The Foundation Stone Meditation in Eurythmy'.

228 See Chapter 12 and Note 213.

229 This sequence is not an expression of the structure of the ritual itself but of the overriding significance of the transformation of the substances in it, around which the other two elements, word and knowledge, are grouped in the spiritual regard.

230 It goes without saying that the element of the word likewise plays an important part in the sacramental communion. Nevertheless, the transubstantiation forms the central point of the sacramental cultus. One can moreover say: In the element of the word we have the proximity of both rituals, but in the sacramental cultus the word takes hold of matter directly and then makes its appearance through them, whereas the word remains in its element in the 'Offering Service' from beginning to end of the ritual.

231 See Note 224.

232 See details about the 'reverse cultus' in GA 257, as well as in *May Human Beings Hear It!*, Supplement VII 'The Reverse Cultus and the Nature of the Foundation Stone'.

233 This stage can also be called the Imaginative one, for on it the 'perception' of ideas is attained, which means that ideas are experienced in perceptual form (pictures).

234 In Rudolf Steiner's biography, this stage corresponds to his supersensible encounter with the Archangel Michael that took place during the Weimar period. See more in *May Human Beings Hear It!*, Chapter 'Rudolf Steiner's Course of Life in the Light of the Christmas Conference'.

235 See details in Chapter 7 as well as in *May Human Beings Hear It!*, Chapter 'Rudolf Steiner's Course of Life in the Light of the Christmas Conference'.

236 In many lectures Rudolf Steiner placed special emphasis on the relation of the Archangels to the word. (See for instance GA 226, 18 May 1923)

237 What is consumption of transformed substances [by humans] on earth, corresponds in the spiritual world to the opposite process, that of receiving the content of the human soul by the spiritual hierarchies.

238   In Earth evolution the three categories of the Third Hierarchy represent the following: The Angels represent the Third Hierarchy in its totality; the Archangels, the Second Hierarchy; the Archai the First. Their combined activity thus corresponds to the general composition of the Foundation Stone Meditation.

239   See GA 15, Chapter III.

240   See Note 224.

241   See Note 224.

242   See GA 265.

243   See Note 235.

244   In the ancient pre-Christian Mysteries, the highest level of initiation was called 'the beholding of the Sun at the midnight hour'. This level was attained only outside the physical body.

List of Works by Rudolf Steiner Referred to in this Book

All emphasis in the quotes, if not noted otherwise, is by Sergei O. Prokofieff.

English titles of works by Rudolf Steiner are given only in cases where a similar (though not always identical) volume to the original German edition from the collected works—the *Gesamtausgabe* (abbreviated as 'GA')—has been published in English translation. In many cases lectures are available in typescript or in print as single lectures or compilations from the collected works. For information on these, contact Rudolf Steiner House Library, 35 Park Road, London NW1 6XT, or similar anthroposophical libraries around the world.

Publishers:

AP:	Anthroposophic Press (USA)
APC:	Anthroposophical Publishing Company (London)
SBC:	Steiner Book Centre (Canada)
RSP:	Rudolf Steiner Press (UK)
TL:	Temple Lodge Publishing (UK)
GAR:	Garber Communications (USA)

Books

GA 4	*The Philosophy of Freedom* (RSP, 1964)
GA 9	*Theosophy* (RSP, 1973)
GA 10	*Knowledge of the Higher Worlds* (RSP; AP: *How to Know Higher Worlds*)
GA 11	*Cosmic Memory* (GAR, 1990)
GA 13	*Occult Science* (RSP; AP: *An Outline of Esoteric Science*)
GA 14	*Four Mystery Dramas* (APC and SBC)
GA 15	*The Spiritual Guidance of Humanity* (AP)
GA 17	*The Threshold of the Spiritual World* (RSP)
GA 26	*Anthroposophical Leading Thoughts* (RSP)
GA 28	*The Course of My Life* (AP)
GA 35	*Philosophie und Anthroposophie* (Collected Articles 1904–1923)
GA 40	*Wahrspruchworte* (Truth-Wrought Words)

Lectures

GA 59	*Metamorphosen des Seelenlebens*
GA 93	*The Temple Legend and the Golden Legend (RSP)*
GA 97	*Das christliche Mysterium*
GA 98	*Natur und Geistwesen - ihr Wirken in unserer sichtbaren Welt*

GA 99	*Theosophy of the Rosicrucian* (RSP)
GA 102	*The Influence of Spiritual Beings Upon Man* (AP)
GA 103	*The Gospel of St John* (RSP)
GA 104	*The Apocalypse of St John* (RSP)
GA 109/111	*The Principle of Spiritual Economy in Connection with Questions of Reincarnation* (AP & RSP)
GA 110	*The Spiritual Hierarchies and Their Reflection in the Physical World* (AP)
GA 112	*The Gospel of St John in Relation to the Other Three Gospels* (AP & RSP)
GA 113	*The East in the Light of the West* (RSP & AP)
GA 114	*The Gospel of St Luke* (RSP)
GA 116	*The Christ-Impulse and the Development of Ego-Consciousness* (AP)
GA 118	*True Nature of the Second Coming* (RSP)
GA 123	*The Gospel of St Matthew* (RSP)
GA 124	*Background to the Gospel of St Mark* (RSP)
GA 127	*Die Mission der neuen Geistesoffenbarung*
GA 129	*Wonders of the World, Ordeals of the Soul, Revelations of the Spirit* (RSP)
GA 130	*Esoteric Christianity and the Mission of Christian Rosenkreutz* (RSP)
GA 131	*From Jesus to Christ* (RSP)
GA 133	*Earthly and Cosmic Man* (RSP)
GA 136	*The Spiritual Beings in the Heavenly Bodies and in the Kingdom of Nature* (RSP)
GA 139	*The Gospel of St Mark* (RSP)
GA 143	*Erfahrungen des Übersinnlichen. Die drei Wege der Seele zu Christus*
GA 148	*The Fifth Gospel* (RSP)
GA 149	*Christ and the Spiritual World and The Search for the Holy Grail* (RSP)
GA 152	*Vorstufen zum Mysterium von Golgotha*
GA 153	*Inner Nature of Man and the Life Between Death and a New Birth* (APC)
GA 155	*Christ and the Human Soul* (RSP)
GA 156	*Occult Reading and Occult Hearing* (RSP)
GA 158	*Der Zusammenhang des Menschen mit der elementarischen Welt*
GA 175	*Bausteine zu einer Erkenntnis des Mysteriums von Golgotha*
GA 177	*The Fall of the Spirits of Darkness* (RSP)
GA 182	*Der Tod als Lebenswandlung*
GA 183	*Die Wissenschaft vom Werden des Menschen*
GA 185	*From Symptom to Reality in Modern History* (RSP)
GA 193	*The Inner Aspect of the Social Question* (RSP)
GA 194	*The Mission of the Archangel Michael* (AP)
GA 202	*Die Brücke zwischen der Weltgeistigkeit und dem Physischen des Menschen*, which includes four lectures available in English: *The Search for the New Isis*
GA 211	*Das Sonnenmysterium und das Mysterium von Tod und Auferstehung*

May Human Beings Hear It!
The Mystery of the Christmas Conference
Sergei O. Prokofieff

'It depends on the human being whether he merely conceives of anthroposophy or whether he *experiences* it.'—Rudolf Steiner

During the Christmas period of 1923–4, Rudolf Steiner refounded the Anthroposophical Society at its headquarters in Dornach, Switzerland. This important event, which has come to be known as the Christmas Conference, can be studied on many levels, and its many mysteries have been central to Sergei O. Prokofieff's anthroposophical research over the years. His beginning point has been an enduring question: What did Rudolf Steiner mean when he called the Christmas Conference the 'start of a World-Turning-point of Time'? In this far-reaching work, the author—working from several different viewpoints—guides the reader towards an answer.

Prokofieff suggests that the impulse of the Christmas Conference can only be reenlivened today through conscious action by individuals to experience its spiritual essence. Rather than offering dogmatic conclusions, he opens up paths of approaching this goal by throwing light on different aspects of the Conference and what lies at its heart: the Foundation Stone and its Meditation. In particular, Prokofieff explores three key perspectives: the connection of the Christmas Conference with humanity's evolution; the inner relationship of each individual anthroposophist to the Christmas Conference; and the significance of the Conference to Rudolf Steiner himself.

Although this is major work of some length, the individual chapters of *May Human Beings Hear It!* are complete in themselves, and can therefore be studied independently of each other.

2004; 944pp; 24 × 16 cm; hardback; £35; ISBN: 1 902636 53 8

The Encounter with Evil and its Overcoming through Spiritual Science
With Essays on The Foundation Stone
Sergei O. Prokofieff

In our everyday lives, we are constantly challenged by the phenomenon of evil in all its many manifestations. But how can we cope with this seemingly eternal hindrance? In the first of these three essays, Sergei Prokofieff suggests that we start by developing a knowledge of the forces of evil in order to learn how they work in human evolution. Such knowledge is, in itself, the beginning of the process of overcoming evil.

In order that members of the Anthroposophical Society might go further along this path, Rudolf Steiner gave them the spiritual 'Foundation Stone of the Good'. This Foundation Stone—which consists of light, imaginative form, and the substance of love—can live in our hearts and souls as a firm foundation for esoteric work, and a creative contribution towards the overcoming of evil. Ultimately it can lead us to a conscious experience of Christ in the etheric realm of the earth.

In the second and third essays, Prokofieff examines further themes relating to the etheric advent of Christ, and its connection with the Foundation Stone of the Good.

1999; 192pp; 21.5 × 13.5 cm; £10.95; 1 902636 10 4